Sire Ratings

1999 - 2000

Pedigrec Update News Volume 11

City Miner Books ◆ Berkeley, California

Copyright © 1999 Michael Helm. All rights reserved including the right of reproduction in whole or in part in any form.

Sire Rating System™ 1994 Michael Helm
Design & Layout: Dayna Goforth
Cover Logo: Don McCartney

Published by City Miner Books, 1999
P.O. Box 176
Berkeley, CA 94701

ISBN 0-933944-24-1

Printed in United States of America
by Consolidated Printers
Berkeley, CA

How to use this book:

THE RATINGS IN THIS VOLUME update and expand the sire ratings previously published as part of *Exploring Pedigree* and *Sire Ratings: 1998-1999*. While veterans of these two books can rely exclusively on the legend which follows for applying these revised ratings to the handicapping process, newcomers are strongly urged to read the analysis and examples provided in *Exploring Pedigree* in order to more clearly understand the optimum conditions under which the pedigree factor is likely to be profitable.

While a horse's pedigree can sometimes be used as an only factor in predicting a winning effort, it is important to emphasize that most often it needs to be integrated with speed and pace and trainer and jockey analysis, as well as a knowledge of the winning par times for each level. Clearly the pedigree factor has the best chance of success when a horse bred for it is trying something for the first time against a field where all the experienced horses are proven losers who have run below par figures and have already failed at the distance or on the surface in question.

Besides increasing the number of individual ratings to more than 24,000, this edition of *Sire Ratings* has been rigorously weighted away from lifetime averages and toward how well a sire's progeny have performed over their last three crops. For example, based on his lifetime FTS average, Storm Cat technically deserves to be a B+-rated debut sire. But over the past three years he only had ten juvenile debut winners from some 90 starters at the top fifty tracks. The reason for this is probably that — given his sharply escalated $150,000 stud fee — breeders can no longer afford to breed to him primarily for sprint speed and are now sending him

stouter mares in the hopes of getting a Classic winner as well as the lucrative breeding fees that are typically associated with success at that level.

Trainers, aware of the economics, have also changed the way they handle their now pricier Storm Cat bloodstock. Rather than push them in the morning with the risk of potential injury, they are more inclined to give them a start or two before asking them to win. The last thing a trainer wants to do is call up a hopeful owner and tell him that his half million dollar Storm Cat colt or filly has just broken down because he was trying to get it to win first time out of the box.

The consequence of these economic and environmental factors — for handicapping purposes — is that Storm Cat, unless he has been bred to a precocious mare is now no better than a C+ rated debut sire who is likely to be overbet based upon inflated lifetime averages that no longer hold. Other sires with high lifetime FTS averages have declined for similar reasons or because bored breeders are sending their better mares to more fashionable younger stallions to see what they can produce.

Besides adjusting for recency, weight has once again been given to parimutuel value in this edition. A select number of sires with a C-rating in the FTS category have been underlined because they have recently produced multiple debut winners at big prices. While handicappers may not score as frequently betting the progeny of these underlined C sires, they should be generously compensated when they do. Additional refinements to the ratings are explained in the legend which follows:

STALLION: Under this category every sire is alphabetically arranged. To find a sire just look for him where you would expect him to appear. When a delta ^ appears after a sire's name, this means he is a freshman stallion whose first crop is racing in l999. A double delta ^^ indicates a stallion whose second crop is racing in 1999. A star * indicates a stallion whose third crop is now racing. When a sire's name is followed by an abbreviated series of letters, that means he stands abroad in such countries as *AUS* (Australia), *FR* (France), *ENG* (England), *IND* (India), *IRE* (Ireland), *JPN* (Japan), *SAF* (South Africa) and so forth.

Veterans of *Exploring Pedigree* and *Sire Ratings: 1998-1999* will note that a number of foreign turf sires and broodmare sires have been added, primarily as an aid to identifying their class and distance abilities. The younger foreign sires have been rated on the performance of their last two crops, adjusted, where possible, to how their runners have done under North American conditions. Fortunately, most of the progeny of these sires will have already shown some foreign form to give us a corroborating hint as whether they are likely to run to their sire's ratings here.

When a sire's name is set off in bold-faced type, such as with **Buckpasser** or **Nijinsky ll**, this means he is a potent broodmare sire and his daughters are more likely than normal to both be and produce successful runners.

SIRE/BROODMARE SIRE: While the *Daily Racing Form* only identifies the sire of each sire, horseplayers can gain significant additional insight into the potential ability of a young horse by also knowing the broodmare sire of the sire. This can be particularly important in identifying potential turf ability in a young sire as illustrated by the success of both Gone West and Groovy whose progeny outperformed their initial turf expectations. Handicappers who appreciated early on that Secretariat was a positive turf broodmare sire influence in Gone West's pedigree and

Northern Dancer a positive one in Norcliffe's, were able to cash some killer tickets before the general public caught on that these two sires were not typical dirt-loving descendants of Mr. Prospector and Buckpasser, respectively.

A broodmare sire's proclivity can also be useful for predicting a horse's precocity as a first time starter. When a horseplayer knows that a precocious broodmare sire influence is at work, such as with a Valid Appeal or a Mr. Prospector mare, he can more confidently back that horse in its debut.

A number of foreign turf broodmare sires have been added to this edition and given an M* turf rating. Most of them have only had a few North American runners, so their data base is quite small. While these broodmare sires are capable of contributing to a winning pedigree, the best use of their ratings is probably in terms of their stamina indexes.

FTS - First-time starters: The A-F ratings in this category measure how successful a sire's progeny are likely to be when they debut in maiden races, with an A rating being the best and an F the worst FTS rating. An A rating indicates that a sire is recently getting 25 percent or more debut winners to starters, B- rated sires generally get 18-24 percent winners, C rated 10-17 percent, D-rated 6-9 percent and F-rated sires get 5 percent or less debut winners to starters.

Sires whose progeny have started less than fifty times generally receive one of three ratings: L for likely, M for maybe and U for unlikely. If the L is underlined this means a sire's first crop has initially proven very precocious. Handicappers should be not be too aggressive when backing the first-time starters of Freshman sires of 1999 as their FTS rating are provisional guesstimates (based on their sire's race record and pedigree) which may or may not be confirmed by results on the track. Last year, for example, we were right in giving Tactical Advantage and L-rating, but wrong with our L-rating for Dehere who was not as precocious as projected.

In a few instances I have gone ahead and given a young sire with less than fifty starts a B or an F rating because the evidence clearly indicates he is either very precocious or not so at all. A sire with ten debut winners from his first thirty starters is unlikely to immediately slow down, while one that is 0-30 is not suddenly going to become a precocious sire.

Spotting a likely debut winner in a maiden race is a tricky business. It generally requires not only a productive FTS sire, but a trainer with a proven history of winning with first-time starters. The most precocious pedigree in the world becomes irrelevant in the hands of a trainer (or owner) who doesn't believe in training his horses for a maximum effort in their first start. Horseplayers who like to play maiden races will profit by ordering a copy of *Debut Winners of 1998* which gives a monthly breakdown for the top fifty tracks around the country of every debut winner according to its age, class, sire, odds, trainer, jockey and owner. Further information about it, as well as *Freshmen Sires of 1999* is provided at the back of this book.

It is worth noting that debut horses that go off as favorites win much less than other types of favorites. Because of their tendency to get agitated during the post parade, break poorly from the gate and/or run greenly around their first turn, it is important to not take too short a price when playing a first-time starter. The most profitable odds range seems to be between 3-1 and 12-1. But some trainer/owner combinations, as can be gleaned from *Debut Winners 1998*, hit regularly with even longer odds debut horses.

CL-Class: The class ratings for each sire have been determined by using the adjusted lifetime median earnings of their progeny, again with serious consideration given to how their last two crops have performed. Median earnings are a much more reliable handicapping factor to use than either stud fees or average earnings because they more accurately represent the typical ability of a sire's progeny.

Though racing is full of examples of horses that transcend and outrun their class levels, the progeny of sires with class ratings of 1-5 will generally be competitive at the Maiden Special Weight level, variously go through their allowance conditions and, if successful there, become stakes horses.

While the progeny of sires with class ratings of 6-7 can win at the Maiden Special Weight, they will more typically win at the high Maiden Claiming level and then go on to be competitive in Allowance and higher claiming races.

The progeny of sires with 8-10 class ratings will typically be most effective in bottom level maiden and claiming events.

Once a horse has a race record, however, it is important to emphasize that his actual race performance supercedes whatever class and other ratings his sire may have initially given him.

When a class rating is followed by an asterisk* this, in most cases, means the sire still has some lower class runners, but that the rating is primarily for him as a broodmare sire where his classier daughters are now contributing to the gene pool. In general when a handicapper is faced with choosing between two otherwise equally-rated horses the nod should go to the classier horse.

TRF - Turf: This is a rating for how well a sire's progeny do on the turf. Sires whose progeny win 20 percent or better of their starts have been assigned an A rating; 15-19 percent a B rating; 10-14 percent a C rating; 5-9 percent a D rating; and 0-4 an F rating. If an A or B sire rating is underlined, this means its runners have been particularly effective their first time on the turf. When a sire is given an A- or B- rating the minus sign indicates his progeny may need a race or two on the turf before winning. Similarly, if a horse is stretching out for the first time, caution is in order, unless it figures to be the lone speed and control the pace or has at least one longer workout and a stamina rating that projects a successful stretch out.

Since opportunities vary considerably around the country for horses on the turf, the best rule of thumb is to invoke the ratings primarily in Maiden Special Weight events as well as NW1 allowance and Claiming events populated by horses that are already proven losers on the grass at the distance in question.

As was the case with maiden first-time starters the progeny of unproven sires with L, M, or U turf ratings should be viewed with caution unless the L is underlined. When a rating is followed by an Y — especially if underlined — this means the sire's progeny are likely to move up on turf courses labeled soft or yielding. When a turf rating is followed by an asterisk * this means the rating applies to the sire as a broodmare sire. A number of more obscure foreign broodmare sires (without their first generation pedigree) have been included in this edition so that handicappers have a good idea at what class level and distance their descendants have won in America.

OT - Off-Track: Establishing useful sire rating for off-track performance is difficult. This is partly because the nature of an off-track can vary considerably not only between tracks, but also at the same track because of a myriad of inconstant environmental factors. Also, with the progeny of so many sons of Mr. Prospector competing on off-tracks, it is much harder to find a single pedigree standout than it used to be.

Still, by adopting more rigorous criteria we have managed to establish sire ratings for two kinds of tracks: wet fast tracks listed as sloppy and muddy and tiring ones where the winner typically finishes six or more ticks slower than par for the level.

Sires whose progeny are running on wet tracks with fast or good times have been rated as follows: A = 22 percent and above winners; B = 19-21 percent; C = 13-18 percent; D =11-12 percent and F = 10 percent or below winners. Users of *Exploring Pedigree* will note that some of the criteria have changed. I have done this to more accurately reflect the fact that too many F-rated sires were winning to keep 12 percent as the upper cut off number for that rating. I have also often assigned a C+ rating for sires whose current performance is either below or above their respective lifetime averages of a B or a C rating.

The T ratings have been revised and expanded based on an additional year of research. In order to avoid using bad races with bad fields in them, I have continued to use only higher claiming, NW2 + allowance and stakes races with fields consisting of multiple winners to establish the tired track ratings. My criteria has been that the races had to be run six ticks or slower than par for the level to qualify as a tiring track and that at least three races on that same card had to meet that criteria. Whether the track was actually wet or not was not the determining factor. Sires with the T underlined represent the cream of the crop.

SI - Stamina Index: This index indicates how far the progeny of a particular sire are *likely* to be able to successfully run. Since breeding and genetics are as yet inexact disciplines, exceptions will occur and handicappers will have to deal with the frustration when a horse outruns its indexes The stamina ratings used here are unique in that they are based on a detailed, crop by crop, look at how far a sire's winning progeny have actually run. This approach is far more useful for handicapping purposes than employing either average winning distances or Dosage numbers. Average winning distances can be deceptive because of the fact that sprints dominate American racing. This not only results in shorter average winning distances for each sire, but also blurs important distinctions beyond a mile. Dosage is limited by its theoretical bent and the fact that sons and grandsons of *chef de races* don't necessarily run to type.

The criteria used for establishing the stamina index ratings are as follows:

An SI rating of 1 means that a sire's progeny have demonstrated the ability to win at 1 1/4 mile or more; a rating of 2 indicates a distance capacity of up to 1 1/8 mile; a rating of 3 suggests a range of up to 1 1/16 mile; an index of 4 means a stallion gets runners able to both sprint and win up to a mile; an SI rating of 5 indicates a distance capacity of 5-7 furlongs.

When a stamina index is underlined this indicates a sire's progeny are particularly effective at that distance. If the 1 is underlined, this means the sire is an extreme source of stamina. If the 4 is underlined, this means that a mile is the most frequent winning distance of a stallion's progeny. An underlined 5 indicates a stallion's progeny are especially brilliant and less likely to win beyond 6 furlongs.

A stamina index of 3 or 4 followed by an asterisk means the sire is a mixer who can contribute enough speed to his progeny to get a sprinter if the broodmare was one or, alternatively enough stamina to get a stayer if she was one. In most cases a sire with a 4* rating (such as Mr. Prospector) will be more precocious than stout. He will get lots of juvenile, sprint and mile winners, but need a mare by a very stout sire to produce a runner than can go further than 1 1/8 mile. Alternatively, a sire with a stamina rating of 3* (such as Seattle Slew) will generally be less precocious, but more likely to get a runner able to stay a 1 1/4 mile.

A stamina index of 1* (such as Kris S. and Theatrical have been assigned) indicates a stallion who is primarily a source of stamina, but who can get a debut sprint winner when bred to a precocious mare. While stallions with SI's of 1* sometimes get 6 furlong winners, their progeny generally are more effective in 6 1/2 and 7 furlong sprints.

It is important to note that the likely distance capacity of a sire's progeny should be adjusted by the stamina index of the broodmare sire, with that index counting roughly half of that of the sire's index because it is one generation further back in the horse's pedigree. Also a stamina index of 2 or 3 for both sire and broodmare sire increases the potential stamina of the foal so that it might run further than either of its parents.

Users of past ratings will note that there are quite a few more sires with SI's of 3 in this edition. This is because the SI 4 category was becoming a catchall — on the one hand including sprint sires barely able to get a mile and on the other hand sires whose progeny were on the edge of getting 1 1/16 mile.

Given the indeterminant nature of breeding, I suggest horseplayers use the SI's in this edition in such a way that no horse is asked to jump two categories from the SI of its sire when stretching out. While the progeny of sires with SI's of 5 can generally be bet against even when asked to get a mile, the 4's may get 1 1/16 mile, but are unlikely to stay 1 1/8 mile. Likewise the progeny of sires with SI's of 3 may get 1 1/8 mile, but are unlikely to stay a classic distance.

AG - Age Bias: The age bias rating indicates how precocious a sire's progeny tend to be. An AB of 2-3 suggests that a sire's runners will break their maidens as both 2 and 3-year-olds. If the 2 is underlined this means a sire's juvenile progeny are very precocious and better than 25% of them will break their maidens as 2-year-olds. If the 3 is underlined that suggests that while some of a sire's runners win as older 2-year-olds, they are more likely to break their maidens as 3-year-olds.

     Sires with AB's of 3-4 are generally not precocious, with the great majority of their progeny breaking their maidens at three and four. A few sire's(such as Devil's Bag) have been assigned AB's of 2-4 which indicates that while they generally mature later, they do hit with a couple of their juvenile first-time starters. each year

     Obviously, the best debut bets in juvenile maiden races are on horses by sires with good FTS ratings and an underlined AB of 2-3. With 3-year-old Maiden races, handicappers should prefer highly rated FTS starters with underlined AB's of 2-3.

The stud fees at the back of this edition reflect what breeders had to pay to breed their mares in 1996. Foals out of those mares represent the 2-year-olds of 1999. Horseplayers can use the stud fees to handicap for owner/breeder intent with first-time starters. If a debuting Wild Again, for example, is being run for a tag in a $8,000 maiden claiming race at Golden Gate Fields, we know something must be amiss. For given Wild Again's $35,000 stud fee in 1996, the owner/breeders are, in effect, publicly stating they are willing to take a huge loss on the horse, not even counting the additional cost of getting the horse to the races. These 1996 stud fees should also be helpful in evaluating late-developing juveniles of 1999 when they debut as 3-year-olds in 2000.

In conclusion I want to reiterate what I said in the preface to *Exploring Pedigree*. These ratings are not etched in stone. My goal has been to create a set of ratings that transcend single misleading statistics and that incorporate vital nuances previously ignored by most pedigree analysts. While I believe the ratings accurate and state-of-the-art, all the while remaining mercifully simple to use, it is important to keep in mind that there will always be an element of mystery when it comes to pedigree and that no ratings can be infallible. The study of pedigree is not now, nor will it ever be a "deterministic" science.

Mike Helm
April 1, 1999
Berkeley, California

METRIC CONVERSION

1200 meters = 6 Furlongs

1600 = 1 mile

1800 = 1⅛ mile

2000 = 1¼ mile

2400 = 1½ mile

Stallion	Sire/Broodmare Sire	FTS	CL	Trf	OT	SI	AB
Aaron's Concorde	Super Concorde/Reviewer	D	6	D	C	5	3-4
Abdos *IRE*	Arbar/Pretty Lady	U	7	M*	M	I	3-4
Abel Prospect	Mr. Prospector/Distinctive	D	7	U	C-	4	3-4
Above Normal*	Great Above/Determine Cosmic	M	6	L	M	4	2-3
Abri Fiscal	The Minstrel/King Emperor	C-	9	D	D	3	3-4
Absent Russian^^	Nijinsky II/Raise a Cup	U	8	L	M	3	2-3
Academy Award	Secretariat/Mr. Prospector	D	7	C+	D	2	3-4
Acallade	Mr. Prospector/Sir Ivor	D	7	C	CT	4*	3-4
Acaroid	Big Spruce/Intentionally	D	6*	C+*	C	3	3-4
Accipter	Damascus/King Island	C	7	C-	D	2	3-4
Accused	Alleged/Admiral's Voyage	C-	9	F	C	4	3-4
Ace of Aces		D	6	C*	D	3*	3-4
A Change For April*	Time for a Change/Alleged	L	8	M	M	4	2-3
Ack Ack	Battle Joined/Turn-to	D	4*	CY*	C	3	3-4
Ack Bold	Ack Ack/Bold Ruler	C	8	C	B	4	3-4
A Corking Limerick^^	Relaunch/Promised Land	M	8	M	L	4	2-3
Across the Field^	Roberto/Never Bend	U	8	L	M	3	3-4
Active Wear	Naskra/Le Fabuleux	U	9	M	M	2	3-4
Adbass	Northern Dancer/What A Pleasure	D	9	D	D	3*	3-4
Adios *ENG*	Silly Season/Crepello	U	7	C-	M	I	3-4
Admiral's Flag	Raise a Native/Good Counsel	M	7	U	U	3	3-4
Admiral's Shield	Crozier/Crafty Admiral	D	8	U	C	2	3-4
Adonijah *ENG*			7*	M*		I	3-4
Adorateur	L'Enjoleur/Up Spirits	U	9	M	M	4	3-4
Advance Man	Crozier/Mirabeau	D	8	D	C-	5	3-4
Advertent	Bold Bidder/Double Jay	D	8	D	C	5	3-4
Advocator	Round Table/Bull Lea	D	7*	C	C	4*	3-4
Advocatum	Advocator/Bold Bidder	D	9	F	C	4	3-4
Aegean's Bolger	Bolger/Aegean Isle	D	8	D	C-	5	3-4
Aferd	Hoist the Flag/Clandestine	D	7	C-	C	3	2-3
Affiliate	Unconscious/Raise a Native	D	7	D	C	2	3-4
Affirmed	Exclusive Native/Crafty Admiral	C	4*	B*	D	3*	3-4
Afleet	Mr. Prospector/Venetian Jester	C-	5	C-	C+T	4*	3-4
African Man	African Sky/Mandamus	D	9	M	F	4	3-4
African Sky *ENG*	Sing Sing/Nimbus	C-	8	C	D	2	3-4
After Eight	Reviewer/Tim Tam	C-	8	C	M	4	3-4
A Funny Grone	Throne/Power of Destiny	M	8	U	M	5	3-4
Again Tomorrow	Honest Pleasure/Northern Dancer	F	8	U	F	5	3-4
Age Quod Agis	Al Hattab/Pavot	D	9	F	F	4	3-4
Aggravatin'	Silent Screen/Damascus	D	8	F	F	3	3-4
Agincourt*	Capote/Conquistador Cielo	D	6	D	LT	4	2-3
Agitate	Advocator/Swaps	C	8	C+*	C	5	3-4
Ahmad *ARG*	Good Manners/Churrinche	C-	5	D	C+	2	3-4
Ahonoora *IRE*	Lorenzaccio/Martial	C	5	C*	C	4*	3-4

Stallion	Sire/Broodmare Sire	FTS	CL	Trf	OT	SI	AB
Air Forbes Won	Bold Forbes/Tobin Bronze	C-	7	C-	C+	3	2-3
Akarad FR	Labus/Abdos	D	7	C	C	2	3-4
Aksar ENG		C	7	C-	M	4	3-4
Akureyri	Buckpasser/Northern Dancer	C	6*	C*	C-	4	3-4
Alarmer	Alydar/Al Hattab	D	10	D	D	3	3-4
Alaskan Frost	Copelan/Far North	C	6	C	C+	3	2-3
Alden's Ace	John Alden/Bold Ambition	D	9	D	D	4	3-4
Alehouse	Porterhouse/Royal Serendade	D	9	C-	D	4	3-4
Alezan Dancer	Nijinsky II/Le Fabuleux	D	8	C-	C	4	3-4
Alfaari	Danzig/Alhambra	M	8	M	M	4	2-3
Alhajras VEN		D	7	C-	M	2	3-4
Al Hareb	El Gran Senor/Prince Tenderfoot	D	8	C-	M	1	2-3
Al Hattab	The Axe II/Abernant	D	6	C-*	C-	3*	3-4
Alias Smith			7	C*		2	3-4
Alibi Ike	Alydar/Roi Dagobert	U	9	U	M	4	3-4
Alhijaz ENG	Midyan/Welsh Pageant	M	7	M	M	4	2-3
Alla Breva	Stop the Music/Third Martini	C-	8	D	C	4	3-4
All Done John	JohnAlden/Pukka Gent	D	9	D	C-	4	3-4
Alleged	Hoist The Flag/Prince John	C-	3*	BY*	C-	1	3-4
Allegedly Wild	Alleged/Cannonade	U	7	M	M	1	3-4
Allen's Alydar	Alydar/Sea Bird	D	7	CY	D	2	3-4
Allen's Prospect	Mr. Prospector/Swaps	C	6	C	C+T	4*	2-3
All For Fun	One For All/Galoot	D	9	D	F	4	3-4
All Gone^	Fappiano/Buckpasser	M	8	U	M	4*	2-3
Allied Flag	Danzig/Hoist the Flag	M	8	M	M	4	3-4
All Kings	King's Bishop/Dead Ahead	D	8	D	C	5	3-4
All of a Sudden	Ramsinga/Tudor Grey	U	8	U	M	4	3-4
All Signs Go	Tilt Up/Our Native	M	8	M	M	4	2-3
All Thee Power	Lines of Power/Al Hattab	C-	7	C	C+	3	3-4
All Worked Up	Cox's Ridge/Full Out	D	8	D	C	3	3-4
Ally Runner	Alydar/Round Table	D	8	D	C-	4	3-4
Al Mamoon	Believe It/Secretariat	C-	8	C+	C	3	2-3
Alnaab*	Mr. Prospector/Hail to Reason	D	8	M	C	3	3-4
Al Nasr FR	Lyphard/Caro	D	7*	C*	C-	2	3-4
Aloha Prospector	Native Prospector/Hawaii	C	6	C-	C	4	2-3
Aloma's Ruler	Iron Ruler/Native Charger	C-	7	D	CT	3	3-4
Along Came Jones	High Tribute/West Coast Scout	C-	8	U	D	3	3-4
Alphabatim IRE	Verbatim/Grey Dawn II	C-	8	C-	D	2	3-4
Al Sabin^	Alydar/Lyphard	M	8	M	M	3	3-4
Altazarr^^	Relaunch/Knights Choice	M	9	M	L	4	2-3
Alwasheek ENG	Sadler's Wells/Habitat	U	6	L	M	1	3-4
Alwasmi GER	Northern Dancer/Bustino	D	6	C+	C	2	3-4
Always Fair FR	Danzig/Buckpasser	M	6	L	M	4*	2-3
Always Gallant	Gallant Romeo/Sadair	C-	8	D*	C	4	3-4
Always Run Lucky	What Luck/Delta Judge	D	8	D	C	4	3-4

Stallion	Sire/Broodmare Sire	FTS	CL	Trf	OT	SI	AB
Alwuhush *GER*	Nureyev/King Emperor	C+	6	C	D	4*	2-3
Alybel^^	Alydar/Graustark	U	10	U	M	3	3-4
Alybrave	Alydar/Bold and Brave	D	9	U	D	4	3-4
Alydad	Alydar/Francis S	D	10	D	D	4	3-4
Alydar	Raise a Native/On-and-On	D	3*	C-*	B	3*	3-4
Aly Dark	Alydar/Jig Time	C-	8	C	C	4	3-4
Alydar's Prophecy	Alydar/Cyane	U	9	U	L	4	3-4
Alydeed *	Shadeed/Alydar	C	6	M	C	4*	3-4
Alyfoe	Alydar/Ridan	D	7	U	C+	3	3-4
Alymagic	Alydar/Never Bend	D	8	C-	C	3	3-4
Alyone	Alydar/Rock Talk	D	9	U	C+	3	3-4
Aly North	Alydar/Northern Dancer	D	7	C+	D	3*	3-4
Alypol	Alydar/Donut King	U	9	U	M	4	3-4
Aly Rat	Alydar/Best Turn	C-	8	D	D	4	3-4
Alysheba	Alydar/ Lt. Stevens	F	6	C+	C	2	3-4
Alytanic	Titanic/Subpet	D	9	M	D	4	3-4
Alzao *IRE*	Lyphard/Sir Ivor	C	4	C+	D	1	3-3
Am All Charged Up	Native Charger/Turn-to	D	10	U	C+	5	3-4
Amazen Cat	Zen/Jungle Savage	U	10	U	M	3	3-4
Amazing Prospect	Fappiano/Lucky Debonair	D	9	D	C	4*	3-4
Amber Morn			8	C*		3	3-4
Amber Pass	Pass Catcher/Somerset	D	6	D	C-	3	3-4
Amber Sioux	Raise a Native/Lyphard	L	7	M	M	4	2-3
Ambessa*	Holy War/Eager Eagle	M	7	U	M	5	3-4
American Artist	Valid Appeal/Flag Raiser	M	10	M	L	5	2-3
American Chance^^	Cure the Blues/Seattle Slew	L	6	M	L	4	2-3
American Diablo	To America/Sibelius	M	8	M	M	5	3-4
American General	Danzig/Creme dela Creme	U	7	U	M	4*	3-4
American Legion	Grey Legion/The Irishman	D	9	F	C	5	3-4
American Standard	In Reality/Bald Eagle	C+	7	D	CT	4	2-3
America's Friend*	Copelan/On-and-On	M	7	U	M	4	2-3
Amerrico Double	Amerrico/Spring Double	D	7	C+	C	2	3-4
Amerrico's Bullet	Amerrico/Gala Harry	M	8	U	M	4	3-4
Americus *IRE*	Sallust/Ragusa	D	7	C+	C	1	3-4
Ameri Valay^	Carnivalay/Amerrico	M	8	M	M	3	2-3
Amorelu	Conquistador Cielo/Nijinsky II	M	9	M	M	4	3-4
A. M. Swinger*	Swing Till Dawn/No Robbery	U	10	M	M	2	3-4
An Act	Pretense/Tatan	D	8	C*	C	2	3-4
A Native Danzig	Danzig/Raise a Native	C-	7	C-	C+	3	3-4
Ancestral *BRZ*	Habitat/Crowned Prince	C	7	C*	C	4	3-4
Ancient Oaks*	Fappiano/Drone	M	9	U	L	4	3-4
Andover Man*	Mr. Redoy/Groton	M	7	U	M	3	2-3
An Eldorado	Vaguely Noble/Double Jay	D	8	D	C	4	3-4
Angel Who	Raise a Native/Fleet Nasrullah	M	10	U	M	4	3-4
Anjiz^^	Nureyev/Foolish Pleasure	M	7	L	M	4	2-3

Stallion	Sire/Broodmare Sire	FTS	CL	Trf	OT	SI	AB
Ankara *SAF*	Northern Dancer/Forli	C	8	C	C-	3*	3-4
Annihilate'em	Hempen/Star Rover	D	8	D*	C	3	3-4
Ann's Intention		U	8	M	U	2	3-4
Another Reef	Plum Bold/Jig Time	C	7	C	C	3	2-3
Anshan *ENG*	Persian Bold/Manado	U	6	M	M	2	3-4
Anticipating	Bold Ruler/To Market	C-	7	D	C	3	3-4
Apalachee	Round Table/Nantallah	C	5*	C+	C	4*	2-3
A. P. Indy*	Seattle Slew/Secretariat	C-	3	B+	C	3*	3-4
Appeal for Justice	Valid Appeal/Mr. Prospector	C-	8	U	C	4	2-3
Apollo^^	Falstaff/Tumble Wind	L	6	M	M	4	2-3
April Axe	The Axe II/Bold Lad	D	10	C	F	3	2-3
Apuron	Mr. Prospector/Prince John	M	8	L	M	3	3-4
Arabian Sheik	Nijinsky II/Damascus	D	9	D	C	4	3-4
Aragon *ENG*	Mummy's Pet/Great Nephew	C-	7	C	U	4	3-4
Aras an Uachtarain	Habitat/Nijinsky II	D	8	C-	C	4	3-4
Arazi	Blushing Groom/Northern Dancer	C-	7	C	M	4*	2-3
Arctic Blitz	Son of Briartic/Prince of Reason	C-	8	D	C	4	2-3
Arctic Groom	Blushing Groom/Bold Lad	C	9	D	CT	5	3-4
Arctic Native	North Tower/Restless Native	M	9	U	M	5	3-4
Arctic Tern *FR*	Sea Bird/Hasty Road	D	6	C+*	F	3	3-4
Ardkinglass *ENG*	Green Desert/Sharpen Up	M	7	C	U	4	2-3
Ardross *ENG*			7	C*		1	3-4
Ariva	Riva Ridge/Bold Ruler	B	8	U	F	4	2-3
Arms and the Man	Salutely/Proudest Roman	D	8	U	T	3*	3-4
Arrived on Time	Codex/King's Bishop	M	10	M	M	4	3-4
Artaius *IR*	Round Table/Stylish Pattern		6	C+*		2	3-4
Artichoke	Jacinto/Hill Prince	D	9	D	CT	3	3-4
Artic Twister	Son of Briartic/Sylarian	M	8	U	L	4	2-3
Artistry *SAF*	Budapest/Casablanca	D	10	C	C	1	3-4
Art of Dawn	Grey Dawn II/Arts and Letter	M	9	M	L	3	3-4
Art of Living^	Alydar/Nervous Energy	M	9	U	M	3	3-4
Arts and Letters	Ribot/Battlefield	F	7*	C-	C	3	3-4
A Run	Empery/Jacinto	D	10	C	D	4	3-4
Asa Yolson *NZ*		D	7*	C*	D	3	3-4
Ascot Knight	Danzig/Better Bee	F	7	C	C	1	3-4
Ask Clarence *PERU*	Buckpasser/Herbager	D	7	D	C	4	3-4
Ask Me	Ack Ack/Tom Rolfe	D	8	C	D	2	3-4
Ask Muhammad	Al Hattab/T.V. Lark	C-	10	D	C-	3	3-4
Aspro	Double Edge Sword/Al Hattab	D	9	D	F	4	3-4
Assagai Jr	Assagai/Revoked	D	8*	C-*	D	2	3-4
Assault Landing	Buckfinder/Solo Landing	F	7*	F	D	4	3-4
Assert *IRE*	Be My Guest/Sea Bird	D	6	B*	D	1	3-4
Assignment Missed	Fire Dancer/Steel Viking	D	9	D	D	4	3-4
Astro	Five Star Flight/Mr. Prospector	M	8	U	L	4	2-3
Astronef *FR*	Be My Guest/Mill Reef	C	7	C+	D	3*	3-4

Stallion	Sire/Broodmare Sire	FTS	CL	Trf	OT	SI	AB
A Sure Hit	Ack Ack/Better Self	D	8	D	D	4	3-4
At Full Feather	Spectacular Bid/Secretariat	D	10	F	C	5	3-4
A Title	Sir Ivor/Swaps	D	8	U	F	4	3-4
Atmosphere	Nijinsky II/Round Table	F	10	F	D	5	3-4
A Toast to Junius	Raise Your Glass/Prince John	C	7	D	F	5	2-3
At the Threshold	Norcliffe/Vertex	D	7	C-	C-	3	3-4
Attribute	Exclusive Native/Minnesota Mac	D	8	D	C	5	3-4
Aubrey's Goal	First and Goal/Taga	C	9	D	D	5	3-4
Auction Ring *IRE*	Bold Bidder/Hooplah	D	7	C*	D	3	3-4
August Agent	Nijinsky II/What Luck	U	9	M	M	3	3-4
Au Point	Lyphard/Princequillo	D	8	C-	CT	3	3-4
Aurium	Mr. Prospector/Creme dela Creme	C	9	D	C	4	3-4
Authenticity	In Reality/Cockrullah	C	7	D	CT	4	3-4
Autocracy	Alydar/Lt. Stevens	D	7	D	C	4	3-4
Avatar	Graustark/Mount Marcy	F	6*	C+*	C-	3	3-4
Avenger M.	Staunch Avenger/Gallant Native	C	8	F	CT	5	3-4
Avenging Storm	Sham/Fleet Nasrullah	D	8	D	F	4	3-4
Avenue of Flags	Seattle Slew/Pass the Glass	B	5	C	C+T	3	2-3
Avies Copy	Lord Avie/Iron Ruler	F	6	D	C-	3	3-4
Avion Francais	Super Concorde/Exclusive Native	C-	7	D	C	4	3-4
Avodire	Nijinsky II/Princequillo	D	8	D	C	3	3-4
Awamasa	Relaunch/Quack	M	7	M	L	3	3-4
Aye's Turn	Best Turn/Mito	C	9	F	C	4	2-3
Ayman	Raja Baba/Dr. Fager	C-	9	D	C	4	3-4
Azzardo	Raise a Native/Tom Rolfe	C-	8	U	C	5	3-4
Baatish*	Slew o'Gold/Key to the Mint	U	8	M	M	3	3-4
Babas Fables *ARG*			6	M*		1	3-4
Baby Slewy	Seattle Slew/Exclusive Native	F	8	D	C	5	3-4
Back Alley	Alydar/Ack Ack	C	10	U	C	4	2-3
Badger Land *SAF*	Codex/Racing Room	C	8	D	CT	3	2-3
Baederwood	Tentam/Northern Dancer	C	6	D	C	4	2-3
Baffle			7	M*		4	3-4
Bag*	Devil's Bag/Mr. Prospector	C+	7	U	CT	4	2-3
Bagdad Road^	Strawberry Road/The Minstrel	M	7	L	M	3*	3-4
Bahri^	Riverman Nijinsky	M	7	L	M	3*	2-3
Bailjumper	Damascus/Royal Vale	D	8	D	C-	3	3-4
Baillamont	Blushing Groom/Shoemaker	D	5*	C	D	1	3-4
Bairn *ENG*	Northern Baby/Sir Ivor	D	7	C	M	2	3-4
Bakharoff *FR*	The Minstrel/Native Royalty	C	6	C	U	4*	2-3
Balderson^	Vice Regent/Olden Times	M	8	M	M	3	3-4
Baldski	Nijinsky II/Bald Eagle	C-	6*	C+Y	C	4*	2-3
Ballachashel *FR*	Vice Regent/Counterpoint	D	7	C	C	1	3-4
Balla Cove *IRE*	Ballad Rock/Sassafras	L	5	L	L	4	2-3
Ballad Rock *IRE*	Bold Lad/True Rocket	C	6	C	M	4	2-3
Ballindaggin	Noble Nashua/Stop the Music	U	7	U	M	4	3-4

Stallion	Sire/Broodmare Sire	FTS	CL	TRF	OT	SI	AB
Ballydoyle	Northern Dancer/New Providence	F	9	D	C-	4	3-4
Ballymore ENG			6	C*		3	3-4
Baltic Dancer	Nijinsky II/Bagdad	D	10	C	D	4	3-4
Balzac BRZ	Buckpasser/Double Jay	D	7*	C*	C	3	3-4
Band Practice	Stop the Music/Young Emperor	C	7	D	C+	3	2-3
Bankbook^^	Mr. Prospector/Private Account	M	8	U	L	3	3-4
Banner Bob ARG	Herculean/Bolinas Boy	D	8	D	C	4	3-4
Banquet Table	Round Table/Barbizon	D	8	C*	C-	3	3-4
Barachois	Northern Dancer/Chop Chop	D	7	CY*	C	1	3-4
Barathea IRE	Sadler's Wells/Habitat	U	5	L	M	1	3-4
Barbaric Spirit	Barbizon/Fleet Nasrullah	D	8	F	F	4	3-4
Barberstown	Gummo/Bolinas Boy	D	7	C	C-	3	3-4
Barcelona	Key to the Mint/Bold Ruler	C	8	D	C	4	3-4
Bargain Day	Prove it/Toulouse Lautrec	C	8	C+	C-	4	3-4
Barkerville	Mr. Prospector/Nijinsky II	U	8	M	M	2	3-4
Barn Wife			7		M	4	3-4
Baron O'Dublin	Irish Ruler/Gyro	D	10	D	C-	4	3-4
Baronius BRZ			6	C		1	3-4
Barrera	Raise a Native/Chieftain	C	7	C*	C	3	3-4
Barswitch	Lombardi/Key to the Mint	U	9	M	M	4	3-4
Barula	Raja Baba/Ribot	D	10	C	C-	4	3-4
Basic Rate	Valdez/Foolish Pleasure	U	9	M	M	4	2-3
Basil Boy ENG	Jimsum/Shiny Tenth	M	7	L	M	4	3-4
Basim^^	Capote/Far North	M	9	M	M	4	3-4
Basket Weave	Best Turn/Buckpasser	D	7	D	C+	4	2-3
Bassenwaithe AUS			6	M*		3	3-4
Bastogne	Sir Ivor/Grey Dawn II	D	7	M	D	3*	2-3
Bates Motel	Sir Ivor/TV Lark	D	6	C+	CT	3	3-4
Batonnier	His Majesty/Dumpty Humpty	C	6	C+	C	3	2-3
Batshoof ENG	Sadler's Wells/Habitat	M	4	C	M	3*	3-4
Battle Call	Native Charger/The Axe II	D	9	D	F	4	3-4
Battle Creek^^	Alydar/Bold Forbes	M	8	U	L	4	3-4
Battle Launch	Relaunch/Battle Joined	C-	9	C-	CT	4	3-4
Battle Play	Nureyev/Quack	M	9	L	M	2	3-4
Batty	Batonnier/The Scoundrel	M	9	C+	M	2	3-4
Bay Express IRE			6	C*		4	3-4
Baynoun FR	Sassafras/Busted	M	4	C+	M	1	3-4
Bayou Hebert	Hoist the Flag/Damascus	C-	7	C	C	3	2-3
B.C. Emblem	Dogwood Passport/Jet Sail	U	9	U	U	4	2-3
Be a Native	Exclusive Native/Cavan	D	8	C-*	F	4	3-4
Be a Prospect	New Prospect/Cyane	C	8	D	B+	4	2-3
Bean Bag	Olympiad King/Inverness Drive	M	8	M	M	4	3-4
Bear Branch	Alydar/Forli	D	9	D	C-	4	3-4
Bear Hunt	Naskra/Gun Bow	D	8	F	C-	4	2-3
Be a Rullah	Raise a Native/Hail to Reason	D	8	D*	DT	4	3-4

Stallion	Sire/Broodmare Sire	FTS	CL	Trf	OT	SI	AB
Beat Inflation	Crozier/Quibu	C	7	F	CT	4	2-3
Beaudelaire *FR*	Nijinsky II/Habitat	F	7	C*	F	1	3-4
Beau Genius	Bold Ruckus/Viceregal	C+	6	CY	C+	3	2-3
Beau Groton	Groton/Beau Purple	C+	7	D	F	4	3-4
Beau's Eagle	Golden Eagle/Maribeau	C-	8	C	F	4	3-4
Beau's Leader	Beau's Eagle/Crowned Prince	U	9	U	C	4	3-4
Beau Monde *IR*		M	7	L	LT	3	3-4
Becker*	Danzig/Secretariat	M	8	M	M	4	2-3
Bedford			7	C*		2	3-4
Bee's Prospector*	Mr. Prospector/King's Bishop	U	7	U	M	4	2-3
Bejilla	Quadrangle/Dancer's Image	D	8	D	D	3	3-4
Bel Bolide	Bold Bidder/Graustark	C	8	C	C	4	3-4
Belek	Irish Tower/Gallant Lad	C	7	M	C+T	4	2-3
Belfort *ENG*	Tyrant/Gilles de Retz	D	8	C-	M	4	3-4
Believe It	In Reality/Buckpasser	D	7	C*	C	2	3-4
Believe the Queen	Believe It/Raise a Native	D-	6	C*	CT	3	3-4
Bello	Stop Gap/Royal Union	M	8	M	M	4	3-4
Bellypha *JPN*	Lyphard/ Le Fabuleux	F	6*	C+*	M	2	3-4
Belmez *FR**	El Gran Senor/Top Ville	D	6	D	M	1	3-4
Belmont			7	C*		4	3-4
Belong to Me^^	Danzig/Exclusive Native	B	5	C+	C	4*	2-3
Belted Earl	Damascus/Nantallah	C-	7	F	C	4	3-4
Be My Chief *ENG*	Chief's Crown/Sir Ivor	D	7	C	D	3*	2-3
Be My Guest *IRE*	Northern Dancer/Tudor Minstrel	D	5*	C+*	D	3*	3-4
Benalidar	Alydar/Maribeau	D	10	U	D	4	3-4
Benefactor	Bold Bidder/Prince John	U	8	M	M	2	3-4
Ben Fab	Le Fabuleux/Nearctic	D	7	C-	D	1	3-4
Benny Q.	Irish River/Sir Ivor	D	9	D	C	4	2-3
Beowulf	Raise a Native/Beau Gar	D	8	F	C	3	3-4
Bering *FR*	Arctic Tern/Lyphard	C	6	C+	F	2	3-4
Bertrando^^	Skywalker/Buffalo Lark	B	6	L	L	4*	2-3
Best Native	Exclusive Native/Get Around	C	6	F	C	5	2-3
Best of Both	J.O. Tobin/Dark Star	C	7	D	C	4	3-4
Best Turn	Turn-to/Swaps	C	7	C-*	C+	2	3-4
Bet Big	Distinctive/Majestic Prince	C	7	D	C+	3	2-3
Bet on the Blurr	Murr the Blurr/Neke Jr.	M	10	M	M	5	3-4
Better Arbitor	Better Bee/Nearctic	D	7	D	C	4	3-4
Bet Twice	Sportin' Life/Dusty Canyon	C-	7	C	CT	3	3-4
Beveled *ENG*	Sharpen Up/High Echelon	C	6	C	C	4	3-4
Beyond the Mint	Key to the Mint/Nijinsky II	D	6	D	C	2	3-4
Bicker	Round Table/Court Martial	D	8	C-*	D	4	3-4
Bidder Be Better	Anxious Bidder/Special Secret	L	7	M	M	4	2-3
Bidding Proud^	Explosive Bid/Proud Birdie	M	8	M	M	3	3-4
Bien Bien^^	Manila/Graustark	U	6	L	M	2	3-4
Big Bold Sefa	Bold Reasoning/Dark Star	C+	7	F	C	4	3-4

Stallion	Sire/Broodmare Sire	FTS	CL	Trf	OT	SI	AB
Big Burn	Never Bend/Sailor	D	7	C*	C	4	2-3
Big Chill	It's Freezing/Cornish Prince	D	9	U	T	4	3-4
Big Event	In Reality/Restless Wind	C-	7	U	C	4	3-4
Big John Taylor	Speak John/Hasty Road	C	8	D	D	4	3-4
Big Kohinoor	Irish Ruler/Crozier	C	8	D	C	5	3-4
Big Lark BRZ			7	C*		4	3-4
Big Leaguer	Bold Bidder/Greek Ship	D	8	C-	F	4	3-4
Big Mukora	Mr. Prospector/Rambunctious	D	6	F	C+	4	2-3
Big Pistol	Romeo/Whitesburg	C	7	C-*	C+	3	3-4
Big Presentation	In Reality/Tatan	C	8	D	C	4	3-4
Big Sal*	In Reality/Olden Times	M	7	M	M	4	2-3
Big Spruce	Herbager/Prince John	D	7	C*	C	1	3-4
Big Stanley	Distinctive Pro/Grey Dawn II	C	7	D	C	4	3-4
Bigstone IRE	Last Tycoon/Posse	M	7	L	M	4	3-4
Big Ted K.	Distinctive/Exceller	L	9	U	L	4	2-3
Big Woods	Vice Regent/Pia Star	U	8	L	U	3	3-4
Bikala FR	Kalamoun/Sea Bird	C	6	C	M	3	3-4
Billy Blue	Sunday Guest/Bold N Bizarre	D	8	D	C	5	3-4
Bimini Captain	Hail to Reason/My Babu	C	8	C	F	4	2-3
Binalong^^	Known Fact/Alydar	M	8	M	L	4	3-4
B. in Time	Don B./Boldnesian	U	7	L	M	3	3-4
Bionic Light	Majestic Light/Best Turn	C-	7	C-*	DT	2	3-4
Bionic Prospect	Miswaki/Best Turn	C+	8	U	M	3	2-3
Birdies Dee Cee	Proud Birdie/Raise a Bid	U	9	M	M	3	3-4
Birdonthewire^	Proud Birdie/Jontilla	M	7	U	M	4	2-3
Biscay AUS			7	M*		4	3-4
Bishop Northcraft	King's Bishop/Northern Dancer	D	6	M	C	4	3-4
Bishop's Choice	King's Bishop/Nearctic	C-	8	B*	C	3	3-4
Bismarck II ENG			7	C*		2	3-4
Black is Beautiful	Quack/Olden Times	D	8	D	C	4	3-4
Black Mackee	Captain Courageous/Six Fifteen	C	8	C	C	4	2-3
Black Moonshine	Mt. Livermore/Cornish Prince	M	8	M	C	4	2-3
Black Prospector	Mr. Prospector/Distinctive	M	9	U	M	4	3-4
Black Tie Affair	Miswaki/Al Hattab	C	6	C+	BT	3*	2-3
Blade	Bold Ruler/Princequillo	C	7	C+*	C	3	2-3
Blair's Cove	Bucksplasher/Kaskaskia	D	7	M	C	3	3-4
Blajic	Blade/Poppy Jay	C-	7	D	D	4	3-4
Blakeney ENG	Hethersett/Hornbeam	D	5*	C+Y	C	1	3-4
Blare of Trumpets^^	Fit to Fight/Northern Dancer	M	7	U	L	3	3-4
Blazing Bart	The Bart/Prove Out	D	7	C+	D	3	3-4
Blazing Ryder	Red Ryder/Tampa Trouble	C	8	C	F	4	3-4
Blazing Saddles AUS	Todman/Lady Simone	U	6	M*	M	1	3-4
Bligh	Damascus/Never Bend	C-	10	U	C-	5	3-4
Blind Spot	Majestic Light/Buckpasser	M	7	C	D	2	3-4
Blini VEN	Nureyev/Hail to Reason	D	7	C-	F	2	3-4

Stallion	Sire/Broodmare Sire	FTS	CL	Trf	OT	SI	AB
Blood Royal	Ribot/Dedicate	D	7	C*	C	2	3-4
Bluebird *IRE*	Storm Bird/Sir Ivor	C-	6	C	D	2	2-3
Blue Bombay	Marfa/Cold Reception	M	8	M	M	3	3-4
Blue Buckaroo	Buckaroo/Sir Ivor	C	7	C-	D	3	3-4
Blue Cashmere *ENG*		M	7*	C*	M	5	3-4
Blue Ensign	Hoist the Flag/Bold Ruler	D	7	C	CT	2	3-4
Blue Eyed Davy	Viking Spirit/Blue Prince	C-	9	F	C	5	3-4
Blue Grass Magic	Cox's Ridge/Tom Rolfe	D	8	D	C+	3	3-4
Blue Heat^^	Explodent/Diplomat Way	M	8	L	M	3	3-4
Blue Orca	Caerleon/Silver Shark	U	10	L	M	2	3-4
Blue Quadrant	Quadrangle/Sword Dancer	D	7	F	D	4	3-4
Blues Parade	Sir Ivor/Dr. Fager	C-	8	C*	C	2	3-4
Blushing Groom	Red God/Wild Risk	C	3*	CY	C+	3	3-4
Blushing John	Blushing Groom/Prince John	D	7	CY	D	2	3-4
Blushing Stage	Blushing Groom/Stage Door Johnny	U	8	L	M	1	3-4
Blush Rambler^	Blushing Groom/Alleged	M	7	L	M	3*	3-4
Bob Back *IRE*	Roberto/Carry Back	U	7	C-	M	1	3-4
Bobby Ben	Our Native/Groton	C	7	C-	C	2	<u>2-3</u>
Bob's Dusty	Bold Commander/Count Fleet	D	7	C*	C	3	3-4
Boca Rio	Mr. Prospector/Native Dancer	D	7	F	C+	4	3-4
Boitron	Faraway Sun/Prudent	D	7	C	D	4	3-4
Bojima	Wajima/Hail to Reason	D	10	D	C	4	3-4
Bold Agent	Bold Bidder/Rasper II	D	7	C*	F	3	3-4
Bold Arrangement *ENG*	Persian Bold/Floribunda	D	7	C	B	3*	3-4
Bold Badgett	Damascus/Never Bend	<u>C</u>	6	U	C	4	<u>2-3</u>
Bold Bidder	Bold Ruler/To Market	C-	7	CY*	C	3	3-4
Bold Conquest	Bold Bidder/Dedicate	D	8	D	C	5	3-4
Bold Dash for Cash	Bold Dash/Rickey Lee	M	8	U	MT	3	3-4
Bold Ego	Bold Tactics/Bullin	C	9	D	C	5	<u>2-3</u>
Bold Executive	Bold Ruckus/Victoria Park	C+	5	C-	C+	3	<u>2-3</u>
Bold Forbes	Irish Castle/Commodore	C-	7	C+*	CT	3	3-4
Bold Hour	Bold Ruler/Mr. Music	C	5*	C+*	C+	1	3-4
Bold Johu	Jolly Johu/Bold Monarch	C	8	D	CT	3	3-4
Bold Josh	Tentam/Boldnesian	C	7	D	C	4	3-4
Bold Lad *IRE*	Bold Ruler/Democratic	C	4	C	C	3*	2-3
Bold Laddie	Boldnesian/Vertex	D	7	D	C+	3	3-4
Bold N Bizarrre	Graustark/Bold Ruler	D	8	D	C	4	3-4
Boldnesian	Bold Ruler/Polynesian	C	6	C*	B	3*	3-4
Bold Pac Man	Nasty and Bold/Our Native	U	8	M	M	3	3-4
Bold Play	Chieftain/Needles	D	8	D	C+	3	2-3
Bold Reason	Hail To Reason/Djeddah	C	7	C	C	4	3-4
Bold Relic	Bold Monarch/Jet Traffic	C	8	D	C	5	3-4
Bold Revenue	Bold Ruckus/I'm for More	D	5	D	C+<u>T</u>	4	2-3
Bold Roberto*	Roberto/Speak John	U	10	L	M	2	3-4
Bold Ruckus	Boldnesian/Raise a Native	C	4	CY	C+	3	2-3

Stallion	Sire/Broodmare Sire	FTS	CL	Trf	OT	SI	AB
Bold Ruler	Nasrullah/Discovery	B	5	C	C	4*	2-3
Bold Run *FR*	Tyrant/Bold Reason	D	7	C-	C	4	3-4
Bold T. Jay	Island Agent/Bold Combatant	D	8	U	C+	4	3-4
Bold Tropic	Plum Bold/Herculaneum	C	8	C+*	C	2	3-4
Bolger	Damascus/Round Table	C	8	C-*	C	3	3-4
Bolting Holme	Noholme II/Tom Rolfe	U	6	M	C+	4	3-4
Bombay Duck	Nashua/Tudor Minstrel	D	7	D	C	3	3-4
Boone's Mill^	Carson City/Secretariat	L	6	M	L	4	2-3
Border Guard	Nureyev/On Your Mark II	M	8	M	M	4	3-4
Borzoi	Round Table/Dr. Fager	D	8	C	C	4	3-4
Boss Koss	Dr. Blum/Stella Aurata	L	9	U	M	5	2-3
Botanic^	Mr. Prospector/The Minstrel	M	8	L	M	4	3-4
Boulder Dam	Seattle Slew/Nijinsky II	C	8	M	C+	3	3-4
Boundary^^	Danzig/Damascus	L	6	L	M	4	2-3
Boundary Ridge^	Broad Brush/Northern Jove	M	6	M	M	3	2-3
Bounding Basque	Grey Dawn II/Jean Pierre	D	7	C-	C	2	3-4
Boundlessly	Marfa/Avatar	U	8	M	M	3	3-4
Bourbon St. Dancer	Staff Writer/King of the Tudors	M	8	M	M	4	2-3
Boutinierre	Bold Forbes/Bagdad	D	9	C-	C-	4	3-4
Bowler's Wharf	Pass the Tab/Soy Numero Uno	M	7	U	M	4	3-4
Boyish Charm	Roberto/Majestic Prince	C	8	M	C	4	2-4
Boys Nite Out	Cutlass/Bolinas Boy	D	8	D	C	4	3-4
Brass Minister	Deputy Minister/Speak John	M	7	M	M	3	3-4
Brave Lad	Damascus/Protanto	C	9	U	C+	4	2-3
Brave Shot *ENG*	Bold Bidder/Sir Gaylord	C	6	C-	C	2	3-4
Bravoure	Recusant/Within Hail	M	8	U	L	3	3-4
Brazen Brother	Boldnesian/Spy Song	C-	7	C-	CT	5	3-4
Breeders Bonus	Seattle Slew/In Reality	C-	6	C+	CT	3	3-4
Breezing On	Stevward/Raise a Native	C	7	F	C	5	2-3
Breezing On *IND*	Breezing On/Hoist the Flag	M	9	U	M	5	3-4
Brent's Danzig	Danzig/Crozier	M	7	M	M	4	2-3
Brett's Lick	No Sale George/Chidester	M	9	U	M	4	3-4
Briartic	Nearctic/Round Table	D	6*	C*	C-	3	2-3
Briar Bend			7	C*		2	3-4
Briar Wind	Briartic/Blakeney	D	9	M	C-	4	3-4
Brief Ruckus	Bold Ruckus/Be My Guest	C	6	B	C	3	3-4
Brief Truce *IRE*	Irish River/Northern Dancer	M	4	L	M	4*	3-4
Brigadier Gerard *ENG*	Queen's Hussar/Prince Chevalier	C	5	C*	C	3*	2-3
Bright Torch	Torsion/Le Fabuleux	F	10	M	C	3	3-4
Brilliant Leader	Irish River/Northern Dancer	M	9	M	M	4	3-4
Brilliant Protege	Secretariat/Ribot	D	8	C	C	2	3-4
Brilliant Sandy	Crimson Satan/Rasper II	D	8	C	C	4	3-4
Brio Cielo	Conquistador Cielo/What a Pleasure	M	6	M	L	4	3-4
Broad Brush	Ack Ack/Hoist the Flag	C+	3	C+	C+T	4*	2-3
Broadway Forli			7	C*		3*	3-4

Stallion	Sire/Broodmare Sire	FTS	CL	Trf	OT	SI	AB
Broadway's Top Gun	Full Pocket/Broadway Forli	M	10	U	M	4	3-4
Brocco^^	Kris S./Aurelius	M	6	M	M	2	2-3
Brogan	Nijinsky II/Round Table	D	7	CY	F	2	3-4
Broken Hearted	Dara Monarch/Busted	D	7	C	M	1	3-4
Brookover	Irish Castle/Commodore	U	8	U	C-	4	3-4
Brother Liam	Hail to Reason/Coco La Terreur	M	8	U	U	4	3-4
Brown Arc	Alleged/Mount Marcy	M	7	C+	M	1	3-4
Brunswick^	Private Account/Mr. Prospector	M	7	U	L	3	2-<u>3</u>
Buck Aly	Prince Aly/Rose Argent	D	7	U	M	5	2-3
Buckaroo	Buckpasser/No Robbery	C	6	C	CT	2	2-3
Buckbean	Buckfinder/Tom Rolfe	U	7	U	M	3	3-4
Buckfinder	Buckpasser/Native Dancer	D	7	C-*	C	3*	3-4
Buckhar^^	Dahar/The Axe II	U	7	L	M	1	2-3
Buck Hill			8	C*		2	3-4
Buck Island	Buckpasser/Olden Times	F	10	C-	D	4	3-4
Buckley Boy	Alydar/Quack	D	7	D	C	2	3-4
Buckpasser	Tom Fool/War Admiral	C	1*	C-*	D	1	3-4
Bucksplasher	Buckpasser/Northern Dancer	C	6	BY	CT	2	3-4
Buddy	Mr. Prospector/Grey Dawn II	M	6	M	L	<u>4</u>	2-3
Buddy Breezin	J.O Tobin/Executioner	M	9	M	M	4	<u>2</u>-3
Buen Jefe	Delaware Chief/No Prevue	D	9	F	M	5	<u>2</u>-3
Buffalo Lark	T.V. Lark/Degage	C	6	C-*	B	2	3-4
Bulldar	Alydar/L'Enjoleur	D	10	M	C	4	3-4
Bumi Bay *CHI*			6*	C		2	3-4
Bupers	Double Jay/War Admiral	C	7*	C-*	C	3*	3-4
Bureau	Secretariat/Ribot	D	8	C	C	2	3-4
Burkaan *FR*	Irish River/Bold Hour	D	6	C+	C	2	3-4
Burn Annie	J. Burns/Figonero	M	9	M	M	5	2-3
Burnt Hills	Conquistador Cielo/Bold Hour	C	7	D	C	3	<u>2</u>-3
Burts Star	Star de Naskra/Bold Monarch	M	8	U	M	5	3-4
Businessisbusiness	Secretariat/Northern Dancer	D	8	C+	C-	2	3-4
Busted *ENG*	Crepello/Vimy	F	4	C*	C	<u>1</u>	3-4
Bustino	Busted/Doutelle	D	6	C-*	D	<u>1</u>	3-4
Buzzards Bay *ENG*	Joshua/Gratitude	F	8	D	M	1	3-4
Bynoderm	Faraway Son/Never Say Die	D	8	C	C	4	3-4
Cabrini Green	King's Bishop/Tudor Minstrel	C	7	D	CT	3	3-4
Cactus Road	Kennedy Road/Bold Bidder	C	9	F	D	3*	3-4
Cad	Timeless Moment/Three Bagger	D	8	F	C	4	3-4
Cadeux Genereux *ENG*	Young Generation/Sharpen Up	C	5	C-*	C	4*	2-3
Caerleon *IRE*	Nijinsky II/Round Table	D	5*	B	D	1	3-4
Caerwent *FR*	Caerleon/Habitat	M	6	L	M	3	3-4
Cahill Road	Fappiano/Le Fabuleux	C	6	C+Y	C	2	3-4
Cajun Prince	Ack Ack/Candy Spots	D	8	C	C-	4	3-4
Caller I.D.	Phone Trick/Ramsinga	C-	6	C-	C-	3	<u>2</u>-3
Calumar	Seattle Slew/On-and-On	D	10	U	C	4	3-4

Stallion	Sire/Broodmare Sire	FTS	CL	Trf	OT	SI	AB
CalTech	Explosive Bid/Shredder	C-	7	C+	C	3	3-4
Cameroon	Grey Dawn II/Arts & Letters	D	9	D	C	4	3-4
Canadian Gil	Northern Dancer/Hill Prince	C	7*	C*	C	3	3-4
Canadian Slew	Seattle Slew/Sassafras	D	7	C+	C-	3	3-4
Can Can Sam	Verzy/	M	8	M	U	4	2-3
Cancun	Tom Rolfe/Buckpasser	C	9	D	F	4	2-3
Candid Cameron^^	Carr de Naskra/Grey Dawn II	M	8	M	L	3	2-3
Candi's Gold	Yukon/Captain Nash	C+	7	C	C+T	3	2-3
Candyman Bee	Raise a Man/Tudor Grey	U	7	U	M	4	2-3
Candy Stripes	Blushing Groom/Lyphard	M	7	L	M	I	3-4
Cannonade	Bold Bidder/Ribot	D	7	C	C	3	3-4
Cannon Dancer	Explodent/Rattle Dancer	D	8	D	C	4	3-4
Cannon Shell	Torsion/Promise	F	8	C	C	4	3-4
Can't Be Slew^^	Seattle Slew/Stop the Music	M	10	M	M	3	2-3
Can You Beat That	In Reality/Tim Tam	M	9	U	M	4	3-4
Cape Storm^^	Storm Cat/Roberto	M	8	L	M	4*	2-3
Capital Idea	Iron Ruler/Arrogate	F	8	C-	D	4	3-4
Capitalimprovement^	Dixieland Band/Buckaroo	L	7	M	M	4	2-3
Capital South	Roberto/Polynesian	D	9	C-	CT	4	3-4
Capote	Seattle Slew/Bald Eagle	C	6	C-	C	4	2-3
Captain Arthur	River Knight/Green Dancer	M	9	M	M	4	3-4
Captain Courageous	Sailor/Bold Ruler	C	7*	C*	C	2	3-4
Captain James	Captain's Gig/Alcide	F	8	D	D	5	3-4
Captain Nick ENG	Sharpen Up/Double Jump	C	7	C*	C	4	3-4
Captain Valid	Valid Appeal/Northerly	M	6	M	M	5	3-4
Capt. Don	Don B./My Host	C	8	C+	C	2	3-4
Capulet's Song	In Reality/Hasty Road	C	8	F	D	5	2-3
Caracolero			7	C*	C	2	3-4
Carborundum	Best Turn/Papa Fourway	D	7	F	DT	4	2-3
Cardoun FR	Kaldoun/Fabulous Dancer	M	6	C	M	4	3-4
Cari Jill Hajji	Cari County/Native Host	L	8	M	M	4	3-4
Carjack	Cojak/Dead Ahead	C	8	D	C	4	3-4
Carload BRZ	Relaunch/Pretense	M	7	M	L	4	3-4
Carnivalay	Northern Dancer/Cyane	C+	6	CY	CT	2	2-3
Caro	Fortino/Chamossaire	F	5*	C+	C	2	3-4
Carodanz	Danzig/Gunflint	M	8	M	M	4	3-4
Carolina Ridge	Cox's Ridge/Groton	M	8	U	U	4	2-3
Caros Love	Caro/Northern Jove	D	7	C	C	3	3-4
Carr de Naskra	Star de Naskra/Cornish Prince	C	6	C-	C	3	3-4
Carson City	Mr. Prospector/Blushing Groom	A	3	C	A	4	2-3
Cartwright*	Forty Niner/What a Pleasure	L	6	M	L	4*	2-3
Casa Dante	Exclusive Native/Delta Judge	D	8	D	C	5	3-4
Case Law IRE	Ahonoora/Reliance II	L	5	L	M	5	2-3
Case the Joint	The Pruner/Nashville	U	9	M	U	4	3-4
Cassaleria	Pretense/Verbatim	D	7	D*	C	3	3-4

Stallion	Sire/Broodmare Sire	FTS	CL	Trf	OT	SI	AB
Casteddu *ENG*	Efisio/Royal Prerogative	L	6	L	M	5	2-3
Castle Guard	Slady Castle/Champion	D	7	F	T	4	3-4
Castle Howard	Slew o'Gold/Alydar	M	9	M	M	4	2-3
Catane	Hatchet Man/Round Table	U	7	U	M	4	3-4
Cathedral Bells	Honest Pleasure/Hail to Reason	U	10	U	C	4	3-4
Cathy's Reject	Best Turn/Decathon	D	8	D	C	4	3-4
Catrail^^	Storm Cat/Majestic Light	M	7	L	M	4*	2-
Caucasus	Nijinsky II/Princequillo	D	7*	C+*	C	2	3-4
Cause For Pause	Baldski/Aureole	C	7	C	C	5	3-4
Cautious Prince			7	M*		1	3-4
Caveat	Cannonade/The Axe II	D	5*	AY	CT	1	3-4
Cee's Tizzy	Relaunch/Lyphard	C+	6	D	C+	4	3-4
Cefis	Caveat/Dancing Champ	U	8	M	U	3	3-4
Celestial Storm *JPN*	Roberto/Ribot	D	8	C-	D	3*	3-4
Centaine *AUS*	Century/Vain	C	7	C+	C	4	3-4
Center Cut	Cutlass/Egg O'Pearl	C	9	C-*	D	3	3-4
Centrust	Mr. Prospector/Hawaii	D	7	C	C	4	3-4
Century Prince	Rollicking/Bold Effort	D	9	F	C	5	3-4
Certain Treat	Affirmed/Grey Dawn II	D	8	C+	C	4	3-4
Chaka	Fifth Marine/Tudor Grey	C	8	U	C	4	3-4
Chalmondilly	Hold Your Peace/Foolish Pleasure	U	9	M	M	3	3-4
Champagneforashley	Track Barron/Alleged	D	8	M	C	3	3-4
Change Takes Time		M	7	M	M	3	3-4
Chapel Creek	Our Native/Cornish Prince	U	8	M	L	3	3-4
Charging Falls	Taylor's Falls/Space Commander	D	7	D	C+	4	3-4
Charlie Barley	Affirmed/Dancing Champ	D	6	C+	C-	3	2-3
Charmer *ENG*	Be My Guest/Round Table	C	8	D	M	4	2-3
Charming Turn	Best Turn/Poker	C	7	D	C+	3	2-3
Chas Conerly	Big Burn/Fair Ruler	C-	8	C+	F	3	3-4
Chateaubay	Raja Baba/Graustark	D	9	D	C+	4	3-4
Chati *IRE*	Terrible Tiger/Sun Lover	D	7	C-	D	1	3-4
Cheer On	Hoist the Flag/Bagdad	D	9	C	D	3	3-4
Chenin Blanc^^	Lypheor/Caro	M	7	L	M	2	2-3
Cheque Froid	Icecapade/Damascus	C	8	U	C	4	3-4
Cherokee Colony	Pleasant Colony/Nijinsky II	C	6	C	CT	1	2-3
Cherokee Fellow	Funny Fellow/Francis S.	C-	6	C*	C	3	2-3
Cherokee Run^	Runaway Groom/Silver Saber	M	6	M	M	2	2-3
Cherry Pop	Explodent/Eurasian	D	8	C-	D	3	3-4
Chicago	Tom Rolfe/Fleet Nasrullah	D	7	C*	C	3	3-4
Chicanery Slew	Seattle Slew/Pretense	M	8	U	M	4	2-3
Chidester	Graustark/Tom Fool	D	9	D	C	4	3-4
Chief Honcho*	Chief's Crown/Riva Ridge	D	8	D	D	2	3-4
Chief of Dixieland	Indian Chief II/Native Dancer	D	7	U	D	4	3-4
Chief Persuasion	Secretariat/Restless Native	U	8	M	M	4	3-4
Chief's Crown	Danzig/Secretariat	D	6	CY	C	3*	3-4

Stallion	Sire/Broodmare Sire	FTS	CL	Trf	OT	SI	AB
Chief Singer *GER*	Ballad Rock/Le Fabuleux	C-	7	C*	M	3	2-3
Chief's Reward^^	Mr. Prospector/Dr. Fager	M	8	U	L	4	2-3
Chief Steward	Chieftain/Deck Hand	C	6	U	C	4	2-3
Chieftain	Bold Ruler/Roman	C	6	C*	C+	4	2-3
Chilicote	Intrepid Hero/Never Bend	M	9	M	M	4	2-3
Chillbang *ENG*	Formidable/Skymaster	C	8	C	M	4	2-3
Chillon *VEN*	Pass the Tab/Aloha Mood	C	8	U	C	4	2-3
Chimes Band^	Dixieland Band/Mr. Prospector	L	6	L	L	4	2-3
Chimineas	In Reality/Chieftain	M	8	M	M	4	3-4
Chinati	Blushing Groom/Reliance	M	9	M	M	4	3-4
Chiromancy	Alydar/Forli	U	10	M	U	4	2-3
Chisos	Alydar/High Perch	C	8	D	C+	4	3-4
Chivalry	Nijinsky II/Sir Ivor	F	10	D	C-	4	3-4
Christopher R.	Loom/Cavan	D	6	C	C	3*	3-4
Chromite	Mr. Prospector/Buckpasser	C-	7	C	C	3	3-4
Chugach	Northern Baby Unconscious	M	9	M	M	4	2-3
Chumming	Alleged/Sea-Bird	D	8	D	C	4	3-4
Churl	In Reality/Tom Rolfe	M	10	M	M	3	2-3
Cien Fuegos	Seattle Slew/Alydar	M	10	M	M	3	2-3
Cipayo *ARG*	Lacydon/Tamerlane	C	5	C+	C	2	3-4
Circle	Round Table/Nasrullah	C-	8	C	C	4	3-4
Circle Home	Bold Bidder/Ribot	C-	8	C+*	C	4	3-4
Circulating^^	Bold Ruckus/Vice Regent	L	8	M	M	4*	2-3
Cisco Road^^	Northern Baby/Secretariat	M	8	M	L	3	2-3
Citidancer	Dixieland Band/Tentam	C	5	C	C+	3	2-3
Claim	Mr. Prospector/Vertex	D	7	C	C+	3	3-4
Clantime *ENG*	Music Boy/Constable	C	7	C-	M	5	2-3
Claramount	Policeman/Cornish Prince	C+	7	D	C+	3	2-3
Classic	Hoist the Flag/Speak John	D	8	C-	C-	4	3-4
Classic Account	Private Account/Arts and Letters	D	8	C	CT	3	3-4
Classic Fame			7	M		2	3-4
Classic Go Go	Pago Pago/Never Bend	C-	8	C-	CT	4	2-3
Classic Pursuit	Miswaki/Dr. Fager	M	8	U	M	4	3-4
Classic Secret	Northern Dancer/Secretariat	D	8	C-	CT	4*	3-4
Claude Monet	Affirmed/Caro	U	8	M	M	2	3-4
Cleone*	Theatrical/Loosen Up	M	7	M	U	3	3-4
Clever Allemont	Clever Trick/Carlemont	D	10	U	D	4	3-4
Clever Champ	Clever Trick/Venetian Court	C	7	C-	C	4	2-3
Clever Gold	Clever Trick/Hard Work	M	8	M	M	4	2-3
Clever Secret	Secretariat/Pia Star	C-	8	M	C	3	3-4
Clev Er Tell	Tell/Swoon's Son	D	9	C	C	4	3-4
Clever Trick	Icecapade/Better Bee	C	5*	C+	C	3	2-3
Coach's Call	Alydar/Velvet Cap	D	9	U	C	4	3-4
Coastal *SAF*	Majestic Prince/Buckpasser	D	7	C+*	C	2	3-4
Coastal Voyage	Coastal/Sir Gaylord	C	7	M	M	3	3-4

Stallion	Sire/Broodmare Sire	FTS	CL	Trf	OT	SI	AB
Coax Me Chad	L'Enjoleur/First Landing	D	7	C	DT	4	3-4
Codex	Arts and Letters/Minnesota Mac	C	6	C*	C	3	3-4
Codified^^	Lear Fan/Messenger of Song	M	8	L	M	3	2-3
Cognizant	Explodent/Dr. Fager	D	7	C	C+	4	3-4
Cohoes	Mahmoud/Blue Larkspur	D	7	F	F	3	3-4
Cojak	Cohoes/Dark Star	D	7	D*	C	4	3-4
Col. Denning	Rock Talk/Grey Monarch	D	8	D	F	5	3-4
Cold Reception GU	Secretariat/Nearctic	D	8	C*	C	4	3-4
Collier	Mr. Prospector/Sir Ivor	D	7	C	C+	4	3-4
Colonel Collins	El Gran Senor/Kenmare	M	8	M	M	3	3-4
Colonel Power	Diplomat Way/Vertex	D	8	C-	D	4	2-3
Colonel Stevens	Lt. Stevens/Bupers	F	8	D	C+	3	3-4
Colonial Affair^^	Pleasant Colony/Nijinsky II	U	5	L	M	1	2-3
Colony Light	Pleasant Colony/Rube the Great	U	7	M	M	2	2-3
Colorful Crew^^	Ogygian/Secretariat	M	8	M	L	4	2-3
Color Me Bold	Bold Lark/Brecon Beacons	M	10	U	L	4	3-4
Combat Ready	Fit to Fight/Native Charger	M	7	C+	LT	3	2-3
Come On Mel	Lucky Mel/Sisters Prince	M	8	U	M	5	3-4
Come Summer	Junius/Sir Gaylord	C-	10	C-	F	4	3-4
Comet Kat	Foreign Comet/Crafty Admiral	D	8	D	C	3	2-3
Comet Shine^^	Fappiano/Vice Regent	M	8	M	M	4*	2-3
Comical Clown	Shecky Greene/Hospitality	D	8	D	D	5	2-3
Commodore C.	Mongo/Call Over	F	8	C	C	4	2-3
Commanche Run IRE	Run the Gantlet/Ratification	D	7	C	M	1	3-4
Commemorate	Exclusive Native/Never Bend	D	8	D	C	3*	3-4
Commissioner	Crozier/Jovial Love	C	8	D*	C	4	3-4
Common Grounds	Kris/Lyphard	C	6	C	F	3	2-3
Community Interest	Forli/Round Table	C	8	U	C	4	3-4
Compelling Sound*	Seattle Slew/Restless Wind	C-	7	M	C-	2	3-4
Compliance	Northern Dancer/Buckpasser	C-	6	C+Y	C-	2	3-4
Compliment	Nijinsky II/Graustark	D	10	D	C	3	3-4
Comrade In Arms ENG	Brigadier Gerard/Birdbrook	D	4	C+	M	2	3-4
Con Brio ARG	Ribot/Petition	C	4	C	C	1	3-4
Concern^	Broad Brush/Tunerup	M	6	M	L	3*	2-3
Concorde Bound	Super Concorde/Iron Ruler	C	8	C	C	4	2-3
Concorde's Tune^^	Concorde Bound/Tunerup	C	7	M	M	4	2-3
Conduction	Graustark/Prince John	D	9	M	C+	4	3-4
Conestoga IR			7	C		1*	3-4
Congolese			7	C*		3	3-4
Connecticut^	Ogygian/Secretariat	M	8	U	L	4	2-3
Conquer	Conquistador Cielo/Royal Ski	M	9	M	M	3	3-4
Conquistador Cielo	Mr. Prospector/Bold Commander	C-	5	B*	C+	3	3-4
Conquistador Oro	Conquistador Cielo/Ack Ack	M	8	M	L	4	3-4
Conquistarose NZ	Conquistador Cielo/Nijinsky II		7	C+		4	3-4
Consigliere ENG	Caerleon/Welsh Saint	U	8	L	M	3*	2-3

Stallion	Sire/Broodmare Sire	FTS	CL	Trf	OT	SI	AB
Contare	Naskra/One Count	C-	7	D	C+	4	3-4
Conte Di Savoya^^	Sovereign Dancer/Fappiano	M	8	M	M	2	2-3
Contempt			7	M		5	3-4
Contested Colors	Conquistador Cielo/Hoist the Flag	C-	7	D	C-	4	3-4
Contortionist	Torsion/Tatan	U	9	U	U	4	3-4
Convention *IRE*	General Assembly/Le Levanstell	D	7	C-	D	4	3-4
Conveyor^	Sharpen Up/What Luck	M	7	L	M	4	2-3
Cool *SAF*	Bold Bidder/Northern Dancer	D	10	D	C-	4	3-4
Cool Corn	Icecapade/Tom Rolfe	C	8	D	C+	4	3-4
Cool Frenchy	French Policy/Persia	D	10	U	C	4	3-4
Cool Halo	Halo/Northern Dancer	D	8	M	C	2	2-3
Cool Joe	Cold Reception/Dancing Count	C	8	C	C	3	2-3
Cool Northerner	Dom Alaric/Northern Dancer	D	7	D	C	4	3-4
Cool Review*	Icecapade/The Minstrel	M	8	L	M	4	3-4
Cool Victor	Tentam/Nearctic	C-	6	D	C+	3	3-4
Copelan	Tri Jet/Quadrangle	C+	6	C*	C+	3	2-3
Corey's Comet	Stalwart/Graustark	M	10	M	M	4	3-4
Cormorant	His Majesty/Tudor Minstrel	C-	5	B-	C	2	3-4
Cornish Prince	Bold Ruler/Eight Thirty	C+	6	D	C+	4	2-3
Corn Off the Cobb	Khaled/Bully Boy	C	8	F	D	4	3-4
Corporate Report	Private Account/Key to the Mint	C-	7	D	CT	3	3-4
Corridor Key	Danzig/Prince John	C-	7	C-	C	3*	3-4
Cortan	Illustrious/Sailor's Guide	D	8	D	C	3	3-4
Corwyn Bay	Caerleon/Crowned Prince	C	7	C-	D	4	3-4
Cosmic Voyager	Gummo/Acroterian	F	10	U	M	5	3-4
Cost Conscious	Believe It/Herbager	C-	8	C	D	3	2-3
Cote d'Ivoire	Sir Ivor/Two Relics	D	7	D	C	4	3-4
Cougar II	Tale of Two Cities/Madara	D	7	C*	C	2	3-4
Cougar's Crown	Vice Regent/Dedicate	C-	6	CY	D	4	3-4
Counsellor Gus	Nodouble/First Balcony	M	8	U	M	3	3-4
Counsellors Image	Dancer's Image/Princequillo	D	8	D	D	2	3-4
Counterfeit Money	Key to the Mint/Buckpasser	F	10	C	C	3	3-4
Count Eric	Riverman/TV Lark	D	9	C+	C	1	3-4
Count Francescui	Barachois/Francis S.	D	9	D	C	4	3-4
Country Light	Majestic Light/Hoist the Flag	C-	8	D	C+	2	3-4
Country Manor	Irish Castle/Hitting Away	F	10	D	F	5	3-4
Country Pine	His Majesty/Vaguely Noble	C+	6	C+	CT	2	2-3
Country Side	Secretariat/Never Bend	D	8	M	D	4	3-4
Country Store	Seattle Slew/Exclusive Native	M	8	M	L	3	3-4
Country Stride	Victory Stride/Swing Pass	D	9	D	C-	4	3-4
Count the Dots	Dancing Count/John Williams	U	10	M	U	4	3-4
Count the Time^	Regal Search/Timeless Moment	M	8	U	M	4	2-3
Coup de Kas	Kaskaskia/Villamor	C	9	D	C	5	2-3
Court Ruling	Traffic Judge/The Doge	D	8	D	C	4	3-4
Court Trial	In Reality/Moslem Chief	D	7	CY*	C	3	3-4

Stallion	Sire/Broodmare Sire	FTS	CL	Trf	OT	SI	AB
Cowboy Posse	Unfurl/Speak John	U	9	M	M	5	3-4
Covert Operation	True Colors/Prince John	U	10	M	T	3	3-4
Cox's Ridge	Best Turn/ Ballydonnell	C	4*	C*	CT	2	3-4
Cox's Time	Cox's Ridge/Olden Times	M	10	U	T	3	3-4
Cozzene	Caro/Prince John	D	5	B-Y	D	1	3-4
C. Poppa Hall	Hold Your Tricks/Exclusive Native	C-	9	C	D	2	3-4
Crafty Native	Native Born/Crafty Admiral	D	8	D	C	4	2-3
Crafty Prospector	Mr. Prospector/In Reality	B	5	C-	B+T	3	2-3
Crawford Special	Bold Street/Crewman	C	8	U	B	4	3-4
Creamette City	In Reality/Native Dancer	C-	9	D	C	4	3-4
Creative Act^^	Spend a Buck/Tentam	M	8	U	M	3	3-4
Creekarosa	Darby Creek Road/Nijinsky II	U	10	M	U	3	3-4
Creme dela Creme		D	7	C*	C	2	3-4
Creole Dancer	Dancing Dervish/Wig Out	C	9	U	C-	4	2-3
Cresta Rider		D	7	C+*	C-	3	3-4
Cresting Water	Cresta Ridge/Buckpasser	U	10	U	M	4	3-4
Cricket Ball IRE	Olden Times/Princely Gift	D	6	C+	C	1*	3-4
Criminal Type JPN	Alydar/No Robbery	F	6	DY	C	2	3-4
Crimson Battle	Crimson Satan/General Don	F	8	D	D	4	3-4
Crimson Satan	Spy Song/Requiebro	C	6	C*	C	3	2-3
Crimson Slew	Seattle Slew/Crimson Satan	M	8	U	C+	4	3-4
Christopher Cool	Luckiness/Big Coroner	M	8	U	L	4	3-4
Critique BRZ	Roberto/Sicambre	F	8	C-	F	4	3-4
Cross Canal	Dedimoud/Blue Counselor	D	8	C	C	2	3-4
Crossed Swords	Alydar/Blade	C	10	U	M	4	3-4
Crow FR	Exbury/Right of Way	D	6	C	C+	3	3-4
Crowning	Raise a Native/Round Table	D	8	D	C+	4	3-4
Crown Pleasure	Foolish Pleasure/Ack Ack	D	7	CY	D	3	3-4
Crown's Wish	Vice Regent/Gunflint	M	7	M	M	3	3-4
Croydon	Conquistador Cielo/Nijinsky II	M	7	M	M	3	3-4
Crozier		C-	7	C-*	C+	3	3-4
Crusader Sword	Damascus/Nijinsky II	C-	7	C	C	2	2-3
Crusoe	The Minstrel/Sir Gaylord	D	8	C	D	3	3-4
Cryptoclearance	Fappiano/Hoist The Flag	C	6	CY	C+	3*	3-4
Crystal Glitters FR	Blushing Groom/Donut King	C	3	C	C	3*	3-4
Crystal Run	Table Run/Anyoldtime	C-	9	D	C	4	3-4
Crystal Tas	Crystal Water/Run of Luck	U	9	U	U	4	3-4
Crystal Water	Windy Sands/T. V. Lark	C	8	C	F	4	3-4
Cuchillo	Blade/Flit-to	M	7	C*	C	2	3-4
Cullendale	Sham/Bold and Brave	D	8	D	C	3	3-4
Cup Challenge^	Mr. Prospector/Knightly Dawn	M	8	M	M	4*	2-3
Cure the Blues	Stop the Music/Dr. Fager	B	6	C	C+T	3	2-3
Current Blade	Little Current/The Axe II	F	7	C*	D	2	3-4
Current Classic	Little Current/Delta Judge	U	10	M	M	3	3-4
Current Hope	Little Current/Warfare	D	7	C	F	3	3-4

Stallion	Sire/Broodmare Sire	FTS	CL	Trf	OT	SI	AB
Cutlass	Damascus/Dunce	C+	6	C-	C+	4	2-3
Cutlass Fax	Cutlass/Greek Sky	C-	8	U	CT	4	2-3
Cutlass Reality	Cutlass/In Reality	C	7	D	C	4	3-4
Cut Shot	Blade/Sunrise County	M	9	U	M	5	2-3
Cut Throat ENG	Sharpen Up/Zimone	C	7	C+	C	4	3-4
Cyane	Turn-to/Beau Pere	C	5	C	C+	3	3-4
Cyrano d'Bergerac IRE	Bold Lad/Brigadier Gerard	C-	6	C	D	4*	2-3
Czaravich GER	Nijinsky II/Linacre	D	7	C-*	C-	2	3-4
Czar Nijinsky	Barrera/Nijinsky II	D	8	D	C	4	3-4
D'Accord	Secretariat/Northern Dancer	C-	7	C	C	1	3-4
Dactylographer	Secretariat/Ribot	D	8	C	C-	2	2-3
Daddy's Mandolin	What Luck/Olden Times	D	10	F	CT	5	3-4
Dahar JPN	Lyphard/Vaguely Noble	D	7	C	C	3*	3-4
Daily Ballot	Mt. Livermore/Cyane	M	7	M	M	3	3-4
Daily Review	Damascus/Reviewer	M	10	U	M	4	3-4
Dallasite	Vaguely Noble/Forli	C	9	C	C	4	3-4
Damascus	Sword Dancer/My Babu	C	4*	C*	B	2	3-4
Dambay	Damascus/Bold Ruler	M	8	U	M	4	3-4
Damister JPN	Mr. Prospector/Roman Line	C-	7	C	C	3*	3-4
Dancebel ENG	Dance in Time/St Crespin II	C	8	C-	C	4	3-4
Dance Bid BRZ	Northern Dancer/Bold Bidder	C	7	C*	D	4*	3-4
Dance Centre	Mr. Prospector/Olympia	C	10	C	C-	4	3-4
Dance Furlough	Nijinsky II/Riva Ridge	U	9	M	M	3	3-4
Dancehall	Assert/Mr. Prospector	U	7	L	M	3	3-4
Dance in My Dreams	Dance Bid/Doctor Hank K.	M	8	M	M	4	3-4
Dance in Time	Northern Dancer/Chop Chop	D	8	C	C+	2	3-4
Dance of Life IRE	Nijinsky II/In Reality	C	6	C	C-	1	3-4
Dance Spell	Northern Dancer/Obeah		7	C*		3*	3-4
Dancewiththedevil		M	7			4	2-3
Dancing Again	Nijinsky II/Round Table	D	8	F	C	4	3-4
Dancing Brave JPN	Lyphard/Drone	C	4	C	C	3*	3-4
Dancing Champ	Nijinsky II/Tom Fool	C	6	C	D	4	2-3
Dancing Count	Northern Dancer/King's Bench	C	6	C+*	C	2	3-4
Dancing Crown	Nijinsky II/Full Pocket	D	7	D	C-	4	3-4
Dancing Czar	Nijinsky II/Hail to Reason	C-	8	D	C+	4	2-3
Dancing Dissident ENG	Nureyev/Raise a Cup	C+	5	C+	D	4*	2-3
Dancing Flight			7	C*		4	3-4
Dancing Minstrel*	The Minstrel/What A Pleasure	U	10	M	M	5	3-4
Dancing Moss			7	C*		3	3-4
Dancing Pirate	Pirate's Bounty/Bold Hitter	D	9	D	C-	5	3-4
Dancing Spree FR	Nijinsky II/Riva Ridge	U	6	M	M	3*	3-4
Dancing Wizard	Northern Dancer/Bold Ruler	C-	9	D	C	3	3-4
Dandy Binge	Draconic/Dandy K	C	8	F	C+	5	2-3
Danebo	Bold Forbes/Sea Hawk	D	9	D	C	4	3-4
Danehill ENG	Danzig/His Majesty	C+	6	B	D	3	2-3

Stallion	Sire/Broodmare Sire	FTS	CL	Trf	OT	SI	AB
Danny's Keys	Dewan Keys/Our Michael	U	9	U	U	4	3-4
Dansil	Silver Hawk/Upper Nile	U	7	M	M	3*	3-4
Danski	Danzig/Pago Pago	C	8	M	C	5	3-4
Dansons	Raise a Native/Turn-to	C-	9	D	C	4	3-4
Danton	Seattle Slew/Majestic Prince	D	10	U	C	3	3-4
Danzatore	Northern Dancer/Raise a Native	C	7	C	C	3	2-3
Danzig	Northern Dancer/Admiral's Voyage	C+	1	<u>A</u>	C	4*	2-3
Danzig Connection	Danzig/Sir Ivor	C	6	CY	C+	3	3-4
Danzig Dancer	Danzig/Tom Rolfe	C	7	D	D	4	3-4
Dapper Danzig	Danzig/Sir Ivor	U	9	M	M	4*	3-4
Darby Creek Road	Roberto/Olympia	C	6	C	C	2	3-4
Dargai	It's Freezing/Master Derby	M	9	U	M	4	3-4
Daring Damascus	Damascus/Amarullah	D	8	D	C	2	3-4
Daring Groom	Blushing Groom/Prince Dare	C-	7	D	C+	4*	3-4
Daring Jim	Daring Marine/Boston Market	D	8	C+	C	4	3-4
Daring Scheme			7	C*		3	3-4
Darly	Alydar/Tom Fool	U	8	U	M	4	3-4
Darn That Alarm	Jig Time/Blazing Count	C+	6	C	CT	3	<u>2-3</u>
Darshaan *IRE*	Shirley Heights/Abdos	D	5	C+	M	1	3-4
Dashing Blade *ENG*	Elegant Air/Sharpen Up	M	7	C+	M	3*	3-4
Dauphin Fabuleux	Le Fabuleux/Viceregal	D	7	C	D	2	3-4
Dave's Reality	In Reality/Knightly Manner	D	9	D	C	4	3-4
Da' White Judge	Whitesburg/Traffic Judge	C	8	F	C	4	3-4
Dawn Flight	Grey Dawn II/Prince John	F	8	C-	C	4	3-4
Dawn of Creation	Raise a Native/Prince John	D	9	D	C	3	<u>2-3</u>
Dawn Quixote	Grey Dawn II/Seattle Slew	C	6	CY	CT	3	<u>2-3</u>
Dawn Revival	Grand Revival/Grey Dawn II	M	9	U	M	5	<u>2-3</u>
Dayjur	Danzig/Mr. Prospector	C	6	C	C	4	2-<u>3</u>
Dealaway	Mr. Leader/Blue Prince	U	8	M	M	3	3-4
Dearborn	His Majesty/My Babu	U	9	M	M	3	3-4
Dearest Doctor	Dr. Fager/Summer Tan	D	9	D	C	3	3-4
Debonair Roger	Raja Baba/Lucky Debonair	C-	8	D	C	4	3-4
De Braak	Mr. Prospector/Dance Spell	U	10	U	M	4	3-4
Debussy	Nijinsky II/Tim Tam	D	8	C	C	3*	3-4
Decidedly			7	C*	C+	3	3-4
Dee Lance	Blade/Swoon's Son	C	9	U	CT	5	3-4
Deep Roots			7	Y*		2	3-4
Deep Saline	Damascus/Tom Rolfe	U	8	U	M	5	2-3
Deerhound	Danzig/Buckpasser	<u>C</u>	7	C	C-	3*	<u>2-3</u>
Defecting Dancer *NZ*	Habitat/Nijinsky II	M	7	C	M	3*	3-4
Defense Verdict	In Reality/ Moslem Chief	C-	9	D	C	3	2-<u>3</u>
Defensive Play	Fappiano/Sham	C	7	C-	C	3*	3-4
Defiance	What a Pleasure/The Axe II	F	9	D	C	4	3-4
Defrere^	Deputy Minister/Secretariat	M	7	M	M	4	2-<u>3</u>
Dehere^^	Deputy Minister/Secretariat	C	6	M	C	4*	2-3

Stallion	Sire/Broodmare Sire	FTS	CL	Trf	OT	SI	AB
De Jeau	Private Thoughts/Rattle Dancer	D	7	D	C	3	3-4
Delaware Chief	Chieftain/Double Jay	C	8	F	C	3	3-4
Delayer	Fappiano/Bold Bidder	C	7	M	CT	3	2-3
Delegant	Grey Dawn II/Vaguely Noble	U	10	M	M	3	3-4
Delineator^^	Storm Cat/Grey Dawn II	L	8	M	L	3	2-3
Delinsky	Nijinsky II/Graustark	U	10	M	U	3	3-4
Delta Flag	Hoist the Flag/Delta Judge	F	8	C-	C	4	3-4
Demidoff^^	Mr. Prospector/Secretariat	M	8	M	M	3	2-3
Democratic ENG	Miswaki/Alleged	M	6	M	M	4*	3-4
Demons Begone	Elocutionist/Halo	D	7	C	D	2	3-4
De Niro^	Gulch/Faraway Son	M	7	M	M	4*	2-3
Departing Cloud^	Talc/Irish Ruler	M	8	M	M	4	3-4
Departing Prints	Dactylographer/Irish Ruler	C-	8	U	C	4	2-3
Deploy ENG	Shirely Heights/Roberto	C	6	C	M	1	3-4
Deposit Ticket	Northern Baby/Mr. Prospector	C	7	C	C+	3*	2-3
Deputed Testimony	Traffic Cop/Prove It	D	6	CY	CT	3*	3-4
Deputy Governor NZ	Master Willie/Vice Regent	D	7	C	M	2	3-4
Deputy Minister	Vice Regent/Bunty's Flight	C	3	C+	CT	1*	3-4
Deputy Regent	Vice Regent/Canadian Champ	D	9	M	C	4	2-3
Derby Wish	Lyphard's Wish/Crozier	C	7	B	C	3	2-3
Derring-Do			7	B*		3	3-4
Desert Classic	Damascus/Never Bend	M	9	CY	M	3	3-4
Desert God	Fappiano/Blushing Groom	M	10	M	L	4*	2-3
Desert Royalty	Desert Wine/King of Kings	L	7	M	M	3	2-3
Desert Secret^^	Sadler's Wells/Secretariat	M	8	L	M	1	2-3
Desert Splendour ENG	Green Desert/Vaguely Noble	M	6	M	M	4	2-3
Desert Wine	Damascus/Never Bend	C	7	C+*	C	2	3-4
Determinant	Norcliffe/Green Ticket	C-	8	U	C	4	2-3
Detour	Kennedy Road/The Scoundrel	M	9	M	M	4	3-4
Deuces Are Loose	Zen/Pampered King II	M	9	U	U	4	3-4
Devil His Due^	Devil's Bag/Raise a Cup	M	5	U	M	1	3-4
Devil on Ice^^	Devil's Bag/Dr. Fager	M	8	U	M	3	2-3
Devil's Bag	Halo/Herbager	C	6	C-	C	2	2-3
Devil's Cry*	Devil's Bag/Sea Bird	M	10	L	M	4	3-4
Devil's Own Time	Devil's Bag/Marshua's Dancer	M	8	U	M	3	3-4
Devil's View	Devil's Bag/Reviewer	M	9	U	M	4	3-4
Dewan	Bold Ruler/Sun Again	C	6	C	C	3	2-3
Dewan Keys THI	Dewan/Royal Union	C	7	C-	C-	4	3-4
D'Hallevant^	Ogygian/Bold Bidder	M	7	M	L	4	2-3
Diablo	Devil's Bag/Cornish Prince	B	6	D	C	4	2-3
Diamondhawke	Meritable/Drum Fire	M	9	M	M	5	2-3
Diamond Prospect FR	Mr. Prospector/Social Climber	C	7	C	D	4*	2-3
Diamond Shoal JPN	Mill Reef/Graustark	D	6	C	C	1	3-4
Diamond Sword	Danzig/Herbager	M	7	M	M	4	2-3
Diazo^^	Jade Hunter/Tyrant	M	6	M	M	3*	3-4

Stallion	Sire/Broodmare Sire	FTS	CL	Trf	OT	SI	AB
Dicken's Hill *IRE*			7	C+*		3	3-4
Dickerson	Grey Dawn II/No Robbery	D	8	C	CT	2	3-4
Dick's Little Man	Crimson Man/Limelight	M	9	U	M	5	3-4
Diction	Elocutionist/Well Mannered	D	10	U	C	4	3-4
Diesis	Sharpen Up/Reliance	C-	6	B	D	1	2-3
Digamist	Blushing Groom/Northern Dancer	D	9	D	D	3	3-4
Digging In^^	Mr. Prospector/Northern Dancer	M	8	L	M	4	2-3
Dignitas^^	In Reality/Tobin Bronze	M	8	U	M	2	3-4
Digression	Seattle Slew/The Axe II	C-	8	C	C-	3*	3-4
Dilum *ENG*	Tasso/Pitcairn	M	5	L	M	4	2-3
Dimaggio	Bold Hitter/Indian Hemp	D	9	C-	C	5	3-4
Dinner Money	Raise a Cup/Herbager	D	9	D	C-	4	3-4
Din's Dancer	Sovereign Dancer/Olden Times	F	6	B	C-	3	2-3
Diplomatic Note	Diplomat Way/Royal Note	C	8	M	D	4	3-4
Diplomat Way	Nashua/Princequillo	D	4	C+	D	1	3-4
Directed Energy	Fit to Fight/Buckpasser	M	9	U	M	4	3-4
Discover*	Cox's Ridge/Mr. Prospector	M	7	U	M	3	3-4
Discretion *FR*	Bold Lad/Worden	D	9	D	F	2	3-4
Dispersal	Sunny's Halo/Johnny Appleseed	C	6	BY	C-	3*	2-3
Distant Day	Fleet Nasrullah/Summer Tan	C	8	D	C+	4	3-4
Distant Heart	Distant Day/Dumpty Humpty	D	8	D	D	4	3-4
Distant Land	Graustark/Bold Ruler	D	8	C*	C+	3	3-4
Distant Relative *ENG*	Habitat/Claude	C	6	C+	M	3	2-3
Distant Ryder	Red Ryder/Tex Courage	C-	7	C	D	4	3-4
Distant View^	Mr. Prospector/Irish River	M	6	L	M	4*	3-4
Distinctive	Never Bend/Requested	C+	6	D	C	4	2-3
Distinctive Pro	Mr. Prospector/Distinctive	C+	6	D	CT	3	2-3
Distinctly Norh *IRE*	Minshaanshu/Distinctive	M	7	M	M	4	2-3
Dixie Brass	Dixieland Band/Sham	C+	5	B	C	4	2-3
Dixieland Band	Northern Dancer/Delta Judge	A	4	C+	CT	4*	2-3
Dixieland Brass	Dixieland Band/Gallant Romeo	C	7	C-	C	3	2-3
Dixieland Heat^	Dixieland Band/Damascus	L	7	L	L	3	2-3
Dixton^^	Dixieland Band/	M	8	M	M	4	2-3
DJ Cat^	Hurontario/Toomuchholme	M	7	M	M	4	3-4
DJ Trump	Raise a Native/Norcliffe	D	8	M	C	4	3-4
Dmitri	Danzig/Raja Baba	C-	8	C+	CT	3	3-4
Doc's Leader	Mr. Leader/Nodouble	D	6	C+	C	3	2-3
Doc Stat	Old Mose/Fleet Nasrullah	C	8	D	C	4	2-3
Doctor's Orders	Tom Fool/Cohoes	D	8	D	C	4	3-4
Dodge *BRZ*	Mr. Prospector/Storm Bird	C-	7	C-	C	3	3-4
Dodington	Forli/Nantallah	D	8	M	C	4	3-4
Dogwood Passport	Silent Screen/Aureole	D	8	D	C	4	3-4
Doinitthehardway	Foolish Pleasure/Lyphard	D	10	M	D	4	3-4
Do It Again Dan	Mr. Leader/Our Michael	C	8	D	CT	3	3-4
Dollar Chili	Moonsplash/Dancing Dervish	M	9	U	C	4	3-4

Stallion	Sire/Broodmare Sire	FTS	CL	Trf	OT	SI	AB
Dolphin Street *FR*	Bluebird/Irish River	M	7	L	M	3	2-3
Dom Alaric	Sassafras/Orsini II	D	6	C*	C	2	3-4
Domasca Dan	Same Direction/Gold and Myrrh	U	6	M	M	4	3-4
Dom Dancer	Dom Alaric/Vice Regent	C-	7	U	C+	4	3-4
Dominated	Exclusive Native/Crafty Admiral	D	7	C	D	2	3-4
Dominator	Secretariat/Windy Sea	F	10	D	D	4	3-4
Domineau *CHI*	Never Bend/Ways and Means		6	C+		1	3-4
Dominion *ENG*	Derring-do/Princely Gift	D	7	C	D	3	3-4
Dominion Royale *SAF*	Dominion/Sharpen Up	C	7	C	D	4*	2-3
Domremy	What a Pleasure/Sir Ivor	D	8	U	D	4	3-4
Don B.	Fleet Nasrullah/Prince John	C	7	C+*	C+	3	3-4
Don Roberto			7	C+		3	3-4
Don's Choice	Private Account/Steward	D	7	D	B	3	2-3
Don Sebastien	Vent du Nord/Jester	D	8	D	C-	4	3-4
Don's Joke	Foolish Pleasure/Court Recess	U	10	M	M	4	3-4
Don't Fool With Me	Tanthem/Forward Pass	U	9	U	M	4	3-4
Don't Forget Me *IND*	Ahonoora/African Sky	C	6	C	C	3*	2-3
Don't Frisk Me Now	Full Pocket/Wallet Lifter	M	8	U	M	4	3-4
Don't Hesitate	Native Uproar/Time Tested	C-	9	F	C	5	3-4
Doonesbear	Doonesbury/Iron Ruler	D	10	U	C+	4	3-4
Doonesbury	Matsadoon/Vaguely Noble	C-	8	C	CT	4	3-4
Double Bed *FR*	Be My Guest/Welsh Saint	M	7	C	M	4*	3-4
Double D. Slew^	Seattle Slew/Fappiano	M	8	M	L	4	2-3
Double Edge Sword	Sword Dancer/Discovery	F	7	F	C	4	3-4
Double Form *IRE*			7	C*		3	3-4
Double Image	Spring Double/Dancer's Image	M	8	M	M	3	3-4
Double Jay	Balladier/Whiskbroom II	C+	5	C	D	4	2-3
Double Jump	Bold Bidder/Vaguely Noble	D	8	C-	C-	3	3-4
Double Leader	Mr. Leader/Carry Back	D	8	C	C	4	3-4
Double Negative	Mr. Prospector/Distinctive	C+	6	D	C	3	2-3
Double Quick	To the Quick/Creme dela Creme	U	9	M	M	3	3-4
Double Reach	Nodouble/Raise a Native	C-	10	D	C-	4	3-4
Double Ready	Nodouble/Eighty Grand	D	8	U	C	4	3-4
Double Riyadh	Anticipating/Double Zeus	M	8	U	MT	3	3-4
Double Schwartz *IRE*	Double Form/Sing Sing	C	8	D	M	3	3-4
Double Sonic	Nodouble/Palestinian	C-	7	C	C	2	3-4
Double Zeus	Spring Double/Ridan	C	8	D	C	3	3-4
Doulab *JPN*	Topsider/Dr. Fager	C-	7	C	M	2	3-4
Dover Ridge	Riva Ridge/Bold Ruler	C	7	F	C	3	3-4
Downing	Our Native/Bolero	M	8	M	M	4	3-4
Dowsing *ENG*	Riverman/Mr. Prospector	C	7	C	C	4	3-4
Doyoun *IRE*	Mill Reef/Kashmir II	C	7	C	M	1	3-4
Dr. Adagio^^	Cure the Blues/Silly Season	M	7	U	MT	4	2-3
Drakus Here	Norcliffe/Times Roman	D	8	M	C	4	3-4
Dramatic Desire	Smooth Dancer/Pago Pago	F	10	D	D	4	3-4

Stallion	Sire/Broodmare Sire	FTS	CL	Trf	OT	SI	AB
Dr. Blum	Dr. Fager/Sir Gaylord	C	7	D	C	4	3-4
Dr. Carter *BRZ*	Caro/Chieftain	D	7	C+	C	3*	3-4
Dr. Dalton	Raise a Cup/Silent Screen	D	10	D	C	3	3-4
Dr. Danzig	Danzig/Dr. Fager	D	7	M	C	4	2-3
Dreadnought	Lt. Stevens/Court Martial	D	8	D	C	4	3-4
Dreams to Reality	Lyphard/Raise a Native	D	8	C-	U	4	3-4
Dream Valley		M	8				3-4
Dr. Fager	Rough 'n Tumble/Better Self	C	3	C	C+	4	2-3
Dr. Geo Adams	Raise a Native/Tom Fool	D	9	F	F	4	3-4
Dr. Jarrell	Pacific Native/Nasrullah	M	8	M	C+	4	3-4
Dr. Koch	In Reality/Bold Ruler	C-	7	U	C	4	3-4
Dr. McGuire	Dr. Fager/Sir Ivor	D	10	F	C	4	3-4
Dr. Nauset	Irish Castle/Malicious	M	10	U	M	4	3-4
Drone	Sir Gaylord/Tom Fool	C	6	C	C+	4	2-3
Drone's Reward	Drone/Double Jay	D	8	D	C+	4	3-4
Drouilly	Mill Reef/Gun Shot	C	7	C+	C	2	3-4
Dr. Reality	In Reality/Dr. Fager	C	8	U	C+	4	3-4
Dr Root	Slew o'Gold/Knightly Manner	C	7	M	C+	3	3-4
Dr. Schwartzman	Florescent Light/Graustark	D	8	C	D	2	3-4
Dr. Secreto	Secreto/Dr. Fager	M	7	M	T	4	3-4
Dr. Spanky	Wardlaw/Pass Catcher	M	8	U	U	4	3-4
Drumalis	Tumble Wind/Coursing	C	8	C+	C	3	3-4
Drum Fire	Never Bend/Ambiorix	C+	7	D	C+	5	2-3
Drum Score	Drum Fire/Envoy	U	10	U	M	5	3-4
Drums of Time	Olden Times/Round Table	D	8	C	C	3	3-4
Dr. Valeri	Gunflint/Andy's Glory	F	9	C	D	3	3-4
Dual Honor	Seattle Slew/Le Fabuleux	D	8	C	C	4	3-4
Duck Dance	Water Prince/Swoon's Son	C	7	F	C	3	2-3
Due Diligence	Steward/Third Brother	F	7	D	C+	2	3-4
Duel's Destiny			7	C*		3	3-4
Duluth	Codex/Key to the Mint	D	8	D	D	<u>4</u>	3-4
Dunant	Sallust/African Sky	U	10	U	C	4	3-4
Dunbeath *ENG*	Grey Dawn II/Irish Castle	D	9	C-	C+	3*	3-4
Dunham's Gift	Winged T./Dead Ahead	C	9	C	C-	4	3-4
Duns Scotus	Buckpasser/Northern Dancer	F	6	C	C-	2	3-4
Dunstable	Nashua/Olden Times	D	7	D	C	3	3-4
Dust Commander	Bold Commander/Windy City II	F	8	C	C-	3	3-4
Dusty Screen^	Silent Screen/Buckfinder	U	7	M	M	2	3-4
Dynaformer	Roberto/His Majesty	C	6	A-Y	CT	3*	3-4
Dynamo Mac	Dynastic/Raise a Native	C	10	F	F	5	3-4
Dynastic	Bold Ruler/Khaled	C	8	C	C	2	3-4
Eager Eagle	T.V. Lark/War Admiral	D	8	C	F	4	3-4
Eager Native	Restless Native/Fleet Nasrullah	C	8	C	C	4	3-4
Eagle Eyed^	Danzig/His Majesty	M	6	<u>L</u>	M	4*	2-<u>3</u>
Early Call	Vice Regent/Petingo	M	7	M	M	4	3-4

Stallion	Sire/Broodmare Sire	FTS	CL	Trf	OT	SI	AB
Early School	Lyphard/Pitskelly	M	9	L	M	4	2-3
Earn Your Stripes	Little Current/In Reality	U	7	C	M	3	3-4
Earthmover	Chieftain/Run Fool Run	D	8	U	C	5	3-4
Eastern Echo	Damascus/Northern Dancer	C+	6	C	CT	3	2-3
Eastern Lord	Nearctic/Sir Gaylord	C	8	D	C	4	3-4
Eastover Court*	Seattle Slew/Grey Dawn II	M	8	M	LT	3	3-4
Easy Approach	Stevward/Crozier	M	9	U	M	4	3-4
Easy Goer	Alydar/Buckpasser	C	5	C-	CT	I*	3-4
Ecliptical	Exclusive Native/Chieftain	C-	7	D	C	4	3-4
Ecole Etage	Disciplinarian/Sunglow	D	7	C	F	4	3-4
Editorial Comment	Staff Writer/Canadian Champ	F	9	U	C	4	3-4
Effervescing	Le Fabuleux/Bold Ruler	D	8	C	C	3	3-4
Efisio ENG	Formidable/High Top	C	6	C+	M	5	2-3
Egg Toss ARG	Buckpasser/Delta Judge	D	5	C	C	2	3-4
Eighty Below Zero	It's Freezing/Pavot	C	7	U	BT	4	2-3
Ela-Mana-Mou IRE	Pitcairn/High Hat	D	5	CY	M	I	3-4
El Baba	Raja Baba/Hail to All	C	6	C*	C	I	3-4
El Barril CHI	Tantoul/Le Petite Roi	C-	8	U	C-	4	3-4
EL Basco			7	C		I	3-4
Elbio IRE	Precocious/Pioneer	M	6	M	M	4	2-3
Elbow Grease	Hard Work/Bold Lark	M	7	L	M	4	3-4
El Casique	Shecky Greene/Cornish Prince	C-	8	C	C	3	3-4
Eldorado Bob ENG	Thatch/Red God	C-	7	C	D	5	3-4
El Dorado Kid	Crazy Kid/Flash o' Night	F	9	F	C	5	3-4
Electric Blue	Cyane/Tibaldo	C-	8	C	C	3	3-4
Elegant Life	Distinctive/Bold Hour	C-	9	D	C+	5	3-4
Eleven Stitches	Windy Sands/My Host	C-	9	C	C	4	3-4
El Gran Senor	Northern Dancer/Buckpasser	C-	6	C+	C	4*	2-3
Elkman	Clever Trick/Tilt Top	C	7	M	M	4	2-3
Elmaamul ENG	Diesis/Roberto	C-	7	C	U	3*	2-3
El Mandingo	Cahasa/Crafty Admiral	C-	10	U	CT	3	3-4
El Mayaguezano	Distant Land/Arachnoid	C-	8	M	T	4	2-3
Elmer L. Brown			7	C*		3	3-4
Elocutionist	Gallant Romeo/Fleet Nasrullah	C	6	C+*	C	3	3-4
El Pitirre			7	C*	C	2	3-4
El Prado	Sadler's Wells/Sir Ivor	B	5	CY	C-	3	2-3
El Raggaas PHI	Northern Dancer/Majestic Prince	D	7	D	D	2	3-4
El Senor JPN	Valdez/Grey Dawn II	U	6	M	M	2	3-4
Embrace the Wind	Regal Embrace/Speedy Zephyr	C-	8	D	C	4	3-4
Eminency	Vaguely Noble/Chieftain	D	9	C-	C-	4	3-4
Emperor Jones ENG	Danzig/Native Royalty	M	4	L	M	4*	2-3
Empery	Vaguely Noble/Postin	D	7	C+*	C	3*	3-4
Empire Glory	Nijinsky II/Fleet Nasrullah	D	9	D	F	3	3-4
Encino	Nijinsky II/Crimson Satan	C-	8	C	C	4	3-4
Endow	Flying Paster/Exclusive Native	C-	8	C-	C	4	2-3

Stallion	Sire/Broodmare Sire	FTS	CL	Trf	OT	SI	AB
End Sweep^^	Forty Niner/Dance Spell	C-	6	M	M	4*	2-3
Ends Well	Lyphard/Stage Door Johnny	C-	6	C+	D	2	3-4
Enemy Number One	Grenfall/Majestic Prince	F	7	U	C	4	3-4
English Harbor ENG			7	C*		2	3-4
Enough Reality	In Reality/Vent du Nord	C	7	C	C	5	2-3
Entitled To	Golden Act/Francis S.	F	9	M	C-	4	3-4
Entropy	What a Pleasure/Intentionally	D	8	C-	B	4	2-3
Environment Friend ENG	Cozzene/Tom Rolfe		7	C+		3*	3-4
Envoy		C	7	C-	C+	4	3-4
Epervier Bleu ENG			7	C		1	3-4
Erin's Isle	Busted/Shantung	F	7	B*	C	1	3-4
Eskimo	Northern Dancer/Dr. Fager	D	7	C	C	3	2-3
Estate	Singh/Damascus	U	10	U	M	5	3-4
Eteelya	Seattle Slew/Sadair	C-	9	U	C	4	2-3
Eternal Prince	Majestic Prince/Fleet Nasrullah	C-	7	C	C	3*	2-3
Eulogize	Roberto/Judger	F	8	C	C-	3	3-4
Evansville Slew^	Slew City Slew/Fappiano	M	7	M	L	4	2-3
Evening Kris	Kris S./Double Hitch	C	7	M	C	3	2-4
Evzone	Peace Corps/Green Ticket	F	8	F	C	2	3-4
Exact Duplicate	Chateaugay/Summa Cum	F	10	U	F	4	3-4
Exactly Sharp	Sharpen Up/Caro	U	8	C+	M	3	3-4
Exbourne*	Explodent/Forum	C	6	C+	C	3	3-4
Excavate^^	Mr. Prospector/Never Bend	L	8	M	M	4	2-3
Exceller	Vaguely Noble/Bald Eagle	D	5*	C+*	C	3*	3-4
Exclusive Darling	Exclusive Native/Spring Double	C-	8	U	C	5	3-4
Exclusive Encore	Exclusive Native/Court Martial	C-	8	D	B	4	3-4
Exclusive Enough	Exclusive Native/Three Martinis	C-	7	C	C	5	2-3
Exclusive Era	Exclusive Native/Nashua	C	8	C	C+	2	3-4
Exclusive Gem	Exclusive Native/Prince John	C	7	D	CT	3	3-4
Exclusive Native	Raise a Native/Shut Out	C-	7	C*	CT	3*	2-3
Exclusive Partner	Exclusive Ribot/Diplomat Way	U	10	M	M	3	3-4
Exclusive Ribot	Ribot/Shut Out	D	8	C*	D	3	3-4
Exclusive's Pride	Apalachee/Shut Out	D	9	C	D	4	3-4
Executive Counsel	Good Counsel/Graustark	C	9	U	C	4	3-4
Executive Intent	Secretariat/Buckpasser	D	9	C	D	2	3-4
Executive Order	Secretariat/Sir Ivor	C	7	C	CT	3	2-3
Executive Pride GER	General Assembly/Majestic Prince	C	8	C	C	2	3-4
Exemplary Leader^^	Vigors/Aristocratic	M	7	M	M	3	3-4
Exile King	Exclusive Native/Hail to Reason	D	7	C	C	4	3-4
Exit Poll	Seattle Slew/Exclusive Native	F	10	D	C-	4	3-4
Expect Greatness	Raise a Native/Dance Spell	M	9	M	M	4	2-3
Expense Account*	Private Account/Riva Ridge	U	10	U	L	3	3-4
Expensive Decision	Explosive Bid/Hydrologist	D	6	C+	C	2	3-4
Explodent	Nearctic/Mel Hash	C	4*	B*	C	2	3-4
Explosive Bid	Explodent/Diplomat Way	C-	6	C	D	2	2-3

Stallion	Sire/Broodmare Sire	FTS	CL	Trf	OT	SI	AB
Explosive Red^	Explodent/Bold Hour	M	6	L	M	2	2-3
Explosive Wagon	Explodent/Conestoga	D	9	D	C+	4	3-4
Expressman	Gaelic Dancer/Olden Times	C	8	C	C+	5	3-4
Exuberant	What a Pleasure/Beau Purple	C-	7	C+*	C-	3	2-3
Ezzoudn IR	Last Tycoon/Claude	M	7	L	M	4	2-3
Fabled Monarch	Le Fabuleux/Princequillo	D	8	C*	C	1	3-4
Fabulous Champ	Somethingfabulous/Shirley's Champion	U	8	M	M	3	3-4
Fabulous Dancer FR	Northern Dancer/The Axe II	C-	5	C+*	D	2	2-3
Fair American*	Mr. Prospector/Jacinto	C	9	U	L	3	3-4
Fair Skies	Storm Bird/Exclusive Native	C	8	M	C-	3	2-3
Fairway Fortune	Northern Dancer/Beau Purple	D	8	C-	C-	4	3-4
Fairway Phantom BRZ	What a Pleasure/Native Dancer	C	8	C*	C	2	3-4
Fairy King IRE	Northern Dancer/Bold Reason	C-	6	C+	C	2	2-3
Falamoun FR	Kalamoun/Tapioca	D	6	C	M	3*	3-4
Faliraki	Prince Tenderfoot/Super Sam	D	8	C*	F	3	3-4
Falstaff	Lyphard/Sir Ivor	C-	8	C	C	4	3-4
Family Doctor	Dr. Fager/Djebe	C-	6	C*	C	3	2-3
Fappavalley BRZ	Fappiano/Road at Sea	C-	8	U	C	4	2-3
Fappiano	Mr. Prospector/Dr. Fager	C+	2*	B*	A	3	2-3
Fappiano Road^	Fappiano/Graustark	M	8	M	M	3	3-4
Fappiano's Dancer	Fappiano/Northern Dancer	D	7	C+	C	3	2-3
Faraway Island	Banquet Table/Our Native	U	10	M	M	2	3-4
Farma Way	Marfa/Diplomat Way	C	7	C+	C	3	2-3
Farnesio ARG	Good Manners/Cardanil II		7	C+*		4	3-4
Far North	Northern Dancer/Victoria Park	D	7	C*	C	3*	3-4
Far Out East	Raja Baba/Ambehaving	C-	7	C	CT	3*	3-4
Fast	Bold Bidder/Commanding II	D	9	D	C-	4	3-4
Fast Account	Private Account/Fleet Nasrullah	D	7	C-	C	3*	3-4
Fast Cure^	Cure the Blues/Pharly	M	7	M	M	4	2-3
Faster Than Sound	Five Star Flight/Turn & Count	F	7	C	C	4	2-3
Fast Foods	Tri Jet/Ack Ack	M	8	M	CT	4	2-3
Fast Forward	Pleasant Colony/Raise a Native	C-	9	D	C	4	3-4
Fast Gold THi	Mr. Prospector/Ack Ack	C-	7	C	C	3*	2-3
Fast 'n' Gold	Fast Gold/One For All	C-	8	M	C	4*	2-3
Fast Passer	Buckpasser/Double Jay	F	10	F	D	4	3-4
Fast Play	Seattle Slew/Buckpasser	C-	7	C-	C	3*	2-3
Fatih	Icecapade/Graustark	D	8	C-	C	4	3-4
Fayruz IRE	Song/Be Friendly	C	7	C-	M	5	2-3
Feather Ridge	Cox's Ridge/Roberto	M	8	U	M	3	3-4
Feel the Power	Raise a Native/Best Turn	C	8	U	CT	4	3-4
Fenter	Rare Brick/Cox's Ridge	C-	8	U	CT	4	3-4
Ferrara^	Capote/Swing Till Dawn	M	7	M	M	4	2-3
Ferdinand JPN	Nijinsky II/Double Jay	F	7	C-	C	3	3-4
Festin	Mat Boy/Con Brio	C-	8	C-	C-	3	3-4
Festival	Damascus/Raise a Native	D	10	U	C	4	3-4

Stallion	Sire/Broodmare Sire	FTS	CL	Trf	OT	SI	AB
Festive	Damascus/Buckpasser	C	7	C-	C	2	2-3
Festive Lad	Alydar/Secretariat	F	8	D	C	3	3-4
Feu d'Enfer	Tentam/Victoria Park	C	7	U	C	4	2-3
Fichte	Never Bend/Hill Prince	C-	7	D	C	4	3-4
Fiddle Dancer Boy	Nice Dancer/Hidden Treasure	C	7	D	C	3	3-4
Fierce Fighter	Fit to Fight/Hitting Away	M	8	U	M	4	2-3
Fiery Best	Sunny North/Diplomat Way	C	7	D	CT	4	2-3
Fiery Special^^	Pass the Line/	U	8	M	M	3	2-3
Fiestero *CHI*	Balconaje/Sun Prince	C	8	D	F	4	3-4
Fiesty Fouts	Northern Jove/Raise a Native	M	9	U	M	4	3-4
Fifth Marine	Hoist the Flag/Princequillo	D	7	C-	D	4	3-4
Fifty Six Ina Row	Dimaggio/Dusty Canyon	D	8	F	F	4	3-4
Fighting Fit	Full Pocket/Nilo	C-	8	F	CT	3	3-4
Fight Over	Grey Dawn II/Raise a Native	C-	7	C	C	4	2-3
Fio Rito	Dreaming Native/Sea Charger	D	8	C*	C	4	3-4
Fire Dancer	Northern Dancer/Native Charger	D	7	D	D	3	2-3
Fire Maker	Fire Dancer/Raise a Native	D	6	C	CT	4	2-3
First Albert	Tudor Grey/Groton	C-	8	D	D	5	3-4
First Landing	Turn-to/Hildene	D	7	C*	C	3*	3-4
First One Up	Johnny Appleseed/Distinctive	U	8	M	M	4	3-4
First Patriot	Salutely/Road at Sea	U	7	M	C+	3	3-4
First Trump *ENG*	Primo Dominie/Valiyar	M	6	L	M	4	2-3
Fit to Fight	Chieftain/One Count	C+	7	C-	C+T	3	2-3
Fitzcarraldo *ARG*	Cipayo/Stallwood	D	7	C	C	3*	3-4
Five Star Flight *MEX*	Top Command/Eddie Schmidt	D	8	D	C	4	3-4
Five Star's Peace	Five Star Flight/Hold Your Peace	M	9	U	M	4	3-4
Flagman Ahead	Riverman/Flag Officer	U	10	M	M	3	3-4
Flag Officer	Hoist the Flag/Bold Ruler	D	7	C*	C	3	3-4
Flare Dancer	Sovereign Dancer/Proudest Roman	D	9	D	C-	2	2-3
Flashy Image	Dancer's Image/Good Shot	D	8	D	F	4	3-4
Flashy Mac	Minnesota Mac/Cagire II	F	10	U	C	4	2-3
Flashy Pocket	Full Pocket/No Robbery	C-	8	U	CT	4	3-4
Fleet Allied	Fleet Nasrullah/Royal Charger	C-	8	C-*	C	4	3-4
Fleet Mel	Lucky Mel/Fleet Nasrullah	C-	8	C	C	4	3-4
Fleet Nasrullah	Nasrullah/Count Fleet	C-	5*	C*	C	4*	2-3
Fleet Swaps	Swaps/Fleet Nasrullah	C-	8	M	C	4	3-4
Fleet Tempo	Fleet Allied/Bright Tiny	C-	8	D	C	4	3-4
Fleet Twist	Fleet Nasrullah/Prince John	D	7	C*	C	3	3-4
Flickering	Summing/Damascus	U	10	U	M	4	3-4
Flight Forty Nine^	Forty Niner/Full Pocket	M	8	U	M	4	2-3
Floating Reserve	Olden Times/Quack	C-	8	D	C	4	3-4
Florez Munoz	Sovereign Dancer/Blazing Count	M	8	M	M	4	3-4
Floriano	Turn and Count/No Robbery	F	9	D	C	3	3-4
Florida Sunshine	Alydar/Quadrangle	D	7	D	C	3	2-3
Flout	Bold Bidder/Ben Lomond	D	10	M	M	5	3-4

Stallion	Sire/Broodmare Sire	FTS	CL	Trf	OT	SI	AB
Flow Technology	Super Concorde/Vaguely Noble	U	7	L	M	1	3-4
Fluorescent Light	Herbager/Ribot	F	8	C+*	C-	1	3-4
Fly a Kite	Be My Guest/Never Bend	D	10	M	D	4	3-4
Fly by Night	Vaguely Noble/Dark Star	U	9	M	M	2	3-4
Flying Continental*	Flying Paster/Transworld	C-	8	M	CT	3	3-4
Flying Flags		D	7	C	U	4	3-4
Flying Granville	Tyrant/Dunce	C-	8	D	C	5	2-3
Flying Paster	Gummo/Acroterion	C	5*	C	C	3	3-4
Flying Pidgeon	Upper Case/Minnesota Mac	D	9	C	D	2	3-4
Flying Target	Ack Ack/Nigromante	F	9	D	C	4	3-4
Flying Victor	Flying Paster/Sir Ivor	C+	7	C-	C	4	3-4
Fly So Free*	Time for a Change/Stevward	C-	7	D	C	3	3-4
Fly Till Dawn	Swing Till Dawn/Carwhite	D	8	C	C-	3	3-4
Fobby Forbes	Bold Forbes/Round Table	D	9	D	F	4	3-4
Foligno	Foolish Pleasure/In Reality	D	6	C	C	3	3-4
Folk's Pride	Turn-to/The Doge	C-	8	D	F	5	3-4
Follow the Drum *THI*	Northern Dancer/Lord Durham	M	7	U	U	4	3-4
Foolish Pleasure	What a Pleasure/Tom Fool	D	6	C+*	C-	3*	3-4
Fools Dance	Rattle Dancer/Tom Fool	F	7	U	C-	4	3-4
Fools Holme	Noholme II/Vaguely Noble	C-	8	C	C	1	3-4
Fool the Experts	Crafty Drone/Zip Pocket	C-	8	C	D	5	3-4
Forbidden Pleasure	Foolish Pleasure/Court Martial	C-	9	C*	D	3*	3-4
Force Fun	Forceten/T.V. Lark	U	9	M	M	3	3-4
Forceten	Forli/On and On	D	8	C*	C	3	3-4
Foreign Holding	Damascus/Buckpasser	U	7	C	M	4	3-4
Foreign Survivor	Danzig/Drone	C-	6	C+	C-	3	3-4
Foretake	Forli/Traffic Judge	D	8	D*	F	4	3-4
Forever Casting	Kaskaskia/Ambiorix	C-	8	D	C	4	3-4
Forever Dancer	Dixieland Band/Herbger	L	8	L	M	4*	2-3
Forever Silver	Silver Buck/Correlation	D	8	U	C-	3	3-4
Forever Sparkle	Secretariat/Ribot	D	7	B*	C	2	3-4
Forever Whirl^	Island Whirl/Forever Sparkle	M	8	U	M	4	3-4
Forget the Showers	Lt. Stevens/Bolero	D	9	D	D	5	3-4
Forli	Aristophanes/Advocate	C	5*	C+	C	3	3-4
Forlion	Forli/On-and-On	D	8	D	C	2	3-4
Forlitano *ARG*	Good Manners/Pardallo	D	5	C+	C	1	3-4
Forli Winds	Forli/Windy Sea	C-	8	C-	D	4	3-4
Formal Dinner	Well Decorated/Hoist the Flag	C+	6	C-	C	3	2-3
Formidable *ENG*	Forli/Raise a Native	D	6	C-*	C-	3*	3-4
For Really	Buckaroo/In Reality	C-	8	U	C	4	2-3
Forsythe Boy	Nodouble/Quadrangle	C	8	C-	C	3	2-3
Fort Calgary	Bold Joey/Calgary Brook	C-	9	D	C-	5	3-4
Fort Chaffee^^	Mr. Prospector/Nijinsky II	M	8	M	M	4	2-3
For The Moment	What a Pleasure/Tulyar	D	7	C	D	4	3-4
Fortunate Moment	For the Moment/Restless Wind	C-	9	D	C	4	3-4

Stallion	Sire/Broodmare Sire	FTS	CL	Trf	OT	SI	AB
Fortunate Prospect	Northern Prospect/Lucky Debonair	C	6	D	CT	3	2-3
Forty Niner JPN	Mr. Prospector/Tom Rolfe	B	5	C-	C+	4*	2-3
Forum	Jaipur/Court Martial		7	C*		3	3-4
Forward	Caro/Commanding II	D	8	C	C	2	3-4
Forward Charger	Native Charger/Royal Note	C-	9	D	D	4	3-4
Forzando ENG	Formidable/King's Troop	C	7	C-	M	4	2-3
Fountain of Gold	Mr. Prospector/Distinctive	C	7	D	C+	4	2-3
Four Seasons^^	Sadler's Wells/Habitat	U	8	L	M	1	3-4
Foxhound^	Danzig/Buckpasser	L	7	L	M	4*	2-3
Foyt BRZ	Raise a Native/On and On	D	7	F	C	3	3-4
Franklin Me	No Sale George/Valdez	C-	7	M	C-	4	3-4
Frankly Perfect	Perrault/Viceregal	C-	8	C-	C	3	3-4
Fraser River^	Forty Niner/Pharly	M	7	M	M	4*	2-3
Fred Astaire	Nijinsky II/Stage Door Johnny	C	7	C+	C-	3*	3-4
Free and Equal*	Nijinsky II/Secretariat	U	8	M	M	2	3-4
Free at Last*	Wild Again/Faraway Son	D	7	U	C-	4	2-3
Freepet			7	M*		3*	3-4
Free Reality	In Reality/Needles	D	8	F	C	4	3-4
Freetex IRE			7	C*		2	3-4
Free Water	Danzig/Tobin Bronze	D	8	C-	C	4	3-4
Freezing Rain	It's Freezing/Well Mannered	D	9	F	C	4	3-4
French Colonial	Tom Rolfe/Sir Gaylord	D	10	C	D	2	3-4
French Deputy^	Deputy Minister/Hold Your Peace	M	6	M	M	3	2-3
French Legionnaire	Grey Legion/Verbatim	D	8	F	C-	3	3-4
Friend's Choice	Crimson Satan/Nashua	C-	8	D	C+	4	3-4
Friul ARG	Good Manners/Pardallo	C-	7	C+	C-	3*	3-4
Frosty the Snowman	His Majesty/Diplomat Way	D	7	C	C	2	3-4
Fruitzig^	Danzig/Quadravan	M	8	L	M	4	3-4
Full Choke	Full Pocket/Never Bend	C	8	C	C+	5	2-3
Full Courage	Mr. Leader/Pretense	U	9	M	M	3	3-4
Full Intent	In Reality/Never Bend	C-	8	F	CT	5	3-4
Full Love BRZ	Figuron/Gabari		7	C		1	3-4
Full of Fools	Full Out/Secretariat	D	9	D	D	4	3-4
Full of Tricks	Clever Trick/Sadair	M	8	M	M	3	3-4
Full Out	Never Bend/Round Table	C	7	C*	C+	4	2-3
Full Partner	Never Bend/Round Table	C	8	D	C	4	2-3
Full Pocket	Olden Times/Summer Tan	C-	7	D	C	3	2-3
Full Swing	Full Out/Youth	M	8	U	M	3	3-4
Fulmar	Northern Dancer/Bolero	C	9	D	C-	4	3-4
Furiously^^	Danzig/Roberto	M	6	L	M	4*	2-3
Future Hope	Our Native/Sir Ribot	C-	7	C	C	3	2-3
Future Storm*	Storm Cat/Sea-Bird	C-	6	C-	C	3	2-3
Fuzzbuster	No Robbery/Hasty Road	D	8	D	C	3*	3-4
Fuzziano	Fappiano/Turn and Count	D	10	D	C-	4	3-4
Fuzzy	It's Freezing/Raise a Native	F	8	D	C	4	3-4

Stallion	Sire/Broodmare Sire	FTS	CL	Trf	OT	SI	AB
Fuzzy Freeze	Icecapade/T.V. Lark	C	10	C	CT	2	3-4
Gaelic Christian	Gaelic Dancer/Intentionally	C	8	D	C	4	3-4
Ga Hai	Determine/Goyamo	D	9	D	F	2	3-4
Gain	Mississippian/Sir Ribot	D	9	F	F	4	3-4
Gala Double	Spring Double/Rasper II	D	8	D	C	3	3-4
Galaxy Guide	Buckfinder/Reviewer	F	9	U	C-	4	3-4
Galaxy Libra	Wolver Hollow/Exbury	D	9	D	D	4	3-4
Galaxy Road	Kennedy Road/Nashua	F	9	C	D	4	3-4
Gallant Best	Best Turn/Gallant Man	C-	8	C-*	C	3*	3-4
Gallant Hour	Bold Hour/Royal Orbit	D	9	D	C	4	3-4
Gallant Man	Migoli/Mahmoud	C-	7	C*	C	3	3-4
Gallant Prospector*	Mr. Prospector/Pharly	C-	7	C-	C-	4*	3-4
Gallant Romeo	Gallant Man/Count Fleet	C	7	C*	C+	3	3-4
Gallapiat	Buckpasser/Sir Gaylord	D	7	C	C-	2	3-4
Gambler's Debt	Storm Bird/A Gambler	U	10	M	M	4	3-4
Ganges *FR*	Riverman/Blushing Groom	M	7	M	M	3*	3-4
Garde Royal *FR*	Mill Reef/Sicambre	D	6	C	M	1	3-4
Garthorn	Believe It/Cyane	D	8	D	C	3	3-4
Gary Jeter	Secretariat/Polyfoto	D	9	C-	C	3	3-4
Gas Energy	Ack Ack/Herbager	D	8	D	D	3	3-4
Gasp	Tinajero/Native Dancer	C-	9	U	C-	3	3-4
Gate Dancer	Sovereign Dancer/Bull Lea	C-	7	C-	C	3	2-3
Gato Del Sol *GER*	Cougar/Jacinto	D	8	D	F	2	3-4
Gaylord's Carousel	Lord Gaylord/Be Somebody	C	9	U	C+	4	3-4
Gay Mecene	Vaguely Noble/Sir Gaylord	D	6	CY*	C	3*	3-4
Gay Old Blade	Hagley/Laugh Aloud	F	9	F	C-	4	3-4
Geiger Counter *AUS*	Mr. Prospector/Nantallah	C-	7	C	CT	4*	2-4
Gemini Dreamer	Great Above/Cool Moon	D	8	C-	C	3	3-4
General *FR*			7	M*	C	3	3-4
General Assembly *GER*	Secretariat/Native Dancer	D	8	C-	C	2	3-4
General Holme *FR*	Noholme II/Count Fleet	C	7	C+	C	3*	3-4
General Jimmy	The Irish Lord/No Prevue	C	10	U	C+	5	3-4
General Meeting	Seattle Slew/Alydar	A	5	C	C-	3	2-3
General Silver	Silver Buck/Count Fleet	C	7	U	C	2	2-3
Generous *JPN*	Caerleon/Master Derby	F	5	C	M	2	3-4
Gentle King	WhatLuck/Nasrullah	C-	8	C*	C	3	3-4
Gentleman Gene	Maribeau/Rico Tesio	D	6	C	C	3*	3-4
Genuine Guy	Gummo/Windy Sands	C-	7	C	C	3	3-4
Georgeff	Raise a Native/Prince John	F	7	D	C-	2	3-4
Georgia's Lyphard	Lyphard/Secretariat	U	8	M	U	4	3-4
Get Around			7	C*		2	3-4
Gettysburg Address	Blushing Groom/Sea Bird	M	10	M	M	3	2-3
Ghaza	Damascus/Hoist the Flag	D	9	D	C	4	3-4
Ghazi^^	Polish Navy/Damascus	C+	8	M	M	1*	3-4
Giboulee	Northern Dancer/Victoria Park	C-	7	C*	C	4	3-4

Stallion	Sire/Broodmare Sire	FTS	CL	Trf	OT	SI	AB
Gift of Gib	Elocutionist/Raise a Native	<u>C</u>	7	U	C	5	2-3
Gilded Age	Tom Rolfe/Bold Ruler	C	8	C+	C	3	3-4
Gilded Time^^	Timeless Moment/What a Pleasure	C+	7	C-	C+	3	2-3
Gills	Secretariat/	U	10	M	M	4	3-4
Ginistrelli	Hoist the Flag/Round Table	C	8	D	C+	3	2-<u>3</u>
Girl's Castle	Slady Castle/Blue Swords	C-	8	D	D	4	3-4
Giuseppe	Fappiano/Graustark	D	8	C	C	3	3-4
Give Me Strength	Exclusive Native/Minnesota Mac	F	8	C+*	D	3	3-4
Give Me Your Ear	Fappiano/Clandestine	D	9	D	C-	4	3-4
Glaros	Sharpman/My Swallow	U	8	U	M	3	3-4
Glassy Dip	Diplomat Way/El Gallo	D	8	D	C-	4	3-4
Gleaming			6*	C+*		3*	3-4
Glide	Mr. Prospector/Northern Dancer	D	7	D	C-	5	<u>2</u>-3
Glint of Gold ENG			7	C*		3	3-4
Glitterman	Dewan/In Reality	B	6	C	B	4	<u>2</u>-3
Globe	Secretariat/Hail to Reason	D	8	C-	C	3	3-4
Glomar	Halo/Etonian	U	8	M	U	3	3-4
Glorious Flag	Secretariat/Hoist the Flag	F	7	C-	D	4	3-4
Glorious Light	On To Glory/Rehabilitate	U	9	M	M	4	3-4
Glossary			7	M*	M	2	3-4
Go and Go	Be My Guest/Alleged	D	7	C	C	2	3-4
Go Exclusive Go	Plenty Old/Exclusive Native	M	10	U	M	4	3-4
Go For Gin^	Cormorant/Stage Door Johnny	M	5	M	M	1	2-<u>3</u>
Go Forth ARG			7	C*		5	3-4
Going Straight	No Robbery/Hasty Road	D	8	D	C	4	3-4
Gold Alert	Mr. Prospector/Arts and Letters	C-	7	C-	C	3	<u>2</u>-3
Gold and Myrrh			7	C*	C+	2	3-4
Gold Blend NZ			7	C+		3	3-4
Gold Crest GER	Mr. Prospector/Northern Dancer	C-	7	C-	C-	3*	3-4
Golden Act	Gummo/Windy Sands	F	8	CY	D	2	3-4
Golden Choice	Val de L'orne/Barachois	D	7	M	D	3	3-4
Golden Derby	Master Derby/Young Emperor	D	7	D	C-	4	3-4
Golden Eagle II	Right Royal/Princequillo	C-	7	C	C	3	3-4
Golden Fleece	Nijinsky II/Vaguely Noble		7	C*		3	3-4
Golden Gauntlet	Golden Eagle II/Dr. Fager	C-	10	U	C	4	3-4
Golden Hill	Tri Jet/Quadrangle	D	7	C	CT	3	3-4
Golden Reserve	Sir Ivor/Round Table	D	8	F	C	4	2-3
Golden Ruler			8	M*	CT	2	3-4
Golden Whirl	Island Whirl/Zulu Tom	M	10	U	M	4	3-4
Gold Exchanged	Blushing Groom/Tom Rolfe	D	8	C	C-	2	3-4
Gold Legend*	Seattle Slew/Mr. Prospector	<u>B</u>	7	C-	C+	4	2-3
Goldlust	Mr. Prospector/Dr. Fager	C	7	D	CT	4	3-4
Gold Meridian	Seattle Slew/Crimson Satan	D	7	C	C	2	3-4
Goldneyev	Nureyev/Riverman	D	8	C	D	3*	3-4
Gold Pack	Relaunch/Mr. Prospector	D	10	U	C	4	3-4

Stallion	Sire/Broodmare Sire	FTS	CL	Trf	OT	SI	AB
Gold Ruler	Mr. Prospector/Bold Ruler	C	7	U	C	5	2-3
Gold Seam	Mr. Prospector/Nijinsky II	C-	6	C-	D	3	2-3
Gold Spring*	Gold Trojan/More Light	D	7	C	C	5	3-4
Gold Stage	Mr. Prospector/Cornish Prince	C-	7	C-*	C	3	2-3
Gold Trojan *ARG*	Gummo/Gipsy Jet		7	C*		3	3-4
Goldwater*	Mr. Prospector/Lyphard	C+	8	M	M	3	2-3
Goliard	Fappiano/Arts and Letters	M	8	M	L	4*	3-4
Go Loom	Loom/Gaelic Gold	C	10	U	C	5	3-4
Gone Digging	Mr. Prospector/Hoist the Flag	M	9	U	M	4	3-4
Gone West	Mr. Prospector/Secretariat	C+	6	BY	C	4*	2-3
Gonzales *GER*	Vaguely Noble/Dark Star	F	9	D	D	3	3-4
Good Bloke *ARG*			7	C+*		3	3-4
Good Counsel			7	C*	C	1	3-4
Good Manners *ARG*	Nashua/The Doge	D	5	C+*	C-	3*	3-4
Good Offense	Amber Pass/Dancing Count	M	9	M	M	4	3-4
Good Rob	Jim J./Faultless	D	8	U	C	5	3-4
Gorky	Key to the Mint/Nice Dancer	D	9	D	C-	3	3-4
Goshen Store	Whitesburg/Mountain Fire	M	9	U	M	4	3-4
Go Step	Bold Reasoning/Native Dancer	D	8	D	C	4	3-4
Gothic Revival	Le Fabuleux/Victorian Era	D	7	B	C	3*	3-4
Go to the Bank			7	M*		2	3-4
Gourami	King's Bishop/Hail to Reason	D	8	D	D	3	3-4
Government Program	Secretariat/Northern Dancer	D	10	D	C	4	3-4
Granacus*	Sweet Candy/Laser Light	M	6	M	L	3	3-4
Grand Allegiance	Pledge Allegiance/Bold Joey	D	8	U	T	5	3-4
Grand Alliance	Vaguely Noble/Shut Out	D	9	D	C	3	3-4
Grand Flotilla *IR*	Caro/Harbor Prince	U	7	M	M	1	3-4
Grand Jette	Timeless Moment/Stevward	M	7	U	M	5	3-4
Grand Jewel^	Java Gold/Alydar	M	7	U	M	3	3-4
Grand Lodge^^	Chief's Crown/Habitat	M	6	L	M	3	2-3
Grand Revival	Native Dancer/Princequillo	F	8	D	CT	4	3-4
Grand Ruler	Mr. Prospector/Pied d'Or	C-	8	U	DT	4	3-4
Gran Zar *Mex*	Raja Baba/Native Charger	C-	7	C-	C-	4	3-4
Gratification	Princely Native/Tumiga	C-	9	D	C-	4	3-4
Graustark	Ribot/Alibhai	D	4	C*	C	2	3-4
Gray Slewpy*	Slewpy/Grey Dawn II	C	7	M	CT	4	3-4
Great Above	Minnesota Mac/Intentionally	C	6	C+	C	3	2-3
Great Commotion *IRE*	Nureyev/Lorenzaccio	D	7	CY	U	3*	3-4
Great Deal	Caro/Raise a Native	D	9	D	C	4	3-4
Great Gladiator	Timeless Moment/Hawaii	C-	7	C	C	3	3-4
Great Neck	Tentam/Dr. Fager	C-	7	C	D	4	3-4
Great Nephew			6	C+*		1	3-4
Great Performance	Nijinsky II/Lt. Stevens	D	10	D	C	3	3-4
Great Prospector	Mr. Prospector/Hail to Reason	C-	7	C-	C	4	3-4
Great Reef	Grundy/Mill Reef	D	8	D	C	3	3-4

Stallion	Sire/Broodmare Sire	FTS	CL	Trf	OT	SI	AB
Great Sun			7	C*	C	2	3-4
Great View	Raja Baba/Dead Ahead	C+	6	U	CT	4	<u>2</u>-3
Greek Costume*	Mt Livermore/Proudest Roman	M	7	M	M	3	3-4
Green Alligator	Gate Dancer/King's Bishop	U	8	M	M	3	3-4
Green Book	Golden Act/Pretense	U	9	M	M	4	3-4
Green Dancer	Nijinsky II/Val de Loir	D	4*	C	C-	3*	3-4
Green Desert *ENG*	Danzig/Sir Ivor	C	5	C	C	4	2-3
Green Forest *IND*	Shecky Green/The Axe II	C-	7	C+	C	3*	3-4
Green Paradise	Vigors/The Axe II	D	9	D	C-	4	3-4
Greensmith *ENG*	Known Fact/Laser Light	C	7	C	M	4	2-3
Green Street	Green Dancer/Majestic Prince	M	8	M	M	2	3-4
Gregorian	Graustark/Dedicate	D	7	C*	C	3*	3-4
Greinton *GER*	Green Dancer/High Top	F	8	C-	C-	2	3-4
Gremlin Grey	Northern Prospect/Explodent	M	9	M	M	4	<u>2-3</u>
Grenfall	Graustark/Swaps	D	8	D	C	3	3-4
Grey Adorn	Grey Dawn II/Bolero	D	8	U	D	4	3-4
Grey Aloha	Grey Dawn II/Hawaii	U	10	M	M	4	3-4
Grey Bucket	Flip Sal/Nilo	D	9	D	C	4	3-4
Grey Dawn II	Herbager/Mahmoud	D	4*	C	C	3*	3-4
Groom Dancer *FR*	Blushing Groom/Lyphard	D	7	C	C	3*	3-4
Groomstick*	Runaway Groom/Francis S	D	7	C+	CT	3	2-3
Groovy	Norcliffe/Restless Wind	C-	7	<u>C</u>	C	4	3-4
Groshawk	Graustark/Jester	D	8	C*	C	3	3-4
Grosvenor *NZ*	Sir Tristam/Hermes	D	6	C+	M	2	3-4
Groton	Nashua/Bimelech	C-	8	F	C	4	3-4
Ground Zero	Silent Screen/Tudor Grey	M	10	U	U	5	2-3
Grub	Mr. Prospector/Never Bend	C-	8	C	C+	4	3-4
Guadalupe Peak	Mr. Prospector/Roman Line	D	8	U	D	4	3-4
Guilford Road	Roberto/Olympia	D	7	C+	D	4	3-4
Guilty Conscience	Court Ruling/Gallant Man	D	8	C+*	C	3	3-4
Gulch	Mr. Prospector/Rambunctious	C-	5	C	C+	4*	<u>2-3</u>
Gumboy	Gummo/Anyoldtime	D	8	D	C	4	2-3
Gummo	Fleet Nasrullah/Determine	C	6	C*	C	3	<u>2-3</u>
Gun Bow	Gun Shot/Ribbons and Bows		7	C*		3*	3-4
Gun Captain	Ack Ack/Crimson Satan	M	9	M	M	4	3-4
Gustoso	What a Pleasure/Native Dancer	U	8	D	C	4	3-4
Habitat	Sir Gaylord/Occupy	C-	6	C*	C	4*	<u>2-3</u>
Habitonia	Habitony/Tudor Minstrel	C	6	D	C+	4	2-3
Habitony	Habitat/Gallant Man	C-	7	C-	C+	3	3-4
Hadeer *ENG*	General Assembly/Crepello	D	7	C	M	1	3-4
Hadif	Clever Trick/Silent Screen	C	7	M	C	4	<u>2-3</u>
Hagley	Olden Times/Jet Action	C-	6	C+*	C	3	3-4
Hagley Mill	Hagley/Mister Buster II	C+	6	U	C	3	3-4
Hagley's Reward	Hagley/Correlation	D	7	D	D	4	3-4
Hail Bold King *PR*	Bold Bidder/Hail to Reason	D	7	C+	C	3	3-4

Stallion	Sire/Broodmare Sire	FTS	CL	Trf	OT	SI	AB
Hail Emperor	Graustark/Bold Ruler	D	7	D*	C+	3	3-4
Hail the Pirates	Hail to Reason/Niccolo Dell'arca	D	7	C*	D	2	3-4
Hail the Ruckus	Bold Ruckus/Hail the Prince	C	7	M	C-	4	2-3
Hail the Truth	Alleged/Le Fabuleux	U	7	M	M	2	3-4
Hail to Buck	Silver Buck/Sea Bird	M	9	U	M	3	3-4
Hail Victorious	King Pellinore/Hail to Reason	M	10	M	M	3	3-4
Hajji's Treasure	Pirate's Bounty/Besomer	D	9	D	D	4	3-4
Half a Year	Riverman/Northern Dancer	C	7	C	CT	4	3-4
Half Term^	Mr. Prospector/Northern Dancer	M	7	L	M	4*	2-3
Halissee^^	Cozzene/Fappiano	U	6	L	M	3	2-3
Halo	Hail to Reason/Cosmic Bomb	D	3*	C*	CT	1*	3-4
Hamas *IRE*	Danzig/Pretense	M	7	L	M	4*	2-3
Hamza *PAN*	Northern Dancer/Val de Loir	D	9	C-	C-	3	3-4
Hansel	Woodman/Dancing Count	D	6	B	CT	3*	3-4
Hapgood	Dance Spell/Jester	D	8	D	C	4	2-3
Happyasalark Tomas	Wonder Lark/Mr. Washington	D	8	D	C	3	3-4
Happy Bid	Spectacular Bid/Raise a Native	D	8	D	C-	4	3-4
Happy Darling	Affirmed/Prince John	C	9	M	U	4	3-4
Happy Escort	Unconscious/Raise a Native	F	10	C-	DT	4	3-4
Happy Hooligan	Rollicking/Swoon's Son	D	10	U	D	4	3-4
Happy Jazz Band^^		L	6	M	L	4	2-3
Happy Trap	Bold LaddieFour-and-Twenty	U	7	U	L	4	2-3
Harbour Bridge	Roberto//Viceregal	U	10	M	M	3*	3-4
Harbor Prince *NZ*	Prine John/Hornbeam		6	C+*		1	3-4
Hardball Bill	Dewan Keys/Naskra	U	8	M	M	2	3-4
Hardwork	Golden Ruler/Sub Fleet	C-	7	C*	C	4	3-4
Harlan^^	Storm Cat/Halo	C	7	M	M	4	2-3
Harmony Creek	Sensitive Music/Barbaric Spirit	M	9	M	M	3	3-4
Harperstown	Devil's Bag/Northern Dancer	M	8	M	CT	4	3-4
Harriman	Lord Gaylord/Restless Native	D	8	U	C-	2	3-4
Harry L.	Olden Times/Never Bend	D	9	U	C	4	3-4
Harvard Man	Crimson Satan/Swaps	F	7	D	C	4	2-3
Hasty Flyer	Misty Flight/One Count	D	8	D	C	4	3-4
Hasty Groom	Blushing Groom/Hasty Road	D	9	M	C+	4	3-4
Hasty Spring	Spring Double/One Count	F	8	D	D	3	3-4
Hatchet Man	The Axe II/Tom Fool	D	7	D	C-	2	3-4
Hawaii	Utrillo II/Mehrail	D	6	C+*	C	3	3-4
Hawkin's Special	Great Sun/Nasomo	C	8	C*	D	3	3-4
Hawkster *JPN*	Silver Hawk/Chieftain	F	8	C	DT	3	3-4
Hay Halo	Halo/Hoist the Flag	C-	6	C	C	2	3-4
Haymaker	Two Punch/Vice Regent	M	7	U	M	3	2-3
Haymarket	Danzig/Halo	C	7	M	C	3*	3-4
Hawaiian Pass*	Pass the Glass/Hawaii	M	8	L	M	4	3-4
Hazaam *FR*	Blushing Groom/Nureyev	U	7	L	M	3*	3-4
Head Games	Clev Er Tell/Roman Line	U	8	U	M	5	3-4

Stallion	Sire/Broodmare Sire	FTS	CL	Trf	OT	SI	AB
Heaven Again	Wild Again/Hawkin's Special	C-	8	M	M	4	3-4
Hechizado ARG	Cambremont/Sideral	C-	7	D	F	2	2-3
Heff	Alydar/Blazing Count	C+	7	U	C+	4	2-3
Hello Gorgeous BRZ	Mr. Prospector/Jet Jewel	D	8	C-	C-	3	3-4
Henbane	Alydar/Chateaugay	C	7	C	CT	3	2-3
Henbit	Hawaii/Chateaugay	D	7	C*	C	4	3-4
Herat	Northern Dancer/Damascus	D	7	C+	D	3	3-4
Herbager	Vandale/Escamillo	D	6	C	C	1	3-4
Here Comes Red	Peace Corps/Stevward	F	9	C	D	4	3-4
Here We Come	Mr. Prospector/The Minstrel	D	7	U	CT	4	3-4
Hermes	Mr. Leader/Hill Prince	M	8	M	T	3	3-4
Hermitage	Storm Bird/Bold Reason	D	8	C	C-	2	3-4
Hero's Honor FR	Northern Dancer/Graustark	C	6	C*	D	3*	2-3
He's a Looker	Raise a Native/Drone	M	8	U	DT	4	2-3
He's Bad	Rambunctious/Djeddah	C	8	D	DT	2	3-4
He's Our Native	Our Native/Incaico	D	8	C-	C	3	3-4
Hey Rob	Tisab/Gaelic Dancer	C-	8	F	C	4	3-4
Hickman Creek*	Seattle Slew/Buckpasser	C	8	M	C	3	2-3
Hickory Ridge	Best Turn/Ballydonnell	D	9	D	C-	3	3-4
High Brite	Best Turn/Forli	C	7	D	CT	4	2-3
High Comedy	The Minstrel/Misty Flight	D	8	D	C-	3	3-4
High Counsel	Apalachee/Court Martial	C-	8	C*	D	4	2-3
High Echelon	Native Charger/Princequillo	C	6	C*	C-	3*	3-4
High Energy	Diamond Prospect/Noblesse Oblige	C	10	C-	C	4*	3-4
High Estate IRE	Shirley Heights/Princely Native	C	5	CY	M	1	3-4
Highest Honor FR	Kenmare/Riverman	C	4	C+	C	1	3-4
High Gold	Mr. Prospector/Irish Lancer	D	7	F	D	4	3-4
High Honors	Graustark/Hail to Reason	F	7	D	C	3*	3-4
Highland Blade	Damascus/Misty Flight	D	7	C+*	C	3	3-4
Highland Park	Raise a Native/Olden Times	C-	8	D	C	4	3-4
Highland Ruckus	Bold Rukus/Victoria Park	C	8	U	C+	5	2-3
High Line ENG	High Hat/Chanteur	C-	3	B*	D	3*	3-4
High Top ENG	Derring Do/Vimy	D	5	C+	D	3*	3-4
High Tribute	Prince John/War Relic	D	7	C	D	2	3-4
Hilal IR	Royal and Regal/Whistling Wind	C	7	C	C	4	3-4
His Majesty	Ribot/Alibhai	D	4*	B	C	1	3-4
Historically	Raise a Native/Dead Ahead	D	9	D	C	4	3-4
Historique FR	Rainbow Quest/Riverman	M	6	L	L	3*	3-4
Ho Choy	Crozier/Northern Dancer	D	7	D	D	5	3-4
Hoedown's Day	Bargain Day/Dance Lesson	C-	8	C+	C-	3	3-4
Hoist the Flag	Tom Rolfe/War Admiral	C-	3	C	C	3*	3-4
Hoist the Silver	Hoist the Flag/Prince John	D	9	C-	C	4	3-4
Hold On Chris	Hold Your Peace/Damascus	M	8	M	L	3	3-4
Hold That Fool	Hold Your Peace/Tom Fool	D	8	U	C	4	3-4
Hold the Sauce	Sauce Boat/Dancer's Image	M	8	M	M	3	3-4

Stallion	Sire/Broodmare Sire	FTS	CL	Trf	OT	SI	AB
Hold Your Peace	Speak John/Eight Thirty	C	6	C*	C	3	2-3
Hollywood Brat	Cannonade/Vaguely Noble	C-	9	C	C	4	3-4
Hollywood Reporter	Saratoga Six/Torsion	M	10	U	L	4	3-4
Holme on Top	Noholme II/Federal Hill	D	8	F	C	4	3-4
Holy Bull^^	Great Above/Al Hattab	M	6	M	M	3	2-3
Holy Mac A Nolley	Flying Paster/Gaelic Dancer	M	9	M	L	3	3-4
Holy War	Damascus/Bold Ruler	C-	9	D	C-	4	3-4
Home at Last	Quadratic/Ack Ack	D	6	C+	C	3	3-4
Homebuilder	Mr. Prospector/Vaguely Noble	C-	6	D	CT	3	2-3
Home Guard			7	C*		I*	3-4
Homestand	Fappiano/Quack	M	10	U	L	4	2-3
Hometown Favorite^	Our Native/Run the Gantlet	U	8	L	M	2	3-4
Honest Note	Honest Pleasure/Native Charger	M	9	U	M	4	3-4
Honest Pleasure	What a Pleasure/Tulyar	D	8	D	C	3	3-4
Honey Jay	Double Jay/Roman	C	7	C*	D	3	2-3
Honeyland	Stop the Music/Drone	C	7	U	C-	4	2-3
Honor Grades	Danzig/Secretariat	C	5	C+	C	3	2-3
Hooched	Danzig/Tom Rolfe	C-	7	C	C-	2	3-4
Hookano JPN	Silver Shark/Sailor	F	9	D	C	3	3-4
Hopeful Word	Verbatim/Mt. Hope	C-	9	CY	C	3	2-3
Horatius	Proudest Roman/Cohoes	C	7	C-	CT	3*	2-4
Hornbeam			7	C*		2	3-4
Horse Flash	Stay for Lunch/Spectacular Bid	U	7	M	M	5	2-3
Hostage BRZ	Nijinsky II/Val de Loir	D	8	C*	C-	3*	3-4
Hot Cop	Policeman/Noholme II	M	8	M	M	3	3-4
Hot Mop Darby		M	9	M	M	3	2-3
Hot Oil	Damascus/The Axe II	D	8	D	C-	4	3-4
Housebuster JPN	Mt. Livermore/Great Above	B	5	C+	C+	4*	2-3
Houston	Seattle Slew/Quadrangle	D	7	C-	C+	3	3-4
Hubble	Seattle Slew/Far North	D	7	M	C	3*	2-3
Huckster	Mr. Prospector/Sir Ivor	F	7	D	C	3	3-4
Huddle Up	Sir Ivor/Never Bend	C-	7	U	C	4	3-4
Huguenot	Forli/Turn-to	C	8	D	C	4	3-4
Hugo's Million		U	8	U	C+	4	3-4
Hula Blaze	Hula Chief/Handsome Boy	C+	8	U	C-	5	3-4
Humbaba	Raja Baba/Crimson Satan	U	10	U	M	4	3-4
Hunting Horn	Northern Dancer/Drone	U	7	M	C+	3	3-4
Hurlingham	Mr. Prospector/Secretariat	D	10	U	D	4	3-4
Hurontario	Halo/Buckpasser	D	8	D	D	4	3-4
Hurricane Ed	Intervener/Dictar	D	7	D	CT	3	3-4
Hurricane Mars	Fichte/Redoubtable	U	9	U	U	5	3-4
Husband^	Diesis/King Emperor	U	6	L	M	I	3-4
Hush Hush Flash	Arctic Flash/Groton	D	9	D	D	5	3-4
Hyannis Port	Kennedy Road/Novarullah	D	9	D	C-	4	3-4
Hyperborean	Icecapade/Prince John	C-	9	C	C-	2	3-4

Stallion	Sire/Broodmare Sire	FTS	CL	Trf	OT	SI	AB
Iades *NZ*	Shirley Heights/Sir Gaylord		7	C		3	3-4
I Am the Game	Lord Gaylord/Dead Ahead	C	7	C	C	4	3-4
Iam the Iceman	Pirate's Bounty/Bold Hitter	C	7	U	C-	4	2-3
I Can't Believe^^	Our Native/Graustark	M	6	M	M	3	2-3
Ice Age	Icecapade/Warfare	C	8	F	BT	4	3-4
Icecapade	Nearctic/Native Dancer	C	5*	C	C	4*	2-3
Ice Hole	Icecapade/Dr. Fager	D	9	U	M	3	2-3
Icehot	Icecapade/Le Fabuleux	U	9	M	M	2	3-4
Ice Power	Icecapade/Lyphard	M	9	M	M	3	3-4
Icy Groom *JPN*	Blushing Groom/Roberto	D	8	C-	C	2	3-4
Idabel	Mr. Prospector/Briartic	C-	8	U	C+	3	3-4
Idaho's Majesty	His Majesty/Raise a Native	D	10	M	D	4	3-4
I Enclose	Cormorant/No Robbery	C-	8	C	C	3	3-4
If This Be So	Secretariat/Olympia	D	7	C*	C-	3	3-4
Ile de Bourbon	Nijinsky II/Roseliere	D	5	CY*	D	1	3-4
Ile de Jinsky	Ile de Bourbon/Sir Ivor	F	7	C	DT	3	3-4
I'll Be Good	Tri Jet/Accipter	M	8	M	M	4	3-4
I'll Raise You One	Far North/Raise a Native	D	6	D	D	3	2-3
Illuminate	Majestic Light/Forli	D	8	C	C-	2	3-4
Illustrious	Round Table/Nasrullah	D	7	D	C	3	3-4
Image of Greatness	Secretariat/Intentionally	D	7	C	C	3	3-4
I'm a Hell Raiser	Raise a Native/I'm for More	B	7	C	C+	5	2-4
I'm a Lyre	The Minstrel/Bold Ruler	D	10	D	D	4	3-4
Ima Teas Dancer	Nureyev/Tom Rolfe	M	9	L	M	2	3-4
Imcaro	Caro/Chieftain	M	7	L	M	3	3-4
I'm Daring	Alydar/In Reality	M	9	U	L	4	3-4
I'm Glad	Liloy/Idle Hour	D	7	D	C	4	3-4
Imperial Falcon	Northern Dancer/Herbager	D	7	C-	DT	2	3-4
Imperial Fling *GER*	Northern Dancer/Buckpasser	C-	9	C-	C+	3	3-4
Imperial Frontier *IRE*	Lyphard/Vaguely Noble	D	8	C	C	3	3-4
Imperial Gold *FR*	Blushing Groom/Prince John	U	7	L	M	1	3-4
Imperial Guard	Northern Dancer/Victoria Park	F	10	D	D	3	3-4
Imperial Napharr *ARG*			7	M		3	3-4
Imperious Regent	Lord Dunham/Vice Regent	U	8	M	U	3	3-4
Implement	Graustark/Chieftain	D	10	D	C	4	3-4
Implore	Sovereign Dancer/Herbager	D	7	C-	C-	3	3-4
Implosion	Explodent/Diplomat Way	C	10	L	M	3	3-4
Impressibility	Our Native/Bold Ruler	C-	9	U	D	4	3-4
Impressive	Court Martial/Ambiorix	C-	7	C+*	C	3	2-3
Imp Society *ENG*	Barrera/Promised Land	D	7	C	C-	2	2-3
In a Walk*	Chief's Crown/Private Account	M	10	M	M	3	3-4
Inca Chief	Mr. Prospector/Minnesota Mac	D	9	C-	M	4	3-4
In Case^	Storm Cat/In Reality	L	6	M	L	4*	2-3
Incense	Gold and Myrrh/Bald Eagle	M	7	M	M	4	2-3
Inchinor *ENG*	Ahonoora/Lomond	U	6	C	M	4	2-3

Stallion	Sire/Broodmare Sire	FTS	CL	Trf	OT	SI	AB
Incinderator	Northern Dancer/Gummo	C	8	C-	C	3	3-4
Incredible Ease	Jacinto/Poker	D	8	D	C-	4	3-4
Indalecio *ARG*	Cipayo/Vervain	M	7	M	M	2	3-4
Indian Detail	Apalachee/Road at Sea	D	9	M	CT	4̲	3-4
Indian Gold	Raise a Native /Fleet Nasrullah	D	9	U	C-	4	3-4
Indian Groom *FR*	Blushing Groom/Graustark	U	7	L	M	I	3-4
Indian Ridge *IRE*	Ahonoora/Swing Easy	C	6	B	M	3	2-4
Indian Trail	Apalachee/Majestic Prince	D	10	D	C-	3	3-4
Indomitable Reb	Nijinsky II/Alleged	U	8	M	M	3*	3-4
Induit	Briartic/Twice Worthy	M	8	M	M	4	2-3
Industry Standard	Spectacular Bid/Gallant Man	D	8	D	D	4	3-4
In Excess*	Siberian Express/Saulingo	C+	7	M	C+	3	2-3
In Fijar	Bold Commander/Martial at Arms	F	8	D	D	3*	3-4
Inflated Ego	Ego Eye/Big Brave	C-	10	U	C	5	3-4
In From Dixie	Isgala/Grey Dawn II	C-	7	U	C	4	3-4
Ingot's Ruler	Diplomat Way/Iron Ruler	D	9	D	D	3	3-4
Inherent Star	Pia Star/Dumpty Humpty	C-	8	C*	C	4	3-4
In House	Riva Ridge/Secretariat	U	9	U	M	3	3-4
Inishpour *IRE*	Nishapour/Tudor Melody	M	8	L	M	4	3-4
Inkosana			6	C*		I	3-4
Innkeeper	Secretariat/Mr. Prospector	D	8	C	C	3	3-4
Inkosana			7	C*		I	3-4
In One Era	Exclusive Era/Reviewer	D	8	D	D	4	3-4
In Reality	Intentionally/Rough 'n Tumble	B	3*	C+*	A	4*	2-3
Inspired Prospect	Woodman/Tell	C-	6	C	C	4*	3-4
Instant Dancer	For the Moment/Dance to Market	D	8	C	C	4	3-4
Instrument Landing	Grey Dawn II/Bold Lad	D	8	C-	D	3	3-4
Interco	Intrepid Hero/Majestic Prince	C-	8	C	C	3	3-4
Interdicto	Grey Dawn II/Ahoy	D	7	C+	D	2	3-4
Interrex *ENG*	Vice Regent/Secretariat	C	7	C	C	4	3-4
In the Slammer	Stiff Sentence/Alley Fighter	C+	7	U	C+	3*	2-3
In the Swing	Blushing Groom/Grey Dawn II	F	8	D	C-	3	3-4
In the Wings *IRE*	Sadler's Wells/Shirley Heights	D	5	CY	M	3*	3-4
In the Woodpile	Raise a Native/Prince John	C-	8	D	C	4	3-4
Intimidation	Sauceboat/Model Fool	D	7	D	C	4	2-3
In Tissar	Roberto/Bold Bidder	D	9	D	C	4	3-4
In Totality	In Reality/Spy Song	C-	8	F	C	5	2-3
Intrusion	Top Command/Kennedy Road	D	9	U	C	3	3-4
Inverness Drive	Crozier/Court Martial	D	7	C	C	3	2-3̲
Iowa Best	Naskra/Tom Rolfe	U	9	M	M	3	3-4
Irish Bard	Tudor Melody/Red God	M	9	U	M	4	3-4
Irish Bear	Lobsang/Tilt Top	U	10	U	M	4	3-4
Irish Castle	Bold Ruler/Tulyar	D	7	C	C	3	3-4
Irish Conn	Buckpasser/Victorian Era	D	10	U	F	4	3-4
Irish Dreamin	The Irish Lord/Any Time Now	M	9	U	M	4	3-4

Stallion	Sire/Broodmare Sire	FTS	CL	Trf	OT	SI	AB
Irish Open	Irish Tower/Buckpasser	C	6	C	C+	4	2-3
Irish River	Riverman/Klairon	C	3*	C	D	3*	3-4
Irish Ruler	Bold Ruler/Bold Irishman	C-	7	C*	C	4	3-4
Irish Scoundrel	The Irish Lord/The Scoundrel	M	8	U	M	5	3-4
Irish Stronghold	Bold Ruler/Tulyar	D	7	C*	C	3	3-4
Irish Sur	Surreal/Irish Dude	C-	6	D	C-	3	3-4
Irish Swords	Raja Baba/Graustark	C-	9	U	DT	4	3-4
Irish Tower	Irish Castle/Loom	C+	6	D	C+	3	2-3
Irish Waters	Norcliffe/National	M	8	M	M	3	3-4
Iron	Mr. Prospector/Buckpasser	C-	7	D	C+	4	3-4
Iron Constitution	Iron Ruler/Hail to Reason	D	6	C*	C	3	3-4
Iron Courage	Caro/Fleet Nasrullah	C-	7	C+	C	2	3-4
Iron Duke *FR*		7		C*		4	3-4
Iron Ruler	Never Bend/Mahmoud	D	8	C+*	CT	3	3-4
Iron Warrior	Native Dancer/Count Fleet	C-	7	C*	C	3	3-4
Ironworks	Hard Work/Bold Bidder	C-	9	M	M	4	3-4
Iroquois Indian	Valid Appeal/Jaipur	M	7	M	M	4	2-3
Iroquois Park	Chief's Crown/Icecapade	C-	7	M	C	3	2-3
Is It True	Raja Baba/Proudest Roman	C-	7	U	CT	3	3-4
Island Champ	Dancing Champ/Search for Gold	C-	8	F	D	4	3-4
Island Sultan	What a Pleasure/Prince John	D	9	F	D	4	3-4
Island Sun	Noble Dancer/Sigebert	D	8	D	D	4	3-4
Island Whirl	Pago Pago/Your Alibhai	C	7	C-	C	3	2-3
Isopach	Reviewer/No Robbery	D	8	C	C	3*	3-4
Itajara *BRZ*	Felicio/Falkland	C	6	C	C+	2	3-4
Italian Connection	Maris/Bley	D	8	U	D	4	3-4
Italian Critic^	Fappiano/The Minstrel	M	9	U	M	4	2-3
It's Acedemic	Sauce Boat/Arts and Letters	D	6	D	D	3	3-4
Itsallinthegame	Herculean/No Robbery	D	10	D	C-	4	3-4
It's Freezing	TV Commercial/Arctic Prince	C	7	C	C	3	2-3
It's the One	Dewan/Hawaii	D	8	D	C	3	3-4
It's True	In Reality/Buckpasser	C-	8	D	C	4	3-4
Ivan Phillips	Sir Ivor/Buckpasser	D	8	U	D	3	3-4
Ivor Street	Sir Ivor/Native Dancer	D	8	U	C-	2	3-4
Ivory Salmon *ENG*		7		C		3	3-4
Iz a Saros	Saros/Bicker	C-	9	C	M	4	3-4
Jack Livingston^^	Deputy Minister/Shecky Greene	M	8	M	M	4	3-4
Jacksonport^	Vigors/Cox's Ridge	U	8	M	L	3	3-4
Jacodra	Highland Park/Green Dancer	M	8	U	M	4	3-4
Jacques Who	Grey Dawn II/Nantallah	C	6	D	D	3	3-4
Jade Hunter	Mr. Prospector/Pharly	C-	6	B	C	1	3-4
Jaklin Klugman	Orbit Ruler/Promised Land	C	7	C	C	4	3-4
Jamiano^	Fappiano/Graustark	M	8	M	M	4	3-4
Jammed Gold	Kentucky Gold/Mito	M	7	U	M	4	3-4
Jane's Dilemma	Master Derby/Hilarious	C-	7	C-	CT	1	2-3

Stallion	Sire/Broodmare Sire	FTS	CL	Trf	OT	SI	AB
Jan's Kinsman	Kinsman Hope/Smart	F	10	U	F	3	3-4
Jareer *IRE*			6	C		1	3-4
Java Gold *GER*	Key to the Mint/Nijinsky II	C-	7	C-	C-	3*	3-4
Jazzing Around	Stop the Music/Jacinto	C+	8	C	C+	4	2-3
Jazz Singer	Silent Screen/Fleet Nasrullah	D	8	F	D	4	3-4
J. Burns	Bold Hour/Double Jay	C-	8	C	C+	3	2-3
Jeblar	Alydar/Lucky Debonair	C+	5	<u>B</u>	C	3	2-3
Jeffers West	Roberto/Nijinsky II	U	9	M	M	3	3-4
Jeff's Companion	Noholme II/Vaguely Noble	C-	9	M	C	3	2-3
Jeloso	Raise a Native/Nijinsky II	D	9	C-	D	2	3-4
Jerimi Johnson	Barachois/Bolinas Boy	D	9	C	C	5	2-<u>3</u>
Jestic	His Majesty/Proud Clarion	D	10	C	C	2	3-4
Jet Diplomacy			7	M*	C	3	3-4
Jetting Home	Tri Jet/Maribeau	M	8	M	L	4	3-4
Jett Sett Joe	Bold Joey/Curandero	M	10	M	M	5	3-4
Jeune Homme	Nureyev/Alydar	M	8	L	M	3	3-4
Jig Time	Native Dancer/Case Ace	C	7	C	C+	4	2-<u>3</u>
Jihad	Damascus/Bold Ruler	D	8	D	C	4	3-4
Jitano	Rattle Dancer/Halter	U	9	M	U	5	3-4
Jitterbug Chief	Sovereign Dancer/Prove It	C-	8	U	C-	3	3-4
Jiva Jima	Wajima/Crimson Satan	M	8	U	M	4	3-4
Joanie's Chief	Ack Ack/Fleet Host	C-	8	C	C	<u>4</u>	3-4
Joey Bob	Bold Hemp/Rough'n Tumble	D	8	C	D	3	3-4
John Alden	Speak John/Nashua	D	7	D	CT	2	3-4
John Casey	Prince John/No Robbery	F	8	C+	C	2	3-4
Johnnie's Story	Lines of Power/Clem	C-	8	U	c-	4	3-4
Johnny Blade	Blade/Saidam	M	9	M	M	5	3-4
John Quincy	Mr. Washington/Tri Jet	M	9	U	M	4	3-4
John Riggins	Virilify/Duc de Fer	M	9	U	M	4	3-4
John's Choice	Friend's Choice/Du de Fer	C	9	D	D	4	3-4
John's Gold	Bold Bidder/Buckpasser	F	7	D	C	3	3-4
Johns Treasure *BRZ*	Exclusive Native/Hoist the Flag	D	8	D	C	3*	3-4
Jokester	Seattle Slew/Spectacular Bid	M	7	C+	M	3	3-4
Jolies Appeal^	World Appeal/Bold Forbes	M	8	M	M	3	2-3
Jolie's Halo* *JPN*	Halo/Sir Ivor	C	6	D	CT	3	3-4
Jollify *FR*			7	M*		2	3-4
Jolly Blade	Blade/T.V. Lark	M	9	U	M	4	3-4
Jolly Johu	Restless Native/Gallant Man	F	7	D	C	4	3-4
Jolly Quick *BRZ*			6	C+		4	3-4
Jon Ian	Our Michael/Catallus	U	10	U	M	5	3-4
Jontilla			7	M*	C	3	3-4
Jose Binn	Vertee/Mr. Randy	C	8	C	C	4	3-4
J.O. Tobin	Never Bend/Hillary	C-	7	C*	C	3	3-4
Journey at Sea	Crozier/Sailor	D	7	C	C	<u>4</u>	3-4
Journey's Joy	Copelan/Exuberant	L	8	M	L	4	2-3

Stallion	Sire/Broodmare Sire	FTS	CL	Trf	OT	SI	AB
Jovial Turn	Northern Jove/Quid Pro Quo	C-	8	D	C	4	3-4
Joyful Charger	Daryl's Joy/Native Charger	C	9	C	C	3	3-4
J.P. Brother	Wig Out/John William	D	9	F	D	5	3-4
Jr. Prospect	Mr. Prospector/Khaled	M	9	U	M	3	3-4
Judgable	Delta Judge/One-Eyed King	D	8	D	C	4	3-4
Judge Lex	Judge Kilday/Citation	C	8	D	C	4	3-4
Judger	Damascus/Sword Dancer	C-	6	C+*	C-	1	3-4
Judge Smells	In Reality/Best Turn	D	7	D	CT	3	2-3
Judiciously	Family Doctor/Diplomat Way	M	10	M	M	4	3-4
Julio Mariner			7	C*		3*	3-4
Jumbo Star	Mombo Jumbo/Octo Boss	M	9	M	T	4	3-4
Jump Over the Moon	Vertex/Sadair	D	8	C-	C-	4	3-4
Junction	Never Bend/Royal Union	F	8	C*	C-	3*	3-4
Jungle Blade	Blade/Jungle Road	C	8	D	CT	3	3-4
Jungle Pocket	Full Pocket/Hillary	C	8	U	C	4	3-4
Jungle Savage	Indian Hemp/Tom Fool	D	7	C	C	4	3-4
Jupiter Island ENG	St. Paddy/Reform	F	8	C	M	1	3-4
Just as Swift^^	Bolger/Lucky Mel	M	8	U	L	4	3-4
Just a Tab	Pass the Tab/Faraway Son	D	10	U	D	4	3-4
Just a Tune	Pass the Tab/Tilt Up	M	9	L	M	3	3-4
Just Plain Tuff	Don-Ce-Sar/Nell's Boy	F	10	U	F	4	3-4
Just Right Classi	Cornish Prince/Blue Prince	D	7	U	D	3	2-3
Just Right Mike	Mastadoon/Windy Sands	C	8	F	D	4	3-4
Just the Time	Advocator/Never Bend	C	8	C+	C	3	2-3
Kabori			7	C*		5	3-4
Kadanour FR	Kaldoun/Baly Rockette	M	6	L	M	4	2-3
Kahyasi IRE	Ile de Bourbon/Blushing Groom	D	6	C	M	1	3-4
Kaintuck	Kentuckian/Rainy Lake	D	8	U	F	5	3-4
Kalaglow IRE	Kalamoun/Pall Mall	D	7	C-	M	1	3-4
Kala Native	Exclusive Native/Kalamoun	D	10	C	F	4	3-4
Kaldoun FR	Caro/Le Haar	C-	3	BY	C	1*	2-3
Kalim	Hotfoot/Lyphard	F	8	C-	C-	4	3-4
Kan D'Oro	Mr. Prospector/Rugged Man	U	8	L	M	3	3-4
Kan Reason	Bold Reason/Mr. Jive	M	9	U	M	4	3-4
Kansas City	Habitony/Sassafras	D	9	M	C	4	3-4
Karabas IRE			7	C*		1	3-4
Kasakov ENG	Diesis/Nureyev	M	6	L	M	4*	2-3
Kashgar	Secretariat/Lyphard	U	8	L	M	3	3-4
Kashmir II	Tudor Melody/Queen of Speed		7	C*		4	3-4
Kasteel ARG	King of the Castle/Le Haar	C	7	C	C	4	3-4
Katahaula County^	Bold Rukus/High Tribute	M	7	M	L	4	2-3
Katowice	Danzig/Prince John	C	7	M	C+	3	3-4
Kautokeino FR			6	B*		2	3-4
Keats	Carapalida/Le Petit Prince		7	C*		3	3-4
Kebrimo IRE	Habitat/Levmoss	C-	9	M	C	5	3-4

Stallion	Sire/Broodmare Sire	FTS	CL	Trf	OT	SI	AB
Keefah *IRE*	Blushing Groom/Vaguely Noble	D	6	C	M	1	3-4
Keen *ENG*	Sharpen Up/Reliance II	U	6	C	L	3*	3-4
Keen Falcon^	Imperial Falcon/Stage Door Johnny	U	7	L	M	2	3-4
Keep It Down	Native Uproar/Cohoes	D	6	U	C	4	2-3
Kendor *FR*	Kenmare/Gay Mecene	C+	4	B	C	4*	2-3
Kenmare *FR*	Kalamoun/Milesian	C	3	C*	C	4	3-4
Kennedy Road	Victoria Park/Nearctic	C	7	C-	C	3	2-3
Kentucky Cookin	Best Turn/Tim Tam	D	9	D	C	4	3-4
Kentucky Gold	Raise a Native/Nashua	D	8	D	C	4	3-4
Kentucky Jazz	Dixieland Band/Restless Wind	C	8	M	C-	5	2-3
Keratoid^	Deputy Minister/Alleged	M	7	L	M	3*	3-4
Kerosene	Devil's Bag/Jacinto	C-	7	U	C	3	2-3
Kessem *NZ*			5	C		1	3-4
Keycolony	Pleasant Colony/Fleet Nasrullah	M	6	M	M	3	2-3
Key Recognition^^	Damascus/Nijinsky II	U	8	M	M	3	3-4
Key to Content	Forli/Princequillo		6	B*		2	3-4
Key to the Carr	Key to the Mint/Cornish Prince	M	8	U	C	4	3-4
Key to the Kingdom	Bold Ruler/Princequillo	D	6	C*	D	2	3-4
Key to the Mint	Graustark/Princequillo	D	3*	C+*	C-	3*	3-4
Key to the Moon	Wajima/Key to the Mint	D	7	C*	C	2	3-4
Kibe	Raja Baba/Frosty Mr.	D	8	U	C	5	3-4
Kid Colin	Baldski/Blade	M	9	M	M	3	3-4
Killarney Road	His Majesty/Damascus	D	8	M	C	3	3-4
Kim's Trick	Clever Trick/Tom Tulle	M	9	M	M	4	3-4
Kind of Hush *ENG*			7	M*		2	3-4
King Alphonse	Ship Leave/Bull Page	D	7	D	C	3	2-3
King Celebrity	Personality/Bold Ruler	C	9	D	C	3	3-4
King Concorde	Super Concorde/Damascus	C-	8	D	D	4	3-4
King Emperor	Bold Ruler/Double Jay	C	7	C	B	4	3-4
King James *IRE*			7	C*		4	3-4
King Jody	Nearctic/Kauai King	C-	8	C-	C	3	3-4
King Lyph	Lyphard/Kauai King	C-	10	D	C-	3	3-4
Kingmambo*	Mr. Prospector/Nureyev	D	7	C	D	3*	3-4
King of Kings	Vaguely Noble/Shut Out	D	8	C-	C	1	3-4
King of Storyland	Graustark/Sailor	D	9	U	F	4	3-4
King of the North	Northern Dancer/Sensitivo	D	8	C	C	3	3-4
King Pellinore	Round Table/Nantallah	D	7	C	D	3	3-4
King's Bishop	Round Table/Fleet Nasrullah	C-	6*	B*	C	1	3-4
King's Canyon	Alydar/Nijinsky II	M	9	M	M	3	2-3
Kings Lake *GER*	Nijinsky II/Baldric	D	6	C*	C	1	3-4
King's Nest	Rollicking/No Robbery	C	7	U	C+	4	2-3
King's Piper			8		T	4	3-4
King's Signet *ENG*	Nureyev/Habitat	M	7	L	M	5	2-3
Kipper Kelly	Valid Appeal/Tentam	C+	5	U	C+	4	2-3
Kirtling			7	C*		3	3-4

Stallion	Sire/Broodmare Sire	FTS	CL	Trf	OT	SI	AB
Kissin Kris^	Kris S./Your Alibhai	M	7	L	M	3	2-3
Kitwood^^	Nureyev/Sea-Bird	M	6	L	M	3*	3-4
Kleven	Alydar/Tudor Minstrel	C	7	D	C	3	3-4
Knight	Mr. Prospector/Jacinto	C	6	D	C+	5	2-3
Knight in Savannah	Knight's Choice/Pass the Glass	C	8	U	C+	4	2-3
Knightly Dawn	Sir Gaylord/Djeddah	D	6	C*	C	3	3-4
Knightly Manner		D	6	C*	C+	1	3-4
Knights Choice	Drum Fire/Turn-to	C+	6	D	C+	4	2-3
Knight Skiing	Snow Knight/Jig Time	C-	9	C	C	4	3-4
Known Fact	In Reality/Tim Tam	C	7	C-	C	4	2-3
Know Your Aces	Call Me Prince/Nahar	F	7	C*	C	3*	3-4
Kodiak	Run For Nurse/Mongo	C	8	D	D	2	2-4
Kokand	Mr. Prospector/Nijinsky II	C	6	M	BT	1*	2-3
Koluctoo Bay	Creme dela Creme/Double Jay	D	8	D	C	3	3-4
Kona Tenor	In Reality/Native Dancer	C-	7	D	C+	3	3-4
Kotani	Wajima/Advocator	D	7	C+	C	4	3-4
Kris ENG	Sharpen Up/Reliance	C	6	C*	C	3*	3-4
Kris S.	Roberto/ Princequillo	C+	5	B-	C	1*	2-4
Kronkkite	T.V. Commercial/Hail to Reason	D	8	D	DT	4	3-4
Kunjar	Fappiano/Minnesota Mac	M	9	M	M	4	3-4
Ky Alta	Good Old Mort/Ky. Lea	C	8	D	C+	4	3-4
Kyle's Our Man	In Reality/Graustark	C-	6	U	C+	3	2-3
Lac Ouimet	Pleasant Colony/Northfields	D	6	C-	CT	2	3-4
Lahab	The Minstrel/Buckpasser	F	10	U	U	4	3-4
Lancastrian ENG	Reform/Molvedo		8	M*		2	3-4
Land of Believe	Believe It/First Landing	F	9	D	C-	4	3-4
Laomedonte	Raise a Native/Toulouse Lautrec	D	9	D	D	2	3-4
Laramie Trail	Swaps/Sir Gaylord	C-	7	C	D	3	3-4
La Saboteur	Seattle Slew/Exclusive Native	C	9	D	C+	4	3-4
Laser Light			7	B*		4	3-4
Lashkari ENG	Mill Reef/Right Royal	D	4	C	U	1	3-4
Lasting Value	In Reality/Nantallah	C-	8	M	C	4	3-4
Last Tycoon JPN	Try My Best/Mill Reef	C	7	C	C	4	3-4
Late Act JAM	Stage Door Johnny/Tom Fool	D	7	C-	C	2	3-4
Latin American*	Riverman/Mr. Prospector	M	8	M	M	2	2-3
Latvia^^	Danzig Connection/Secretariat	M	8	M	M	2	3-4
Launch a Dream	Relaunch/Chieftain	M	7	U	L	4	3-4
Launch a Leader	Relaunch/Caro	D	7	M	C	4	3-4
Launch a Pegasus	Relaunch/Pago Pago	C	8	C	C	4	3-4
Launching	Relaunch/Cougar	U	10	M	M	3	3-4
Lawmaker	Round Table/Victoria Park	D	7	C*	C	3	3-4
Law Me	Wardlaw/Ridan	M	7	U	M	3	3-4
Law Society IRE	Alleged/Boldnesian	D	6	CY	M	1	3-4
Lazaz	Blushing Groom/Shoemaker	U	8	M	M	3	3-4
L.B. Jaklin	Jaklin Klugman/Rising Market	M	9	M	L	4	3-4

Stallion	Sire/Broodmare Sire	FTS	CL	Trf	OT	SI	AB
Leadership	The Minstrel/Hasty Road	D	10	U	C	4	3-4
Leading Hour	Bold Hour/Mr. Leader	D	9	U	C	3	3-4
Lead on Time *GER*	Nureyev/Lorenzacio	C	6	C	M	3	2-3
Lear Fan	Roberto/Lt. Stevens	C	6	C+	C-	3*	2-3
Le Chanceau	Le Fabuleux/Victorian Era	D	7	C	C	2	3-4
Le Danseur	Lord Durham/Dancer's Image	D	8	D	C	3	3-4
Leematt	Turn-to Reason/Bull Briar	D	6	F	C	3	3-4
Le Fabuleux	Wild Risk/Verso II	F	5*	C+*	D	1	3-4
Legacy of Love	Giacometti/Bold Skipper	D	9	D	C	3	3-4
Legal Bid	Spectacular Bid/Boldnesian	F	8	M	DT	4	3-4
Legal Prospector	Mr. Prospector/First Landing	C	7	U	C	4	3-4
Legatee	Foolish Pleasure/Dr. Fager	D	7	M	F	4	3-4
Le Glorieux *FR*			6	C+*		2	3-4
Le Gosse	Nijinsky II/Bagdad	U	8	M	U	4	3-4
Le Johnstan			7	C*		3	3-4
Lejoli *ITY*	Cornish Prince/Sir Ivor	C-	7	D	C	4	3-4
Lemhi Gold *GER*	Vaguely Noble/Candy Spots	F	8	D	F	2	3-4
L'Emigrant *FR*	The Minstrel/Vaguely Noble	F	7	C*	C	2	3-4
L'Empire	The Minstrel/Vaguely Noble	U	7	L	M	4	3-4
L'Enjoleur	Buckpasser/Northern Dancer	D	6	CY	DT	2	3-4
Lens*	Spectacular Bid/Forli	U	8	M	M	3	3-4
Leo Castelli	Sovereign Dancer/Raise a Native	C+	6	C-	C+	3	2-3
Leprechaun's Wish	Lyphard's Wish/Nashua	D	9	M	D	3	3-4
Leroy S	Honest Pleasure/Dr. Fager	C	9	D	F	3	3-4
Les Apres	Riverman/Cadmus	D	9	C	F	4	3-4
Let's Go Blue	Bob's Dusty/Amber Morn	U	7	U	T	3	3-4
Liberty Lane	Great Sun/Barbizon	D	7	D	F	4	3-4
Lieutenant's Lark	Lt. Stevens/Knightly Dawn	D	8	C+	F	1	3-4
Life Interest	Private Account/Bold Ruler	M	8	U	M	3	3-4
Light Cavalry *ENG*	Brigadier Gerard/Relko	C	6	C	C	3*	3-4
Light Idea	Majestic Light/Hail to Reason	D	8	M	D	4	3-4
Lightning Leap	Nijinsky II/First Landing	D	7	C-	C	3	3-4
Light of Morn*	Alleged/Olden Times	M	7	M	M	1	3-4
Light Years	Explodent/Sunny	F	7	U	C	3	3-4
Lil E. Tee*	At the Threshold/For the Moment	C	7	C	D	3*	3-4
Lil Fappi	Fappiano/What a Pleasure	D	7	C-	C-	3	3-4
Liloy *SAF*	Bold Bidder/Spy Song	C	7	C+*	C	3	3-4
Lil Tyler	Halo/T.V. Lark	F	8	C	D	3	3-4
Limited Practice	Dearest Doctor/Alley Fighter	M	9	U	M	5	3-4
Linamix *FR*	Mendez/Breton	C	4	B	M	1	2-3
Lincoln Park	Pappagallo/Turn-to	U	10	M	M	3	3-4
Lin D. Charger	Native Charger/Graustark	C-	9	D	DT	4	3-4
Line in the Sand*	Mr. Prospector/Northern Dancer	C-	6	B-	C-	3	2-3
Lines of Power	Raise a Native/Bold Ruler	C-	7	C*	C+	4	3-4
Linkage	Hoist the Flag/Cyane	D	6	C	C	3	3-4

Stallion	Sire/Broodmare Sire	FTS	CL	Trf	OT	SI	AB
Lion Cavern *ENG*	Mr. Prospector/Secretariat	M	6	L	L	4*	2-3
Lion D'or *IRE*	Secretariat/Northern Dancer	D	9	F	C	4	3-4
List	Herbager/Double Jay	D	7	C+	C	3	3-4
Litchi	Jacinto/Graustark	F	9	U	U	4	3-4
Literati	Nureyev/Bleep-Bleep	D	10	C-	D	3	3-4
Little Current	Sea Bird/My Babu	D	6	C	C	1	3-4
Little Missouri	Cox's Ridge/Jacinto	D	7	F	C	3	2-3
Little Secreto	Secreto/Dike	D	9	M	C	4	2-3
Little Shecky	Shecky Greene/Tim Tam	M	9	U	M	4	3-4
Lively One *JPN*	Halo/The Axe II	C	6	C-	C	3*	2-3
L'Natural	Raise a Native/Seaneen	C-	8	C-	C	5	3-4
Loach^^	Lines of Power/Rainy Lake	M	7	U	M	3	2-3
Lobsang *IRE*	Petingo/Sir Ivor	C	8	C	C	3*	3-4
Local Suitor *ENG*	Blushing Groom/Vaguely Noble	D	6	C	C	4*	3-4
Local Talent	Northern Dancer/Vaguely Noble	C	7	C	C-	3	3-4
Lockjaw	Raise a Bid/Roman Line	D	9	D	C-	4	3-4
Lode *ARG*	Mr. Prospector/Sir Ivor	D	5	C+	C	3*	3-4
Loft	Roberto/What a Pleasure	C	7	M	C	4	3-4
Lombardi	Northern Dancer/Herbager	D	6	C	C-	4	3-4
L'Ombre	Laomedonte/Bold Ruler	F	10	D	D	4	3-4
Lomond *ITY*	Northern Dancer/Poker	C	8	C	C-	2	3-4
London Bells *AUS*	Nijinsky II/Raise a Native	C	7	D	F	5	3-4
London Company	Tom Rolfe/Bolero	F	8	D	C	4	3-4
Long Row *ENG*			7	M*		1	3-4
Lone Star Bar	Mr. Prospector/Handsome Boy	C-	8	F	CT	4	3-4
Look See*	Conquistador Cielo/Danzig	L	8	M	L	4	2-3
Loom	Swoon's Son/Beau Pere	C+	7	F	C+	5	2-3
Loose	Bailjumper/Misty Flight	M	9	U	M	4	3-4
Loose Cannon	Nijinsky II/Graustark	F	7	C*	D	2	3-4
Loosen Up			7	C*		3	3-4
Lord at Law^^	Lord Carlos/Tri Jet	L	7	M	M	4	2-3
Lord at War	General/Con Brio	C+	4	A	C+	2	3-4
Lord Avie	Lord Gaylord/Gallant Man	C-	5	BY	C-	2	3-4
Lord Calvert		M	8	M	L	4	3-4
Lord Carlos	Lord Gaylord/Bold Legend	C-	7	U	C	4	2-3
Lord Chilly	Lord Durham/Nearctic	C-	8	U	C-	5	3-4
Lord Charmer*	Our Native/Seattle Slew	M	8	L	M	3	3-4
Lord Double Gate	Lord Gaylord/Groton	D	7	D*	C-	2	3-4
Lord Durham	Damascus/Summer Tan	C-	8	C*	C	4	3-4
Lordedoc	Lordedaw/Regal and Royal	M	8	M	M	3	3-4
Lord Gayle	Sir Gaylord/Sticky Case	D	8	C	D	3	3-4
Lord Gaylord	Sir Gaylord/Ambiorix	D	7	C+*	D	2	3-4
Lordly Love	Lord Harry L./Umbrella Fella	C-	9	D	C	4	3-4
Lord of All	Seattle Slew/Restless Native	F	9	D	C+	2	3-4
Lord of the Apes	Alydar/Jungle Cove	U	8	M	M	4	3-4

Stallion	Sire/Broodmare Sire	FTS	CL	Trf	OT	SI	AB
Lord of the Night	Lord Avie/Northern Dancer	D	7	C+	D	4	3-4
Lord of the Sea	Torsion/Cyclotron	C	7	C-	CT	3	2-3
Lord Pleasant*	Lord Avie/Roberto	U	8	L	M	3	3-4
Lord Rebeau	Maribeau/Call Over	C	8	D	C	4	3-4
Lord Treasurer	Key to the Mint/Sir Gaylord	F	9	D	C	4	3-4
Lorenzaccio	Klairon/Phoenissa	C-	6	C+*	D	2	3-4
Lost Atlantis	Northern Dancer/Swaps	D	9	C	D	3	3-4
Lost Code	Codex/Ack Ack	C	6	B-	C+T	3	2-3
Lost Mountain^^	Cox's Ridge/To the Quick	U	8	M	M	4	3-4
Lost Opportunity	Mr. Prospector/Buckpasser	C-	8	U	C	3	3-4
Lothario	Nashua/Tom Fool	D	8	C-*	C-	4	3-4
Loto	Icecapade/Search For Gold	M	10	U	M	4	3-4
Lot o' Gold	Lothario/Young Emperor	D	7	C	C	3	3-4
Louisiana Slew	Seattle Slew/New Policy	C	8	F	C	4	3-4
Loustrous Bid	Illustrious/Cannonade	C-	6	C-	C	3	3-4
Lovely Dancer IRE			7	M*		2	3-4
Lover Boy Leslie	Raise a Native/Round Table	D	9	D	C-	4	3-4
Lover's Cross	Explodent/Lucky Debonair	M	9	M	M	2	3-4
Love That Mac	Great Above/Irish Ruler	C-	9	C	C	4	3-4
Loverue	Ruffinal/Turk's Delight	M	8	M	M	3	3-4
Loyal Double	Nodouble/Royal Ascot	D	7	C+	D	3	3-4
Loyal Pal	Caro/Sailor	U	7	M	C	1	3-4
Lt. Stevens	Nantallah/Gold Bridge	C-	6	C	C+	4	2-3
Luck's Reality	In Reality/The Axe II	M	10	M	M	3	3-4
Lucky Larry	Parade of Stars/Bold Bidder	M	9	M	M	4	3-4
Lucky Legend	Secretariat/New Policy	D	8	F	C-	3	3-4
Lucky North	Northern Dancer/Olden Times	D	7	C	CT	3	2-3
Lucky Point	What Luck/Olden Times	C-	9	F	C	5	2-3
Lucky Prospect	Mr. Prospector/What Luck	D	8	U	D	5	3-4
Lucky Sec*	Secretariat/Nijinsky II	U	8	L	M	3	3-4
Lucky So n' So	Alydar/Nashua	C	7	U	C	4	2-3
Lucy's Axe	The Axe II/Turn-to	D	9	C*	C	2	3-4
Lugnaquilla IRE	Mill Reef/Ballyogan		7	C+Y		2	3-4
Luguna Beach ENG	Tumble Wind/Blakeney	D	6	C	M	4	2-3
Lunar Ray	Roberto/Princequillo	F	9	D	D	3	3-4
Lure^^	Danzig/Alydar	L	5	L	L	4	2-3
Lustra SAF	Danzig/Buckpasser	M	7	M	M	3	2-3
Luthier	Klairon/Cranach	C	5*	C*	C	1	3-4
Lycius IR	Mr. Prospector/Lyphard	C	6	C+	M	3	2-3
Lydian FR	Lyphard/Bon Mot	C	6	B*	C	2	3-4
Lympstone	Lyphard/Bold Lad	C	8	C-	D	3	3-4
Lyphaness	Lyphard/Ridan	C-	9	U	C	3	3-4
Lyphard	Northern Dancer/Court Martial	C	3*	B*	F	3*	3-4
Lyphard's Ridge	Lyphard's Wish/Riva Ridge	C	6	D	CT	3	3-4
Lyphard's Wish JPN	Lyphard/Sensitivo	D	7	C+Y	D	3	3-4

Stallion	Sire/Broodmare Sire	FTS	CL	Trf	OT	SI	AB
Lypheor *ENG*	Lyphard/Sing Sing	C	6	C+*	C	3	3-4
Lytrump	Lypheor/Bold Bidder	C-	8	C-	C-	3	3-4
Macarthur Park	First Balcony/Conjure	D	8	F	C	3	3-4
Mac Corkle	Jig Time/Saggy	D	8	U	C	3	3-4
Mac Diarmida	Minnesota Mac/Tim Tam	C	8	C	C	3	3-4
Machiavellian *ENG*	Mr. Prospector/Halo	C	6	C	M	4*	2-3
Macho Hombre	Raise a Native/Sir Gaylord	C	7	D	C	4	3-4
Mad Scientist	Quack/Windy Sands	M	8	M	M	4	3-4
Maelstrom Lake *IRE*	Auction Ring/Skymaster	C	6	C-	C	2	3-4
Magesterial	Northern Dancer/Bold Lad	C	7	CY	C	3*	2-3
Magical Mile	J.O. Tobin/Magesterial	C	7	U	C	5	2-3
Magical Wonder *IRE*	Storm Bird/Crimson Satan	C	6	C	C	4*	3-4
Magic Banner	Hoist the Flag/Cyane	C	8	D	C	2	3-4
Magic Level	Alydar/Nodouble	U	8	M	M	3	3-4
Magic Moment II	American Native/Gentle Art	C-	9	C	C	4	3-4
Magic North	North Sea/Impressive	D	9	D	F	4	3-4
Magic Partner	Partner's Hope/Dunfee	C	8	D	C	3	3-4
Magic Prospect	Mr. Prospector/Cox's Ridge	M	7	M	L	3	3-4
Magic Rascal	Raise a Native/Ack Ack	D	9	U	C	5	3-4
Magic Ring *ENG*	Green Desert/Empery	M	6	C	M	4	2-3
Magic Sound *CHI*	Lyphard/Trevieres	D	7	C	C	1	3-4
Magloire	Exceller/Round Table	C-	7	C	C-	3	3-4
Maha Baba	Raja Baba/No Robbery	D	8	F	C	4	3-4
Maheras	Walker's/Ambiopoise	C	10	C*	C-	4	3-4
Main Debut	Seattle Slew/Bold and Brave	D	8	D	C	4	<u>2-3</u>
Main Reef			7	C*		1	3-4
Majesterian*	Pleasant Colony/Northern Dancer	U	7	L	M	3*	3-4
Majestic Fun	Majestic Prince/Prince John	D	8	D	C-	3	3-4
Majestic Honor	Majestic Prince/Nijinsky II	C-	8	M	C	3	3-4
Majestic Light	Majestic Prince/Ribot	D	6	B-Y	D	1	3-4
Majestic Prince	Raise a Native/Royal Charger	C	8	C	C	3*	3-4
Majestic Reason	Majestic Prince/Hail to Reason	M	9	U	M	4	3-4
Majestic Shore	Majestic Prince/Windy Sands	C	9	D	C	3	3-4
Majestic Style^	Nureyev/Riva Ridge	U	7	L	M	3	3-4
Majestic Venture *PR*	Majestic Prince/Illustrious	C-	7	C	C	3	3-4
Majesty's Imp	His Majesty/Stonewalk	U	7	M	M	2	3-4
Majesty's Prince	His Majesty/Tom Fool	D	8	C*	C	2	3-4
Majesty's Time	Majestic Prince/Torsion	M	8	M	M	3	2-3
Major Account	Seattle Slew/Vaguely Noble	C-	8	D	C	3	3-4
Major Impact*	Roberto/In Reality	C-	6	M	C	3	<u>2-3</u>
Major Luck	What Luck/Hilarious	C-	6	D	C-	4	3-4
Major Moran	Colonel Moran/Irish Ruler	D	7	C-	C	3	<u>2-3</u>
Make Luck^^	Strike Gold/Lyphard	L	8	M	M	4	<u>2-3</u>
Malagra	Majestic Light/Vice Regal	C	7	C-	D	3	3-4
Malinowski	Sir Ivor/Traffic Judge	F	7	C-	C-	3*	3-4

Stallion	Sire/Broodmare Sire	FTS	CL	Trf	OT	SI	AB
Mamaison	Verbatim/Groton	C	8	D	D	3	3-4
Mambo	Northern Dancer/Bold Ruler	C-	8	C	C	4	3-4
Manado	Captain Gig/Sing Sing		7	C*		3*	3-4
Manastash Ridge	Seattle Slew/Crewman	D	7	C-	C	3	3-4
Mane Magic	Hawaii/Lt. Stevens	M	9	M	M	4	3-4
Mane Minister	Deputy Minister/In Reality	C-	7	C	D	3	3-4
Man from Eldorado*	Mr. Prospector/Youth	D	10	M	C-	3*	3-4
Mangaki	Olympiad King/Isle of Greece	D	10	C	C-	4	3-4
Manila TUR	Lyphard/Le Fabuleux	D	7	C+	C	2	3-4
Manlove	Mr. Prospector/Hoist the Flag	C+	7	C+	C-	3*	2-3
Mannerism	Grey Dawn II/Knightly Manner	D	8	D	F	4	3-4
Man of Vision	Exclusive Native/Warfare	U	9	M	U	4	3-4
Mansfeld BRZ			7	Y*		1	3-4
Mansonnien FR	Tip Moss/Margouillet		6	C		1	3-4
Many a Wish	Lyphard's Wish/Riva Ridge	M	7	M	MT	3	3-4
Manzotti	Nijinsky II/Tom Rolfe	C	8	C+	C-	3*	2-3
Mara Lark	T.V. Lark/First Fiddle	C	7	C	C	4	3-4
Marasid	Forli/Habitat	D	8	C	C	4	3-4
Marcellini	Never Bend/Pretense	D	9	C-	C-	3	3-4
Marco Bay	Copelan/Bailjumper	M	8	U	M	4	2-3
Marco Ricci	Herbager/Double jay	D	7	D	D	3	3-4
Marfa	Foolish Pleasure/Stratmat	C	7	C	CT	3	3-4
Maribeau	Ribot/Cosmic Bomb	D	7	C	C	4	3-4
Marignan ENG			7	M		1	3-4
Marine Brass	Fifth Marine/In Reality	C	7	D	CT	3	3-4
Marine Patrol	Sail On Sail On/Rasper II	C-	8	F	C	5	3-4
Mari's Book	Northern Dancer/Maribeau	C	6	C+	C	3*	3-4
Marju IR^^	Last Tycoon/Artaius	L	5	C+	M	3	2-3
Mark Chip	Our Blue Chip/Windsor Ruler	C	8	D	C-	4	3-4
Marked Tree^^	Forty Niner/Apalachee	M	7	M	M	4*	2-3
Market Control	Foolish Pleasure/Drone	D	8	D	D	3*	3-4
Mark in the Sky	Graustark/Hasty Road	F	10	U	C-	3	3-4
Mark of Nobility	Roberto/On Your Mark II	D	7	C+	C-	3	2-3
Marquee Universal IRE	Home Guard/Pampered King II	D	7	C	DT	2	3-4
Marquetry*	Conquistador Cielo/Vice Regent	C+	6	C-	C	3*	3-4
Marsayas	Damascus/Round Table	C	7	D	C	3	2-3
Marshua's Dancer	Raise a Native/Nashua	D	7	C*	CT	3	3-4
Martial Law	Mr. Leader/Round Table	D	8	D	C-	3	3-4
Martian Spell	Dance Spell/Damascus	D	8	U	C-	4	3-4
Marvin's Policy	L'Natural/New Policy	D	8	C	D	4	3-4
Masakado	Native Charger/Beau Gar	C-	8	D	C	4	3-4
Masked Dancer SWE	Nijinsky II/Spy Song	D	7	C	F	1	3-4
Maskrullah	Never Listen/CarryBack	C	9	D	D	4	3-4
Masked Native	Raise a Native/Spy Song	C	9	D	D	4	3-4
Masqued Dancer			7	M*		1	3-4

Stallion	Sire/Broodmare Sire	FTS	CL	Trf	OT	SI	AB
Masterclass *IRE*	The Minstrel/Sir Ivor	U	7	L	M	1	3-4
Master Derby	Dust Commander/Royal Coinage	D	9	C*	C	3	3-4
Masterful Advocate	Torsion/Grey Dawn II	D	8	U	C-	4	3-4
Master Hand	Bold Ruler/Spy Song	C	7	C*	C	4	3-4
Master Willie *GER*	High Line/Set Fair	D	7	C+*	D	3*	3-4
Mastery	Damascus/Buckpasser	D	8	D	C-	3	3-4
Mat-Boy	Matun/Pastiche	D	5	C	C+	1	3-4
Matchlite	Clever Trick/Sir Ivor	D	7	D	C+	3	2-3
Matsadoon	Damascus/Prince John	C-	8	D	C+	4	3-4
Matter of Honor	Conquistador Cielo/Venetian Jester	D	6	U	C	3	2-<u>3</u>
Maudlin	Foolish Pleasure/Dr. Fager	D	6	C+	CT	3*	2-3
Mawsuff *ENG*	Known Fact/Dancer's Image	M	7	M	M	4	3-4
Maxistar	Pia Star/To Market	C-	10	C	C-	4	3-4
Mayanesian	Bold Hour/T.V. Lark	D	8	D	C	4	3-4
Mazilier *ENG*	Lyphard/Exbury	C-	7	C-	M	4	2-3
McCann	Forli/Better Bee	F	7	C+*	D	4	3-4
McCracken	Pretense/Swaps	C-	8	F	C-	4	3-4
McKim	Roberto/Exclusive Native	D	9	C+	C-	2	3-4
M. Double M.	Nodouble/New Policy	D	8	C	C-	2	3-4
Meadowlake	Hold Your Peace/Raise a Native	C	5	D	C+T	4	2-<u>3</u>
Medaille D'Or	Secretariat/Northern Dancer	D	8	C*	C	4*	3-4
Media Starguest	Be My Guest/Sea-Bird	D	7	C-	C	2	3-4
Medieval Man	Noholme II/Tim Tam	C-	7	C+*	C	3	2-<u>3</u>
Medieval Victory	Medieval Man/Bold Native	M	6	L	M	4	2-3
Medifast*	Bold Ego/Gaelic Christian	M	10	U	M	4	3-4
Megaturn *PR*	Best Turn/Vertex	D	8	F	C+	3	3-4
Mehmet	His Majesty/Swaps	D	7	C-	CT	3	3-4
Mehmetori	Mehmet/Jungle Savage	U	9	M	M	<u>4</u>	3-4
Mellon			7		L		3-4
Melodisk	Alydar/One for All	C-	8	C	CT	3	3-4
Meloy	Liloy/Forli	U	10	M	M	3	3-4
Melyno *NZ*	Nonoalco/Boran	D	7	C	D	3*	3-4
Memo^^	Mocito Guapo/Chairman Walker	L	7	M	M	3	3-4
Memorized^	Ziggy's Boy/Bold Hour	U	8	L	M	2	3-4
Menderes	Noholme II/Baybrook	F	9	C	C	4	2-<u>3</u>
Mendez *FR*	Bellypha/Miss Carina		7	M*		4	3-4
Meneval	Le Fabuleux/Nashua	D	8	D	F	3	3-4
Menocal	Graustark/Bold Ruler	D	8	D	C	2	3-4
Mercedes Won	Air Forbes Won/Roman Line	C	6	C	CT	3*	2-4
Meritable	Round Table/Bold Ruler	C	8	C-	C	4	2-<u>3</u>
Mertzon	Mr. Prospector/Damascus	C-	8	D	CT	4	2-3
Meshach	Icecapade/Prince John	D	9	D	DT	4	3-4
Messenger of Song	Envoy/Tudor Minstrel	D	8	C*	CT	3	3-4
Metfield	Seattle Slew/Hail to Reason	D	8	C-	C	3	3-4
Metrogrand	Queen City Lad/Dedicate	D	9	U	C-	4	3-4

Stallion	Sire/Broodmare Sire	FTS	CL	Trf	OT	SI	AB
Metropolis	Bold Reasoning/Round Table	F	10	D	C	4	3-4
Mia's Boy	D'Accord/Mr. Leader	U	8	L	M	3	3-4
Michelozzo ENG	Northern Baby/Luthier	U	6	L	M	1	3-4
Mi Cielo^^	Conquistador Cielo/Thatch	D	8	C	C	4	2-3
Mickey Le Mousse			8	C*	M	4	3-4
Mickey McGuire	T.V. Lark/Determine	D	7	C*	C+	4	3-4
Midnight Prospect	Tank's Prospect/Northern Dancer	M	8	M	M	4	3-4
Midway Circle	Alydar/Round Table	C	8	D	C	3	3-4
Midyan FR	Miswaki/Ribot	C-	7	C-	C-	2	3-4
Mighty Adversary	Mr. Redoy/New Charger	C-	8	D	C	4	2-3
Mighty Appealing	Valid Appeal/Roi Dagobert	C-	7	D	C	5	3-4
Mighty Courageous	Caro/Seaneen	C	9	M	C	4	3-4
Mileage Miser	Brazen Brother/Beau Prince	F	10	U	C	5	3-4
Milesius GR	Alleged/Tropical Breeze	U	6	M	M	1	3-4
Milford JPN	Mill Reef/Queen's Hussar	D	8	C*	D	3	3-4
Militron	Marfa/Lt. Stevens	M	10	M	M	3	2-3
Mill Balles FR	Mill Reef/Elizinha		7	C		3	3-4
Mill Native	Exclusive Native/Mill Reef	F	9	C-	C-	3	3-4
Mill Reef ENG	Never Bend/Princequillo	D	5*	C	C	3*	3-4
Mineral Ice^^	Diamond Prospect/ Crimson Satan	M	8	M	M	3	3-4
Miner's Mark^^	Mr. Prospector/Private Account	M	6	U	L	4*	2-<u>3</u>
Mining JPN	Mr. Prospector/Buckpasser	B	6	D	C	3	2-3
Minneapple	Riverman/Umbrella Fella	C-	8	C	C	4	3-4
Minnesota Mac	Rough'n Tumble/Mustang	C-	7	C	C	4	3-4
Minshaanshu Amad ENG	Northern Dancer/Chieftain	D	8	C-	C-	4*	3-4
Minstrel Dancer	The Minstrel/Gallant Man	M	8	M	L	4	3-4
Mirabeau	Sharpen Up/Princely Gift	D	8	D	D	<u>4</u>	3-4
Mi Selecto	Explodent/Ribot	D	8	C	C	2	3-4
Missed Flight ENG	Dominion/Overskate	M	5	L	M	4	3-4
Missionary Ridge*	Caerleon/Salvo	C+	6	M	C-	3*	<u>3-4</u>
Mississipian			7	C*	C+	2	3-4
Mister Baileys ENG^	Robellino/Sharpen Up	U	6	L	M	4*	3-4
Mister Frisky	Marsayas/Highest Tide	C-	7	C	C	3	2-3
Mister Jolie^	Valid Appeal/Sir Ivor	L	7	M	M	4	2-3
Mister Lorenzo	Tentam/Nijinsky II	M	9	M	M	3	3-4
Mister Modesty VEN	Nijinsky II/Dr. Fager	M	9	M	M	3	3-4
Mister Slippers^^	Miswaki/Lyphard	M	9	M	M	4*	2-3
Mister Wonderful ENG	Mummy's Pet/Petingo	C-	8	D	D	5	3-4
Miswaki	Mr. Prospector/Buckpasser	C	3*	C	CT	3	<u>3-4</u>
Miswaki Gold	Miswaki/Lt. Stevens	U	9	U	M	4	3-4
Miteas Well Laff	Vertex/Crafty Admiral	D	8	F	C	4	3-4
Mixed Pleasure	Sucha Pleasure/Windy Sea	M	8	M	M	4	2-3
Mocito Guapo CHI	Good Manners/Right of Way	C	5	C+	C	3*	3-4
Mogambo JPN	Mr. Prospector/Rainy Lake	D	8	C+*	D	4	3-4
Mohamed Abdu IRE	Rusticaro/Welsh Pageant	M	7	M	M	4	2-<u>3</u>

Stallion	Sire/Broodmare Sire	FTS	CL	Trf	OT	SI	AB
Mokhieba	Damascus/Royal Vale	C	8	C	D	I*	3-4
Mombo Jumbo	Jungle Savage/Iron Peg	C-	6	D	CT	4	3-4
Moment of Hope	Timeless Moment/Baffle	C-	7	C-	C	3	3-4
Moment of Triumph	Timeless Moment/T.V. Lark	M	8	M	L	3	3-4
Momsfurrari	Elecutionist/Cornish Prince	M	7	M	C+	3	3-4
Monarch	Best Turn/Round Table	D	8	D	D	4	3-4
Monetary Crisis	Buckpasser/Sailor	C-	8	D	C-	4	3-4
Monetary Gift	Gold and Myrrh/Dancing Dervish	C-	6	U	C	4	2-3
Money by Orleans	L'Enjoleur/Outing Class	U	8	M	M	4	3-4
Mongo			7	C*		3	3-4
Mongo Drums	Drum Fire/Mongo	M	8	U	L	5	2-3
Mongo's Image	Mongo/Major Portion	D	8	F	C	5	2-3
Monongahela *AUS*			6	C+		3	3-4
Monsieur Champlain	Cutlass/Good and Plenty	D	8	F	C-	4	3-4
Montagnet	To the Quick/Ribot	C-	8	C-	C	2	3-4
Montbrook^^	Buckaroo/Jet Diplomacy	C+	6	L	M	3	2-3
Monteverdi *IRE*	Lyphard/Match II		6	C+*		4	3-4
Mon Tresor *ENG*	Longleat/ My Swallow	C	7	C	M	4	3-4
Moon Prospector	Northern Prospect/Sky High II	D	8	D	C-	5	3-4
Moonsplash	Boldnesian/Roughn' Tumble	D	9	C	C	4	3-4
Moon Up T.C.	Sharpen Up/Roberto	M	9	M	M	4	2-3
More Pleasure	Princely Pleasure/Correlation	M	7	U	M	4	3-4
Morstan *IRE*	Ragusa/Windmill Girl		7	M*		4	3-4
Morning Bob	Blushing Groom/The Axe II	D	7	C-	C	2	3-4
Morning Charge	Battle Joined/Eight Thirty	F	8	U	C	4	3-4
Moro	Full Out/Mito	F	9	D	C	3	3-4
Moscow Ballet	Nijinsky II/Cornish Prince	C-	7	C-	CT	4	3-4
Most Welcome *ENG*	Be My Guest/Habitat	C	6	C	M	I	2-3
Mountain Cat*	Storm Cat/Key to the Mint	C-	7	D	C	3	3-4
Mountain Express	Caro/Warfare	D	10	C	F	3	3-4
Mountain Lure	Rock Talk/To Market	C-	8	D	C-	4	3-4
Mountain Native	Our Native/Groton	C-	8	C	C	4	2-3
Mount Hagen	Bold Bidder/Tom Fool	D	8	C	C	3*	3-4
Mount Sterling *VEN*			7	C+*		3	3-4
Mr. Agitator	Mr. Prospector/Ambernash	U	8	U	U	3	3-4
Mr. Badger	Mr. Leader/Pago Pago	C-	10	U	C-	4	3-4
Mr. Brilliant	Brilliant Sandy/Mr. Leader	M	7	U	L	4	3-4
Mr. Classic	Mr. Prospector/Board Marker	M	9	U	M	3	3-4
Mr. Crimson Ruler	Secretariat/Crimson Satan	F	9	U	C-	4	3-4
Mr. Expo	Explodent/Red Ryder	M	9	M	M	3	3-4
Mr. Goldust	Mr. Prospector/Crepello	D	8	CY	DT	4	3-4
Mr. Greeley^	Gone West/Reviewer	L	6	M	L	4	2-3
Mr. Howard	Mr. Prospector/What a Pleasure	C-	8	D	C	4	3-4
Mr. Integrity	Mr. Prospector/Nijinsky II	C	8	M	C	3	3-4
Mr. J.C.'s Mons	Tarboosh/Etonian	C	8	U	D	4	2-3

Stallion	Sire/Broodmare Sire	FTS	CL	Trf	OT	SI	AB
Mr Justice *SAF*	Nijinsky II/Matador	C	6	C*	C	4	3-4
Mr. Leader	Hail To Reason/Djeddah	D	4*	C*	CT	2	3-4
Mr Napton	Mr. Prospector/	M	9	M	M	4	3-4
Mr. Nasty*	Raised Socially/Quack	M	6	U	M	4	3-4
Mr. Procrastinator	Hard Work/Balance of Power	C	7	U	C	3	3-4
Mr. Prospector	Raise a Native/Nashua	B	2*	C*	C+T	4*	2-3
Mr Prosperous	Mr. Prospector/Bold Commander	D	9	U	D	4	3-4
Mr Ralph	Catullus/Nickey W.	C-	9	F	C	5	3-4
Mr. Redoy	Grey Dawn II/Pocket Ruler	D	8	D	CT	3	3-4
Mr. Sparkles	Deputy Minister/Buckpasser	C+	7	C-	C	4	2-3
Mt. Livermore	Blushing Groom/Crimson Satan	C	5	C	C+	4*	2-3
Mt. Magazine	Mr. Prospector/Damascus	D	8	U	C-	4*	3-4
Mtoto *ENG*	Busted/Minicio	D	6	C	C	1	3-4
Much Fine Gold	L'Natural/Drone	D	10	U	D	5	3-4
Much the Best	In Reality/Boldnesian	M	8	M	L	4	3-4
Mufti	Nodouble/Prince Taj	D	9	C	D	3*	3-4
Mugassas *VEN*	Northern Dancer/Round Table	D	7	C	C	3	3-4
Mugatea	Hold Your Peace/Olden Times	C	7	D	C	3	3-4
Muhayaa^	Danzig/Jean Pierre	M	7	L	M	4*	2-3
Mujtahid *IRE*	Woodman/Mill Reef	C	7	C	M	3*	2-3
Mukaddamah *IRE*	Storm Bird/Never Bend	U	6	C	C	2	2-3
Mummy's Pet *ENG*	Sing Sing/Grey Sovereign	C-	7	C	C-	5	2-3
Murrtheblurr	Torsion/Cornish Prince	C	9	C	C-	5	2-3
Muscovite	Nijinsky II/Raise a Native	D	9	CY	D	3*	3-4
Musical Fappi	Fappiano/In Reality	C+	7	U	C	3	2-3
Music Master	Marshua's Dancer/Western Sky II	C-	9	U	C-	4	3-4
Music Prince	Stop the Music/Call Me Prince	F	7	M	D	4	3-4
Musketeer *CHI*			7	M*		2	3-4
Mute Dancer*	Sovereign Dancer/The Axe II	M	7	M	M	3	3-4
Muttering	Drone/Gamin'	D	9	F	F	4	3-4
My Boy Adam	Encino/Pontoise	C-	7	M	D	2	3-4
My Dad George	Dark Star/Mabekky	C	6	C*	C	3	3-4
My Favorite Moment	Timeless Moment/Dragante	M	9	U	M	4	3-4
My Gallant	Gallant Man/Nashua	C	6	D	C	4	2-3
My Habitony	Habitony/Dogoon	F	7	F	C+	4	3-4
My Memoirs*	Don't Forget Me/Track Spare	M	8	C	M	4*	3-4
My Prince Charming	Sir Wimborne/Stage Door.Johnny	C	7	D	C	3	3-4
Mystery Storm^	Storm Bird/Affirmed	M	7	L	M	3	2-3
Mythical Ruler	Ruritania/Victorian Era	C	6	C*	C+	3	3-4
Nabeel Dancer	Northern Dancer/Foolish Pleasure	D	8	D	F	4	3-4
Naevus	Mr. Prospector/Bold Lad	C	7	C	BT	4	3-4
Naevus Star^^	Naevus/El Pitirre	M	8	M	L	4	3-4
Nain Bleu	Lyphard/Tanerko	D	8	C	F	3	3-4
Naked Sky	Al Hattab/Forli	D	7	C	C	2	2-3
Nalees Man	Gallant Man/Nashua	D	7	C*	CT	3	3-4

Stallion	Sire/Broodmare Sire	FTS	CL	Trf	OT	SI	AB
Nantequos	Tom Rolfe/Nantallah	D	8	C	C	4	3-4
Napa Sonoma	Our Native/Little Current	U	8	L	M	3	3-4
Nashamaa FR	Ahonoora/Balidar	C	7	C	M	4	3-4
Nashua	Nasrullah/Segula	C	6	C-*	C	2	3-4
Nashwan ENG	Blushing Groom/Bustino	C	4	C	C	3	2-3
Naskra	Nasram/Le Haar	C	5*	CY*	C+	3*	3-4
Nassau Square		M	8	M	L	3	3-4
Nassipour AUS	Blushing Groom/Aureole	C	6	C	C	1	3-4
Nasty and Bold	Naskra/Boldnesian	C	7	C*	C	3	3-4
Nataraja	Nijinsky II/Admiral's Voyage	F	10	C	F	3	3-4
Nathan Detroit	Drone/Forli	D	9	U	C	4	3-4
National Match	Seattle Slew/Hold Your Peace	M	8	M	L	3	3-4
Nation's Pic			7		CT	4	3-4
Native Aid			7	C*		3	3-4
Native Bidder	Raise a Native/Bold Bidder	D	9	D	C	4	3-4
Native Charger	Native Dancer/Heliopolis	C	7	C*	C	3	3-4
Native Factor*	Foolish Pleasure/Sinister Purpose	D	8	U	D	4	2-3
Native Host	Raise a Native/Sword Dancer	C	8	D	C	4	3-4
Native of Seattle	Raise a Native/Ambiopoise	M	7	U	M	4	3-4
Native Over Tilt	Fight Over/Tilt Up		7		MT	4	2-3
Native Prospector	Mr. Prospector/Carlemont	C	7	C	CT	4	3-4
Native Royalty	Raise a Native/Nasrullah	D	6	C*	C-	3*	2-3
Native Supreme	Mock Bird/Roibbean	M	10	U	M	5	3-4
Native Tactics	George Navonod/Delta Judge	C	9	C	C	4	2-3
Native Uproar	Raise a Native/Never Bend	C	7	C	C	4	3-4
Native Wizard	In Reality/Northern Dancer	C+	8	C-	C+	3	3-4
Natomas	Secretariat/Windy City II	D	10	D	F	4	3-4
Natural NZ			7	C		3	3-4
Naturals Grand	L'Natural/Aberion	M	9	U	M	3	3-4
Navajo	Grey Dawn II/Double Jay	D	6	C	D	2	3-4
Navarone^^	Irish River/Round Table	U	7	L	M	1	3-4
Navy Admiral	Mr. Prospector/Crafty Admiral	D	10	U	C	4	3-4
Nebbiolo	Yellow God/Novara		6	B*		3	3-4
Neckar GER			7	C*		2	3-4
Needles	Ponder/Jack High	D	7	C*	T	3	3-4
Negative	Lucky North/Raja Baba	D	7	D	F	4	3-4
Negotiated Account	Private Account/Hoist the Flag	D	9	U	C-	3	3-4
Nelson^^	Seattle Slew/Mr. Prospector	L	8	M	L	4*	2-3
Nepal	Raja Baba/Grey Dawn	C-	7	C-	C	3	3-4
Nephrite	Majestic Light/Never Bend	U	7	M	M	3	3-4
Neptuno	Ahmad/Prepenador	M	6	M	L	4	3-4
Nerud^	Forty Niner/Rich Cream	M	8	U	M	4*	2-3
Neveda Reality	In Reality/Have Tux	C	9	D	C	4	3-4
Never Bend ENG	Nasrullah/Djeddah	C+	4*	C*	C	4*	2-3
Never Company	London Company/King of Tudors	U	9	M	U	4	3-4

Stallion	Sire/Broodmare Sire	FTS	CL	Trf	OT	SI	AB
Never Cry	Never Bend/Sea Bird	D	8	C	D	3	3-4
Never Cye	Cyane/Never Bend	C	7	M	C	4	3-4
Never Hi	Never Bend/Polynesian	F	9	F	F	5	2-3
Never Lark	Buffalo Lark/Never Bend	C	7	D	C+	4	3-4
Never So Bold *ENG*	Bold Lad/Habitat	D	7	C	C	4*	3-4
Never Tabled	Never Bend/Round Table	C-	7	C	C	3	2-<u>3</u>
Never Wavering^	Wavering Monarch/United Holme	U	8	L	M	3	3-4
New Circle	Circle/Bald Eagle	U	10	M	U	3*	3-4
New Prospect	Neve Bend/Hasty Road	C	8	C*	C	3	3-4
Newscast	Irish Tower/Try Sheep	M	8	U	L	4	3-4
New Years Grapes	Arachnoid/Scout Leader	D	9	U	C	4	3-4
Nias	Secretariat/Northern Dancer	F	9	C-	F	3	3-4
Nice Catch	Pass Catcher/Chateaugay	D	8	D	C	4	3-4
Nice Pirate	Hail the Pirates/Graustark	F	8	D	D	4	3-4
Nicholas	Danzig/Tom Rolfe	D	7	C	C-	4*	3-4
Nickel Slot	Plugged Nickel/Majestic Light	U	8	M	U	3	3-4
Night Invader	Misty Flight/Sun Glow	C	8	D	C	5	3-4
Night Mover	Cutlass/Nantallah	C	9	U	C	4	3-4
Night Shift *IRE*	Northern Dancer/Chop Chop	C	7	C	D	3*	2-3
Nijinsky II	Northern Dancer/Bull Page	D	3*	C+*	C	3*	3-4
Nijinsky's Secret	Nijinsky II/Raise a Native	F	8	C-	C-	3*	3-4
Nijinsky's Table	Nijinsky II/Round Table	M	10	M	U	3	2-4
Nines Wild*	Wild Again/Honest Pleasure	M	9	M	M	4	3-4
Nininski *ENG*	Nijinsky II/Tom Rolfe	D	7	C	C	1	3-4
Nishapour *ENG*	Zeddan/Aureole	D	7	C-*	M	1	3-4
Nisswa	Irish River/Mr. Prospector	M	8	L	M	4	3-4
Noactor	Theatrical/Silent Screen	C+	6	C	C+	3	2-3
No Bend	Never Bend/Traffic Judge	C-	8	D	D	3	3-4
Noble Assembly	Secretariat/Damascus	D	9	D	C	4	3-4
Noble Dancer *ENG*	Prince de Galles/Sing Sing	C	7	CY*	C	3*	3-4
Noble Jay			7	C*		3	3-4
Noble Monk	African Sky/Mandamus	D	9	C	C-	4	3-4
Noble Nashua	Nashua/Vaguely Noble	D	7	C*	C	2	3-4
Noble Novice	Wardlaw/Fleet Nasrullah	D	7	D	CT	3	3-4
Noble Patriarch *ENG*	Alzao/Bold Lad	M	6	L	M	3*	3-4
Noble Saint	Vaguely Noble/Santa Claus	D	8	C	D	4	3-4
Noble Savage *IRE*	Caerleon/Astec	U	7	L	M	2	3-4
Noble Table	Vaguely Noble/Round Table		7	C*		3	3-4
No Budget	Spend a Buck/Sir Ivor	M	7	M	M	3	3-4
No Distress	Vaguely Noble/Guerrero	D	9	D	D	3	3-4
Nodouble	Noholme II/Double Jay	C-	5*	C*	C	3	3-4
No Excuses	Damascus/Reneged	C	8	U	C	5	3-4
Noholme II	Star Kingdom/	C+	4	C*	C	4*	2-3
Noholme Way	Noholme II/Fleet Nasrullah	C	8	C-	C	3	3-4
No House Call	Dr. Fager/Olden Times	D	8	F	C	4	3-4

Stallion	Sire/Broodmare Sire	FTS	CL	Trf	OT	SI	AB
Noir et Or *ENG*			7	C+*		3*	3-4
No Louder *IND*	Nodouble/Quadrangle	D	6	C	C-	2	3-4
No Marker	Grey Dawn II/Drone	M	10	M	M	3	3-4
Nomination *ENG*	Dominion/Rarity	C	7	C	M	4	2-3
No Pass No Sale	Northfields/Djakeo	D	7	C	C	1	3-4
No Points	Miswaki/Amerigo	D	7	C	C	3	3-4
Norcliffe	Buckpasser/Northern Dancer	D	7	C+*	C	4	3-4
Nordic Legend *VEN*	Northern Dancer/Riverman	D	7	D	C	3	3-4
Nordico *IR*	Northern Dancer/Gallant Man	C-	8	D	D	4*	3-4
Nordic Prince	Nearctic/Hill Prince	D	7	D	C	3	3-4
No Robbery	Swaps/Bimelech	C-	7	C-*	C	3*	3-4
Norquestor	ConquistadorCielo/NorthernDancer	C+	6	C	C+T	3	2-4
Northern Baby	Northern Dancer/Round Table	C-	7	C*	C	3*	3-4
Northern Baron	Northern Jove/Young Emperor	C-	10	D	D	5	3-4
Northern Bay		C-	8	C	C	3	3-4
Northern Birdie	Proud Birdie/Norcliffe	D	7	U	C	3	3-4
Northern Blazer	Northern Dancer/Vaguely Noble	D	10	D	CT	3	3-4
Northern Classic	Danzig/Summer Tan	C-	7	C-	C	4	3-4
Northern Crystal *FR*	Crystal Glitters/Green Dancer	M	6	L	M	1	3-4
Northern Dancer	Nearctic/Native Dancer	C	2*	B*	C	3*	2-3
Northern Flagship	Northern Dancer/Raise a Native	C	7	C+	C	3	2-3
Northern Fling	Northern Dancer/Hasty Road	C	7	C*	C	3*	3-4
Northern Horizon	Northern Dancer/Court Harwell	D	8	D	C-	4	2-3
Northern Ice	Fire Dancer/Vertex	D	9	D	F	3	3-4
Northern Idol	Northrop/Explodent	C-	6	M	C+	4	2-3
Northern Jay	Northern Jove/Warfare	D	9	C	D	4	3-4
Northern Jove	Northern Dancer/Sun Again	D	5*	B*	D	3*	3-4
Northern Magus	Olden Times/Exclusive Native	C-	8	D	C	4	2-3
Northern Majesty	His Majesty/Northern Dancer	D	8	C-	D	3	3-4
Northern Match	Nearctic/Raise a Native	C-	8	D	C-	4	3-4
Northern No Trump*	Vice Regent/Spectacular Bid	D	7	U	C+	4	3-4
Northern Park *ENG*	Northern Dancer/Great Nephew	M	6	L	M	3*	2-3
Northern Passage	Northern Dancer/Cyane	D	8	D	C+	4	3-4
Northern Prospect	Mr. Prospector/Northern Dancer	C	7	C-	CT	4	2-3
Northern Raja	Raja Baba/Northern Dancer	D	6	C-	C	4	3-4
Northern Ringer	Northern Dancer/Round Table	F	8	C-	DT	3*	3-4
Northern Score	Northern Dancer/Halo	C-	6	C	C	3	3-4
Northern Smartee	Northern Bay/Fleet Nasrullah	C-	8	F	C-	3	2-3
Northern Spell	Dance Spell/Bolero	D	10	D	F	4	3-4
Northern Supremo	Northern Dancer/Habitat	D	9	C-	C	3	3-4
Northern Treat			7	C*		2	3-4
Northern Wolf	Wolf Power/Northern Fling	C	7	D	C+	3	3-4
Northfields	Northern Dancer/Occupy	D	4*	C*	F	3*	3-4
North Forest*	Imperial Guard/Victory Mom	U	10	U	M	4	3-4

Stallion	Sire/Broodmare Sire	FTS	CL	Trf	OT	SI	AB
Northjet *GER*	Northfields/Fortino II	F	6	C	D	3*	3-4
North Lad	Far North/Gallant Lad	C-	8	M	C	4	3-4
North Pole	Northern Dancer/Canadian Champ	C-	7	C	C	3	3-4
North Prospect	Mr. Prospector/Northern Dancer	C-	8	C+	DT	4	3-4
Northrop	Northern Dancer/Warfare	D	8	C	C	3*	3-4
North Sea			7	C+*		3	3-4
North Tower	Northern Dancer/Hill Prince	C	9	C*	C	3	3-4
Northwest Passage	Nearctic/Native Dancer	C-	9	C-	C	3	3-4
North Woodsman^	Woodman/Bailjumper	M	8	U	M	3	3-4
No Sale George	Raise a Native/Jacinto	B	6	D	B	3	3-4
Nostalgia	Silent Screen/Herbager	F	9	C	C	2	3-4
Nostalgia's Star	Nostalgia/Big Spruce	C-	7	C	C	3	3-4
Nostrum	Dr. Fager/Native Dancer	D	7	D	C+	3	3-4
Notebook	Well Decorated/Tom Rolfe	C+	5	C	C+T	3	2-3
Not For Love^	Mr. Prospector/Northern Dancer	M	7	L	M	4*	2-3
Not Surprised	His Majesty/Never Bend	D	8	M	C	3	3-4
Nova Scotia	Nureyev/Reviewer	D	8	C	D	3	3-4
Novel Nashua	Noble Nashua/Prince John	U	6	U	C+	2	3-4
Now Listen *BRZ*	Miswaki/Envoy	C	6	M	CT	3	3-4
Numchuek	Riverman/Olympiad	D	10	C	D	4	3-4
Numerous^	Mr. Prospector/Nijinsky II	M	7	M	M	4*	2-3
Nureyev	Northern Dancer/Forli	C-	3	B	D	4*	2-3
O Big Al	Don B./Traffic Judge	C-	8	D	C	4	3-4
Obligato	Northern Dancer/In Reality	C-	7	D	D	4	3-4
O'Brannigan	Clever Trick/Advocator	M	10	L	M	4	3-4
Obraztsovy	His Majesty/Nashua	D	9	C-	F	3	3-4
Ocala Slew	Seattle Slew/Diplomat Way	C-	8	C	C-	3	2-3
Ocean Crest^	Storm Bird/Seattle Slew	U	7	M	M	2	2-3
Ocean Trick	Clever Trick/Sham	D	8	U	C	4	2-3
Oedipus Appeal	Valid Appeal/Rexson	M	8	U	M	5	3-4
Ogygian *JPN*	Damascus/Francis S.	C	6	C	CT	3	3-4
Oh Say	Hoist the Flag/Cyane	C	6	C	C	3	3-4
O.K. By You	Buck's Bid/Stevward	D	8	C	C-	5	3-4
Olantengy *FR*	Riverman/Snob		7	M*		2	3-4
Old Broadway	Broadway Forli/Hail to Reason	D	9	M	D	4	3-4
Olden Times	Relic/Djebel	C-	6	D	C+	3	2-3
Old Stories	Cox's Ridge/Olden Times	D	8	U	C	3	2-3
Old Vic *ENG*	Sadler's Wells/Derring-do	D	6	C	F	1	3-4
Ole'	Danzig/Verbatim	C-	6	C	C-	3	3-4
Ole Bob Bowers	Prince Blessed/Bull Lea	D	7	C+*	C	4	3-4
Olympiad King	Curragh King/Big Game	C	7	C*	C	4	3-4
Olympic Native	Raise a Native/Olympiad King	C	8	U	C+	4	3-4
Olympic Victory	Nijinsky II/Bold Ruler	D	10	C-	D	3	3-4
Olympio	Naskra/Whitesburg	C+	6	U	C+	4	2-3
Once Wild	Baldski/What a Pleasure	C	7	C	C+	3	2-3

Stallion	Sire/Broodmare Sire	FTS	CL	Trf	OT	SI	AB
One Drink^^	Never Tabled/T.V. Lark	M	9	M	M	4	3-4
Onefinesilverbuck	Silver Buck/Tri Jet	M	8	U	L	3	3-4
One For All	Northern Dancer/Princequillo	D	7	B*	C-	3*	3-4
One in a Mil	Crafty Drone/First Landing	F	8	C-	D	4	2-3
One More Brother	Naskra/Groton	D	8	D	C-	3	3-4
One More Slew	Seattle Slew/Caro	F	8	C-	F	3*	3-4
Ongoing Mister	Valdez/Hagley	D	10	U	M	4	3-4
Onion Juice PR	Quartermaster/Victoria Park	D	6	U	C	4	3-4
Only Bold	Nasty and Bold/Blade	M	9	M	M	3	3-4
Only Dreamin	Raise a Native/Prince John	D	9	D	C-	3*	3-4
On Report^	Fappiano/Roberto	M	8	M	M	4*	3-4
On Target^	Forty Niner/Al Hattab	M	8	U	L	4	2-3
On the Sauce	Sauceboat/Mito	D	7	D	C-	3	2-3
On to Glory	Bold Lad/Native Dancer	D	5	C*	C	3	2-3
Onyxly	Rock Talk/Creme dela Creme	D	8	F	C-	1	3-4
Opening Lead	Flush/Insubordination	D	8	D	C-	4	3-4
Opening Verse	The Minstrel/Grey Dawn II	C	6	CY	C-	2	2-3
Opposite Abstract	Alydar/Bold Commander	U	10	M	C	2	3-4
Oraibi	Forli/Northern Dancer	C-	7	D	C	3	3-4
Orange Sunshine	Linkage/In Reality	U	10	U	M	4	3-4
Orbit Dancer	Northern Dancer/Gun Shot	C	7	C-	C	3	3-4
Orbit Ruler	Our Rulia/Royal Orbit	D	8	C-	D	5	3-4
Orbit's Scene	Orbit Dancer/Pachuto	D	10	U	C	3	2-3
Order	Damascus/Reviewer	D	9	F	C-	4	3-4
Ormonte	Danzig/Nodouble	D	8	C-	C	4	3-4
Orono THI	Codex/Gallant Man	D	8	C	D	3*	2-3
Orpheus Island	Blushing Groom/Judger	D	9	D	D	3	3-4
Our Bold Landing	Bold Forbes/First Landing	C-	8	U	D	5	3-4
Our Captain Willie BRZ	Little Current/Ribot	D	7	C	F	3*	3-4
Our Gary	Our Michael/Catullus	C	8	U	C	4	3-4
Our Hero	Bold Ruler/Aristophanes	D	9	C-	C	4	3-4
Our Liberty	Raise a Native/Round Table	C-	6	D	C+	3	2-3
Our Michael	Bolero/Tribe	D	8	D	C	4	2-3
Our Native	Exclusive Native/Crafty Admiral	D	4*	C+*	C+	3*	2-3
Our Talisman	Cornish Prince/Arrogate	C	9	C	C-	4	3-4
Outdoor Celebrity	Cresta Rider/Blushing Groom	M	9	M	M	4	3-4
Out of Place	Cox's Ridge/Damascus	C+	6	C-	C	3	2-3
Out of the East	Gummo/Windy Sands	C	8	C	C	4	3-4
Over Arranged	Staunchness/Royal Union	D	9	D	C	4	3-4
Overdressed	Tom Rolfe/Stage Door Johnny	D	10	D	D	3	3-4
Overpeer	Overskate/Impressive	C	8	D	C	4	3-4
Overskate	Nodouble/Speak John	D	6	C+	D	1	3-4
Over the Rainbow	Alydar/Distinctive	D	6	C-	C	3	3-4
Owens Troupe	For the Moment/Drone	M	8	U	U	3	3-4
Pachuto	Lt. Stevens/Summer Tan	D	8	C	D	3	3-4

Stallion	Sire/Broodmare Sire	FTS	CL	Trf	OT	SI	AB
Pacific Native	Raise a Native/Jet Pilot	C-	8	C+*	C	4	3-4
Page Nijinsky	Nijinsky II/Graustark	U	9	U	U	3	3-4
Pago Pago	Matrice/Abbots Fall	C	8	D	C	4	3-4
Pair of Deuces PR	Nodouble/Your Alibhai	D	8	D	D	3	2-3
Palace Music JPN	The Minstrel/Prince John	D	7	C	D	3*	3-4
Palace Panther	Crystal Palace/Val de Loir	F	7	C	F	I	3-4
Palmers Tex	Vertex/Ambehaving	C	10	C	D	4	3-4
Pancho Villa	Secretariat/Crimson Satan	C-	8	C-	C	4	2-3
Panoramic FR	Rainbow Quest/Roberto	M	6	B		3	3-4
Papa Banks	Prince Og/Prince Mito	D	8	D	C-	5	2-3
Pappagallo	Caro/Hard Sauce	F	8	C-	C	3	3-4
Pappa Riccio	Nashua/Raise a Native	C	7	F	C+	4	3-4
Parade Marshall ARG	Caro/No Robbery	D	6	C+	M	2	3-4
Parade of Stars	T.V. Lark/Dedicate	C	7	C	C	4	3-4
Paramount Jet	Tri Jet/Quadrangle	D	8	C-	D	3	3-4
Paranoide Arg ^	Friul/Country Doctor	M	7	L	M	4	3-4
Parfaitement	Halo/The Axe II	D	7	D	CT	4	3-4
Par Five	Icecapade/Vertex	D	9	U	C	4	3-4
Paris Dust	Dust Commander/Ambiorix	D	8	D	C	4	3-4
Paris House IRE*	Petong/Artaius	M	7	M	M	5	2-3
Paris Song	Hurok/Stop the Music	M	8	U	M	4	3-4
Parlay Me	Irish Tower/Native Charger	D	7	F	C-	4	2-3
Parochial	Mehmet/Hail to Reason	M	8	U	M	2	3-4
Parramon	Lyphard/Cyane	M	9	M	U	4	3-4
Partez	Quack/Tim Tam	C-	9	C-	C-	4	3-4
Particular Item	Affirmed/Northern Dancer	D	10	M	D	3	3-4
Partner's Hope	T. V.Lark/Yildiz	F	8	C-	C-	4	3-4
Pas de Cheval	Nijinsky II/Bold Ruler	F	10	C	F	4	3-4
Paskanell	Bold Forbes/Candy Spots	C-	9	M	DT	4	2-3
Pass Catcher	All Hands/Flaneur	D	7	C-	D	4	3-4
Pas Seul	Northern Dancer/Bold Ruler	D	8	C+	C	3*	3-4
Passing Zone	Buckpasser/Round Table	D	9	C-	F	3	3-4
Pass'n Raise	Raise a Native/Alibhai	D	8	U	U	5	2-3
Pass the Glass	Buckpasser/Amerigo	C-	8	C-	C	3	3-4
Pass the Line	Pas Seul/Roman Line	D	8	C+	C	3	3-4
Pass the Tab	Al Hattab/Gray Phantom	C-	8	C*	C	3	2-3
Patch of Sun	Sunny Clime/Illustrious	C	10	U	C	5	3-4
Patchy Groundfog	Instrument Landing/Olden Times	M	7	U	LT	4	3-4
Patrick McFig	Figonero/Fleet Host	F	10	U	C-	5	3-4
Patriotically	Hoist the Flag/Amerigo	C-	8	C	CT	3	2-3
Pauper Prince	Majestic Prince/Round Table	D	10	C	D	3*	3-4
Pax Nobiscum	Hold Your Peace/Fleet Kirsch	C-	7	D	D	4	3-4
Peace Arch	Hoist the Flag/Restless Native	C-	9	C	C	4	3-4
Peace Corps	Restless Native/Rosemont	D	8	C	C	2	3-4
Peaked		M	7		M	4	2-3

Stallion	Sire/Broodmare Sire	FTS	CL	Trf	OT	SI	AB
Pembroke^	Gone West/Boldnesian	L	6	L	M	4	2-3
Pencil Point	Sharpen Up/Hill Clown	C-	8	C-	C	4	2-3
Penine Walk SWS	Persian Bold/Thatch	F	7	C-	M	4	3-4
Pentaquod	London Company/Drone	C	9	D	C	4	3-4
Pentelicus	Fappiano/In Reality	B	6	C+	C+T	4*	2-3
Peppermint Schnaps	Annihilate'em/In Reality	M	9	M	L	5	3-4
Pep Up		M	7	M	L	4	2-3
Percifal	Riverman/Round Table	D	9	C	C+	2	3-4
Perfect Delivery	Swift Delivery/Prince Alert	U	8	M	M	3	3-4
Perfecting	Affirmed/Cornish Prince	C	7	C-	C-	3	3-4
Perfect Parade ARG	Alleged/Dr. Fager	U	7	M	C+	3	3-4
Perforce	Seattle Song/Nantallah	U	9	U	U	4	3-4
Perkin Warbeck	Vaguely Noble/Quack	D	6	C+	C-	1	3-4
Perpendicular ENG	Shirley Heights/Priamos	U	4	L	M	1	3-4
Perrault ENG	Djakao/Court Martial	D	7	C+	C-	1	3-4
Persevered VEN	Affirmed/Never Bend	F	9	D	D	3	3-4
Persian Bold IRE	Bold Lad/Relko	C-	6	B	D	3*	3-4
Persian Emperor	Damascus/Lt. Stevens	D	8	F	C-	4	2-3
Personable Joe	Seattle Slew/No Robbery	M	9	M	T	3	3-4
Personal Flag	Private Account/Hoist the Flag	C-	7	CY	C	3*	3-4
Personal Hope*	Storm Bird/Alydar	D	8	C-	D	2	3-4
Persuasive Leader	Mr. Leader/Speak John	D	10	U	M	4	3-4
Pertsemlidis	Naskra/Buckpasser	D	6	B	C-	3	3-4
Petardia IRE	Petong/Mummy's Pet	U	7	M	M	5	2-3
Peterhof	The Minstrel/Cornish Prince	C	8	D	C	4	3-4
Petersburg	Danzig/Icecapade	C-	8	M	C	5	2-3
Peteski*	Affirmed/Nureyev	C	7	C-	C-	3*	2-4
Petong ENG	Mansingh/Linacre	C-	7	C-	C	5	3-4
Petorius IRE	Mummy's Pet/Club House	C-	6	C-	C-	4	2-3
Petoski ENG	Niniski/Petingo	D	8	C-	U	1	3-4
Petra Forbes	Bold Forbes/The Axe II	U	8	U	M	3	3-4
Petral's Flight*	Storm Bird/Acroterion	U	10	M	M	3	3-4
Petrone	Prince Taj/Wild Risk	D	8	C	C	2	3-4
Petronisi			7	C*		3	3-4
Phantom Jet	Tri Jet/Mr. Prospector	M	8	M	M	4	2-3
Pharly ENG	Lyphard/Boran	C-	6	C+*	D	3*	3-4
Pharostan NZ			7	C		3	3-4
Philosopical	Horatius/Silver Badge		7	M		4	3-4
Phone Order	Fappiano/In Reality	C	7	U	C+	3	2-3
Phone Trick	Icecapade/Finnegan	C+	6	C-	C	4	2-3
Piano Jim			7	C*		1	3-4
Pia Star	Olympia/Mahmoud	C	7	C	C+	4	3-4
Piaster	Damascus/Round Table	C-	7	C	C	4	3-4
Piccolino	Fappiano/In Reality	C	6	U	C	4	2-3
Pick Axe	Mr. Prospector/Sham	M	10	U	M	4	3-4

Stallion	Sire/Broodmare Sire	FTS	CL	TRF	OT	SI	AB
Pick Up the Phone^^	Phone Trick/Coastal	L	8	U	M	4	2-3
Piece of Pacific	Pacific Native/Third Brother	U	9	U	L	5	3-4
Piedmont Pete	Son of Bagdad/Uncle Percy	D	8	D	D	4	3-4
Piker *PH*	Mr. Prospector/Iron Ruler	D	8	F	C	5	3-4
Pilgrim	Northern Dancer/Victoria Park	D	7	C*	D	3	3-4
Pilot Ship	Hoist the Flag/Sir Gaylord	F	8	D	C	3*	3-4
Pine Bluff	Danzig/Halo	C	6	C+	C	4*	2-3
Pine Circle	Cox's Ridge/Gallant Man	D	7	C-	C-	2	3-4
Pink *FR*	Northern Dancer/Never Bend	C	7	C	C-	3	3-4
Pineing Patty^	Country Pine/Fabled Monarch	U	7	M	M	2	2-3
Pip's Pride *IRE*	Efisio/Relkino	U	6	M	M	5	2-3
Pirate Army *AUS*	Roberto/Lt. Stevens	U	7	M	U	3	3-4
Pirateer	Roberto/Chieftain	D	9	C	C	4	3-4
Pirate's Bounty	Hoist The Flag/Steward	C-	7	C	C	4	3-4
Pirouette	Best Turn/White Gloves II	C-	8	F	F	3	3-4
Pistolet Bleu *IRE*			7	C		2	3-4
Pistols and Roses^^	Darn that Alarm/Princely Pleasure	M	6	U	L	2	2-3
Plain Dealing	Northern Dancer/Intentionally	<u>C</u>	7	C	C+	4	2-3
Play Fellow	On the Sly/Run For Nurse	C-	7	C-	CT	3	3-4
Play On *VEN*	Stop the Music/Impressive	C	6	C-	C-	3*	3-4
Pleasant Colony	His Majesty/Sunrise Flight	C	4	B-Y	C-	I	3-4
Pleasant Prospector^	Pleasant Colony/Mr.Prospector	U	8	M	M	4	3-4
Pleasant Tap	Pleasant Colony/Stage Door Johnny	C-	6	C	D	2	3-4
Pleasure Appeal^^	Valid Appeal/What a Pleasure	L	9	M	L	4	2-3
Pleasure Bent	What a Pleasure/Rasper II	C-	8	F	C	5	2-3
Pleasure Prize	What a Pleasure/Swoon's Son	D	8	C-	C	4	3-4
Pleasure Three	Honest Pleasure/Le Haar	U	8	M	U	4	3-4
Pledge Card	Quack/Damascus	U	9	U	L	4	2-3
Plentyofit^	Mr. Prospector/Full Pocket	M	8	U	L	4	2-3
Plinth	Tom Rolfe/Double Jay	D	9	F	D	3*	3-4
Plugged Nickel *SAF*	Key to the Mint/Buckpasser	C-	8	C-	C	3	3-4
Pluie's Sylvester	Verbatim/Lt. Stevens	D	8	D	CT	3	3-4
Ply the Sea	North Sea/Turn-to	D	10	C	D	4	3-4
Pocket Book	Full Pocket/Amberoid	M	9	U	M	4	3-4
Pocketful in Vail	Full Pocket/Jungle Road	C-	8	D	C	4	3-4
Pocket Phone	Phone Trick/Full Pocket	M	8	U	LT	4	2-3
Pocket Park	Verbatim/Jet Pilot	F	8	D	C-	3	3-4
Pocket Zipper	Full Pocket/Jungle Road	C-	9	D	D	4	3-4
Poison Ivory	Sir Ivor/Northern Dancer	D	8	C-	D	3	3-4
Poker	Round Table/Glamour	D	5	C+	C	I	3-4
Polar Falcon *ENG*	Nureyev/Jefferson	M	6	C	M	3*	3-4
Poleax	The Axe II/Ambiorix	D	9	D	C+	3	3-4
Pole Position	Draft Card/Wallet Lifter	C-	7	F	C	4	2-3
Poles Apart	Danzig/Cyane	D	6	D	C+T	3*	2-3
Police Car	Nearctic/Menetrier	D	8	C+	C	4	3-4

Stallion	Sire/Broodmare Sire	FTS	CL	TRF	OT	SI	AB
Police Inspector	Police Car/Winning Shot	D	9	C+	F	4	3-4
Policeman	Riverman/Barbare	C-	7	C	C	4	3-4
Polish Navy JPN	Danzig/Tatan	C-	7	C	C	I	3-4
Polish Numbers	Danzig/Buckpasser	B	4	A	C+T	4*	2-3
Polish Pro^	Mr. Prospector/Danzig	L	7	L	L	4*	2-3
Polish Patriot	Danzig/Filaberto	M	6	M	M	4*	2-3
Polish Precedent ENG	Danzig/Buckpasser	C+	6	C+	M	3	3-4
Political Ambition	Kirtling/Round Table	D	7	C+	C	3	3-4
Polka	In Reality/Chieftain	M	7	U	T	4	3-4
Pollinize	Buckpasser/Better Self	C-	9	D	C	4	3-4
Polski Boy FR	Danzig Connection/Tom Fool	M	6	M	M	4	3-4
Polynesian Flyer	Flying Lark/Best Dancer	D	9	D	C	4	3-4
Polynesian Ruler	Manifesto/Polynesian	F	9	U	F	4	3-4
Pontoise	Cornish Prince/Battlefield	C-	8	F	C	4	3-4
Port Authority	Delta Judge/Cohoes	C	10	D	C	5	3-4
Port Eades	Big Joker/El-Zahbl	F	8	D	D	5	3-4
Port Master	Raise a Native/Lt. Stevens	D	8	C	C	3	3-4
Posen IR	Danzig/Best Turn	M	7	M	M	4	3-4
Position Leader	Pole Position/Mr. Leader	U	9	U	M	4	3-4
Positiveness	Exclusive Native/Alcibiades II	C-	7	D	C	3	3-4
Positive Step	Mr. Leader/Prince Dare	M	9	U	T	4	3-4
Posse			7	C+*		3	3-4
Potentiate	Foolish Pleasure/Northern Dancer	D	8	D	C	3	3-4
Powder Horn	Tom Rolfe/My Babu	C-	7	C-	C-	4	3-4
Power Boat			7		M	3	3-4
Power of Mind	Mr. Prospector/Youth	M	8	U	L	4	3-4
Power Ruler			7	C*		3	3-4
Practicante		C	6*	C*	C	3	3-4
Practitioner	Dr. Fager/Round Table	D	7	D	D	3	3-4
Precocious ENG	Mummy's Pet/Reform	F	7	C-	M	4	3-4
Preemptive	Tri Jet/Quadrangle	M	8	U	U	3	3-4
Premier Ministre	Cannonade/Sonadore	F	10	C	C	4	3-4
Premiership	Exclusive Native/Never Bend	C	7	C-	B	3	2-3
Preponderant FR	Arctic Tern/Djakao	D	8	M	F	4	3-4
Present Value	Halo/Vice Regal	C-	7	U	CT	3	2-4
Presidium ENG	General Assembly/Reliance	D	7	C	C-	4	3-4
Press Card^^	Fappiano/Never Bend	L	8	M	LT	4	2-3
Presto Lad	Nijinsky II/Buckpasser	C-	8	D	C	3	3-4
Preston	Fabulous Dancer/Relko	M	7	L	M	3	3-4
Pretense	Endeavor II/Hyperion	C	6	C+*	C	4	3-4
Primo Dominie ENG	Dominion/Swanee	C	7	C	M	4	2-3
Prince Alydar	Alydar/Northern Dancer	M	7	M	LT	3	3-4
Prince Astro	Dancing Dervish/Naiur	F	8	C*	C	4	3-4
Prince Card	Prince John/Royal Charger	C	9	C+	C	3	3-4
Prince Colony	Pleasant Colony/Cornish Prince	U	8	M	M	3	3-4

Stallion	Sire/Broodmare Sire	FTS	CL	TRF	OT	SI	AB
Prince Cox^^	Cox's Ridge/Gallant Man	M	9	M	M	3	3-4
Prince Dantan			7	C*		2	3-4
Prince Don B	Don B./Grey Dawn II	C	8	D	C	3	3-4
Prince Forli	Broadway Forli/Jungle Road	C-	9	F	C	4	3-4
Prince Hague	Nijinsky II/Key to the Mint	D	7	C+	C	I	3-4
Prince John	Princequillo/Count Fleet	D	4*	C+	C+	I	3-4
Princely Native	Raise a Native/Francis S.	C	7	CY	C	3	3-4
Princely Pleasure	What a Pleasure/Prince John	C-	6	C*	C	3	2-3
Princely Ruler	Foolish Pleasure/Prince John	C	9	D	C	5	3-4
Princely Verdict	Prince John/Hail to Reason	D	8	D	F	4	3-4
Prince of Fame	Fappiano/Secretariat	C	7	M	C	4	3-4
Prince Rupert *IRE*	Prince Tenderfoot/Vaguely Noble	C	7	C-	M	I	3-4
Prince Siam			7	C+*		3	3-4
Prince Sabo *ENG*	Young Generation/Song	C	7	C	M	5	2-3
Prince Street	Nijinsky II/Native Dancer	D	8	C	D	4	3-4
Prince Tenderfoot		D	6	C*	D	I	3-4
Prince Valid	Valid Appeal/Klem	D	9	D	C	4	3-4
Priolo *FR*	Sovereign Dancer/Irish River	D	6	C+	M	3	3-4
Private Account	Damascus/Buckpasser	C-	5*	C-	C+	2	3-4
Private Admirer*	Private Account/Danzig	M	9	L	M	3	2-3
Private Express	Pass the Tab/El Macho	D	7	U	C-	5	3-4
Private Key	Private Account/Key the Mint	C-	7	C+	C	4	2-3
Private School*	Bates Motel/Torsion	U	8	U	M	3	3-4
Private Talk	Private Account/Mill Reef	U	6	C+	D	3	2-3
Private Terms	Private Account/Bold Ruler	C	6	CY	C+T	2	2-3
Private Thoughts	Pretense/Bagdad	D	5	D	C	3	3-4
Private Tudor	Tudorich/Octopus	D	9	D	C	4	3-4
Private Venture	Private Account/One For All	U	6	U	M	4	3-4
Prized	Kris S/My Dad George	B	6	C	C	3	2-4
Prize Ring	Buckpasser/Turn-to	C-	7	F	C	3	3-4
Probable	Codex/Intentionally	F	9	U	D	4	3-4
Procida *IND*	Mr. Prospector/Distinctive	C-	8	C-	C	3	3-4
Pro Consul	Vice Regent/Bing	D	7	C-	D	3*	3-4
Proctor	Graustark/Bold Ruler	D	9	D	C	3	3-4
Productivity	Windy Sands/Fleet Nasrullah	C	9	D	C	4	3-4
Professor Blue	Northern Dancer/Delta Judge	D	8	D	D	4	3-4
Pron Regard	Speak John/Cavan	D	10	D	C	3	3-4
Proof	Believe It/Court Martial	D	7	C	D	I	3-4
Properantes	Protanto/My Babu	D	8	C-	C	3	3-4
Proper Challenge			10		M	4	3-4
Proper Reality	In Reality/Nodouble	C	6	C	C+	3	3-4
Propico *ARG*	Dorileo/Pronto	D	7	C-	C-	I	3-4
Prospective Star	Mr. Prospector/Distinctive	C-	8	C-	CT	4	3-4
Prospect North	Mr. Prospector/Northern Dancer	D	8	D	C+	4	3-4
Prospector Jones^	Mr. Prospector/Nijinsky II	M	8	M	M	3	3-4

Stallion	Sire/Broodmare Sire	FTS	CL	TRF	OT	SI	AB
Prospector's Bid	Mr. Prospector/Crimson Satan	C-	7	D	C	4	3-4
Prospectors Gamble	Crafty Prospector/Sunny South	C+	6	DY	C+	4	2-3
Prospector's Gold	Mr. Prospector/Diplomat Way	D	10	D	D	3	3-4
Prospector's Halo	Gold Stage/Halo	C	6	D	C+T	3	2-3
Prospector's Music*	Mr. Prospector/The Minstrel	C	7	M	C	3	2-3
Prospector's Pick	Mr. Prospector/What a Pleasure	M	7	U	M	4	2-3
Prosper Fager	Mr. Prospector/Dr. Fager	C-	6	D	C	3	3-4
Prosperous	Mr. Prospector/Sadair	D	7	D	C	3	2-3
Proud Appeal	Valid Appeal/Proudest Roman	C	6	C	C	3*	2-3
Proud Arion			7	C*		3*	3-4
Proud Birdie	Proud Clarion/Bolero	C	6	C-	C+T	3*	2-3
Proud Clarion	Hail to Reason/Breath O'Morn	D	7	C*	C	3*	3-4
Proudest Doon	Matsadoon/Nail	U	9	U	M	4	3-4
Proudest Duke	Regal and Royal/Proudest Roman	C-	7	D	C	3	3-4
Proudest Roman	Never Bend/Roman	C-	6	C+*	C+	3	2-3
Proud Irish	Irish River/Delta Judge	C-	8	M	C-	3	2-3
Proud Ling	Proud Clarion/Icecapade	D	8	C+	C	2	3-4
Proud Northern	Northern Jove/Jaipur	C-	8	U	C	4	3-4
Proud Pocket	Full Pocket/Sailor	D	8	D	D	4	3-4
Proud Truth PAN	Graustark/Summer Tan	D	6	C+	C	1	3-4
Prove It	Endeavor II/Khaled	C-	7	C-	C	4	3-4
Prove Out	Graustark/Bold Venture	F	7	D	C	3	3-4
Providential	Run the Gantlet/Primera	C-	8	C	D	1	3-4
Prowess Prince	Cornish Prince/Irish Lancer	D	7	D	C	4	3-4
Pruning	The Pruner/Chieftain	D	7	D	C	4	3-4
Publicity	Bold Hitter Terrang	D	8	C	C-	3	3-4
Puissance ENG	Thatching/Balidar	C	6	C	C	5	2-3
Pulsate	Explodent/Nashua	U	9	M	M	2	3-4
Pulverizing^^	Well Decorated/Explodent	M	8	M	L	3	3-4
Puntivo	Restivo/Beau Gar	D	8	F	C	3*	3-4
Purdue King	Dimaggio/Truxton Fair	U	7	U	M	4	3-4
Purely Pleasure	Secretariat/Pass Catcher	C-	8	C	C-	3	3-4
Purple Comet	Kohoutek/Beddard	C-	7	M	D	3	3-4
Pursuit	Never Bend/Prince John	D	9	C	C-	4	3-4
Pursuit of Love ENG	Groom Dancer/Green Dancer	U	7	C	M	3	2-3
P Vik	Petrone/Viking Spirit	F	9	C*	C	2	3-4
Pyrite	Mr. Prospector/Northern Dancer	C-	9	D	D	4	3-4
Quack	T. V. Lark/Princequillo	D	6*	C	C	3*	3-4
Quadrangle	Cohoes/Bull Lea	D	7	D	C	2	3-4
Quadratic	Quadrangle/Quibu	D	7	C-	CT	3	2-3
Queen City Lad	Olden Times/Royal Union	C+	7	D	C	4	3-4
Queen's Gray Bee^^	Drone/Sham	U	9	U	M	4	2-3
Queen's Minister	Bold Lad/Sword Dance	D	8	D	F	4	3-4
Quest for Fame	Rainbow Quest/Green Dancer	U	6	BY	M	3*	3-4
Quibble	Mongo/Quadrangle	M	8	M	M	3	3-4

Stallion	Sire/Broodmare Sire	FTS	CL	TRF	OT	SI	AB
Quick Dip	Vigors/One for All	C	9	C+	C	4	2-4
Quicksilver	Navajo/Bold Reasoning	M	8	U	U	4	3-4
Quick Style	To the Quick/Cornish Prince	D	10	D	F	4	3-4
Quiet American	Fappiano/Dr. Fager	D	6	C	C	3*	2-3
Quiet Enjoyment^^	Ogygian/Wig Out	M	8	U	M	4	2-3
Quiet Fling		7*	c*			2	3-4
Qui Native	Exclusive Native/Francis S.	C	8	C	C	3	3-4
Quite Special*	Danzig/First Landing	M	10	M	M	4	2-3
Quintillion *IRE*	Rusticaro/Habitat	M	7	C+	M	3	3-4
Quinton	Damascus/Never Bend	D	9	U	C	4	3-4
Quip	Hoist the Flag/Needles	C-	8	D	C-	4	2-3
Raba Road	Raja Baba/Road House	D	10	D	C	3	3-4
Racconto		7	C*			4*	3-4
Racing Star *COL*	Baldski/Imasmartee	D	7	C	C-	3	3-4
Raconteur	The Minstrel/Stage Door Johnny	D	8	C	D	2	3-4
Raft	Nodouble/Round Table	C-	8	C	C-	2	3-4
Ragtime Band *SWS*	Northern Dancer/Delta Judge	M	7	M	M	3	3-4
Rahy	Blushing Groom/Halo	C-	5	B	C	2	3-4
Rail^	Majestic Light/Believe It	U	7	L	M	3	3-4
Rainbow Quest *ENG*	Blushing Groom/Herbager	D	5	B	L	1	3-4
Rainbows First	Star Nasrullah/Semi Pro	M	9	M	M	4	2-3
Rainbows For Life *IRE*	Lyphard/Halo	M	5	M	M	1*	3-4
Rainy Lake *IR*	Royal Charger/War Admiral	C-	6	C*	C	3	3-4
Raise a Bid	Raise a Native/Double Jay	C-	7	C-	C	3	2-3
Raise a Champion	Raise a Native/Ack Ack	C	8	D	C+	4	3-4
Raise a Cup	Raise a Native/Nashua	C	5	C*	C+	3*	3-4
Raise a Man	Raise a Native/Delta Judge	C-	8	C-	C	4	3-4
Raise a Native	Native Dancer/Case Ace	C+	5*	C*	B	4	3-4
Raise a Rascal	Raise a Native/Nashua	M	10	M	M	5	3-4
Raised on Stage	Raise a Man/Stage Director	C-	8	D	C-	3	3-4
Raised Socially	Raise a Native/Never Bend	C-	7	D	CT	4	2-<u>3</u>
Raised Well	Raise a Native/Well Mannered	C-	8	U	C-	4	3-4
Raise Your Glass	Raise a Native/Barbizon	M	8	U	M	5	2-3
Rajab	Jaipur/Princequillo	C-	7	C*	C	3	2-3
Raja Baba	Bold Ruler/My Babu	C	5*	C*	B	4*	3-4
Raja Native	Raja Baba/Native Charger	C-	7	F	D	4	3-4
Raja's Best Boy	Raja Baba/Icecapade	C-	8	D	C-	4	2-3
Raja's Revenge	Raja Baba/Northern Dancer	C-	7	BY	C	4	3-4
Rakeen^^	Northern Dancer/Halo	M	8	L	M	3*	3-4
Rambling Rector	Blushing Groom/Hail to Reason	C	7	D	C+	3*	<u>2</u>-3
Rambo	Northfields/Sea Bird	D	8	F	C	3	3-4
Rambo Dancer *ENG*	Northern Dancer/Chateaugay	C-	7	C	M	3*	2-3
Rambo Phil	Nodouble/In Reality	U	7	M	T	4	3-4
Rambunctious	Rasper II/The Solicitor II	C	6	F	C+	3	<u>2</u>-3
Ramirez	T. V. Lark/Dedicate	D	8	C*	D	4	3-4

Stallion	Sire/Broodmare Sire	FTS	CL	TRF	OT	SI	AB
Rampage	Northern Baby/Vaguely Noble	D	8	C	CT	2	3-4
Ramplett	Fappiano/Crimson Satan	C+	7	U	C	4	2-3
Ransack	Search for Gold/Snob	C-	8	F	C	4	3-4
Rare Brick	Rare Performer/Mr. Brick	C+	7	C-	C+T	4	2-3
Rare Dancer	The Minstrel/Vaguely Noble	U	8	M	M	3	3-4
Rare Performer	Mr. Prospector/Better Self	C	6	CY	C+T	4	2-3
Rarerullah	Rollicking/Towson	D	9	F	D	4	3-4
Ratification	Forli/Sir Gaylord	D	8	C	C	4	3-4
Rattenburys Bank	Verbatim/Flip Sal	U	10	M	M	3	3-4
Raykour^^	Dalsaan/Charlottesville	M	8	L	M	3	3-4
Ray's Word	Verbatim/Etonian	D	8	C	C	4*	3-4
R.B. Chesney FR	Brigadier Gerard/Vienna	D	7	C	C	1	3-4
Reach for More	I'm for More/Villamor	C+	7	U	BT	4	2-3
Re Ack	Ack Ack/Mister Jive	M	7	U	M	3	3-4
Reading Room	Ribot/Shut Out	F	8	D	C-	3	3-4
Real Courage DR	In Reality/Key to the Mint	C	8	DY	C	3	2-3
Reality and Reason	In Reality/Boldnesian	D	8	C-	C+	5	3-4
Real Landing	In Reality/First Landing	C	9	D	C-	3	3-4
Really Awesome	Mr. Prospector/Le Fabuleux	C	8	D	D	3	2-3
Really Cooking	Hilarious/Beau Gar	C-	9	C*	D	3	3-4
Really Golden*	In Reality/Raise a Native	M	10	U	L	4	3-4
Really Secret	In Reality/Bold Ambition	C	7	D	C	3	3-4
Real Supreme			7	C*		3	3-4
Real Value	In Reality/Rocky Royale	C-	8	D	C	5	3-4
Real Way	In Reality/Diplomat Way	C-	8	M	C	4	3-4
Real West^	Gone West/Relaunch	L	8	M	L	4	2-3
Reap	Royal Ski/Vent du Nord	M	9	MY	M	3	3-4
Reb's Golden Ale	Reb's Policy/Donut King	D	10	M	C	5	3-4
Recital Hall	Stop the Music/Dr. Fager	C-	8	D	D	3*	3-4
Recognized	Raise a Native/Reviewer	C-	9	C-	C	4	3-4
Record	Delta Oil/Gallant Romeo	M	9	U	M	5	3-4
Record Catch	What Luck/Tom Fool	D	9	D	C	3	3-4
Rectory	King's Bishop/First Landing	F	9	C-	D	3	3-4
Recusant	His Majesty/Cornish Prince	F	7	F	C	3	3-4
Red Anchor	Damascus/Swaps	D	9	D	D	5	3-4
Red Attack	Alydar/Buckpasser	F	7	CY	C	2	3-4
Red Bishop^	Silver Hawk/Silly Season	U	5	L	M	1	3-4
Red Clay Country	Master Derby/Carry Back	F	7	D	D	3	2-3
Red Ransom	Roberto/Damascus	C	6	B	DT	3*	3-4
Red Ryder SAF	Raise a Native/Nashua	D	7	C-	C	3	3-4
Red Sunset IRE	Red God/Tampion	C	7	C	L	3*	3-4
Red Tempo	Mussorgsky/Small Time	U	8	L	M	3	3-4
Red Wing Bold	Boldnesian/Rocky Royale	C+	8	C	C	5	2-3
Reel on Reel	Nijinsky II/Cyane	U	7	M	L	4	3-4
Reference Point ENG	Mill Reef/Habitat	F	6	C	C	1	3-4

Stallion	Sire/Broodmare Sire	FTS	CL	TRF	OT	SI	AB
Reflected Glory	Jester/Palestinian	D	8	C*	C	4	3-4
Refleet			7	C*		3	3-4
Regal Affair	His Majesty/Dr. Fager	C-	7	C-	C-	3	3-4
Regal and Royal	Vaguely Noble/Native Dancer	C-	7	C+*	C	3	3-4
Regalberto	Roberto/Roi Dagobert	D	8	C	C	3	3-4
Regal Classic	Vice Regent/Nodouble	C	5	C	D	3	2-3
Regal Conquest	Conquistador Cielo/Viceregal	M	8	M	M	4	3-4
Regal Embrace	Vice Regent/Nentego	D	8	F	C	3	3-4
Regal Flier	Majestic Light/Damascus	D	8	C-	C-	3	3-4
Regal Humor	Regal and Royal/Diplomat Way	F	8	C	DT	3	3-4
Regal Intention	Vice Regent/Tentam	D	6	C	C	3	3-4
Regal Remark	Northern Dancer/Speak John	C-	8	M	C+	4	2-3
Regal Search	Mr. Prospector/Dr. Fager	C+	6	C+	D	3	2-3
Regal Song	Vice Regent/Norcliffe	U	7	M	M	4	3-4
Regent Cat	Vice Regent/Cougar II	D	8	D	D	3*	3-4
Rehaan*	Storm Bird/Buckpasser	D	9	M	M	3	3-4
Rehearing	Valid Appeal/Creme dela Creme	M	8	U	M	4	3-4
Reign Road*	Sovereign Dancer/Gallant Man	U	9	M	M	2	3-4
Reinvested	Irish Castle/Crafty Admiral	D	8	C	D	2	3-4
Relaunch	In Reality/The Axe II	C+	4	C+	B	4*	2-3
Relaunch a Tune	Relaunch/Don B.	C	7	M	C	4	3-4
Religiously *IRE*	Alleged/Admiral's Voyage	U	8	M	M	2	3-4
Remedial	Ramadan/Nearctic	C	8	U	C	4	2-3
Reno City	Fappiano/Lt. Stevens	M	8	M	L	4	3-4
Repriced^^	Roberto/Quack	U	7	L	M	4	3-4
Reprimand *ENG*	Mummy's Pet/Nonoalco	C	6	C	M	4*	2-3
Restivo	Restless Native/Palestine	C-	8	D	C-	2	2-3
Reprized	Kris S./My Dad George	L	7	L	M	3	2-3
Restless Con	Restless Native/Wallet Lifter	C	8	U	M	3	2-3
Restless Native	Native Dancer/Bull Lea	C	7	C	C	4*	2-3
Restless Run	Restless Native/Northern Dancer	C	8	C*	C	4*	3-4
Retsina Run	Windy Sands/Pia Star	C	8	M	C+	4	3-4
Returnee	Secretariat/Riva Ridge	U	8	M	M	3	3-4
Reve Du	Gallant Best/Fleet Nasrullah	U	10	U	L	2	2-3
Reverse Mulligan		D	7	U	C+	3	2-3
Reviewer	Bold Ruler/Hasty Road	C	6*	C	C+	4	2-3
Rewana	Relaunch/Envoy	C-	9	C	C-	4	3-4
Rex Imperator	King Emperor/Imbros	F	6	C-	C+	4	3-4
Rexson	Bold Bidder/Turn-to	F	7	F	C+	4	3-4
Rexson's Hope *PR*	Rexson/Abe's Hope	F	8	C-	C	3	2-3
Rheingold			7	C*		4	3-4
Rhinflo	Shecky Greene/Rheingold	D	8	M	F	4	3-4
Rhodes	Mr. Prospector/Bold Ruler	M	8	C	M	3	3-4
Rhythm *JPN*	Mr. Prospector/Northern Dancer	M	7	M	M	4*	2-3
Ribblesdale *IRE*			7	M*		3	3-4

Stallion	Sire/Broodmare Sire	FTS	CL	TRF	OT	SI	AB
Rich Cream	Creme dela Creme/Turn-to	C-	7	C	C-	4	3-4
Rich Doctor	Doc Scott J./Rich Gift	M	10	U	C-	4	3-4
Riches to Riches	Fappiano/Hill Rise	D	10	C-	D	4*	3-4
Richman*	Bet Big/Super Concorde	C	7	M	C+	4	2-3
Ricky Horn	Bold Bidder/Damascus	D	9	F	C-	4	3-4
Ridgewood High	Walker's/Curragh King	U	9	U	U	5	3-4
Riflery*	Turkey Shoot/Cornish Prince	C	7	M	M	4	2-3
Right Con	Beau Buck/Unconscious	U	9	U	M	4	3-4
Ringaro ARG	Caro/Outing Class	D	7	C*	M	2	3-4
Ringside	Sir Ivor/Speak John	C	7	D	C	3	3-4
Rinka Das^	Nureyev/Gregorian	U	7	L	M	3	3-4
Rinoso	Noble Sun/Ridan	C	8	C	D	5	2-3
Rio Bravo			7	M*		1*	3-4
Rio Carmelo	Riverman/Alycidon	F	8	C	F	3	3-4
Rio's Lark	Rio Carmelo/Knightly Dawn	D	8	C	C	2	3-4
Risen Star	Secretariat/His Majesty	F	7	C	CT	1	3-4
Rising Market	To Market/War Admiral	C	6	C*	C	4	3-4
Rising Raja THI	Raja Baba/Pia Star	D	9	C-	C-	4	3-4
Riva Pass	Riva Ridge/Val de l'orne	D	8	M	CT	3	3-4
Riva Ridge	First Landing/Heliopolis	C	7	C*	C	2	3-4
River Crest	Riverman/Hoist the Flag	D	8	C	D	4	3-4
River Daj	Riverman/Royal Note	F	9	D	C-	4	3-4
River Falls ENG	Aragon/Morstan		6	M		4	3-4
Riverhill CHI			7	C		4	3-4
Riverman	Never Bend/Prince John	C-	4*	C+*	D	3*	3-4
River of Kings	Sassafras/Sovereign Path	D	8	C+	D	3	3-4
River Special TUR*	Riverman/Nijinsky II	M	8	L	M	3	3-4
Rixdal			7	C+*		4	3-4
Rizzy^	Afleet/Topsider	L	7	M	M	4	2-3
Road Rush^	Broad Brush/Private Account	M	8	U	L	3	2-3
Roan Drone	Drone/John's Joy	F	8	U	C-	4	3-4
Roanoke	Pleasant Colony/Sea-Bird	C-	7	C	DT	2	3-4
Roanoke Island	Cyane/Never Say Die	D	8	C-*	C	4	3-4
Roan Rocket			7	C		5	3-4
Roaring Camp^	Forty Niner/Nijinsky II	L	8	M	M	4*	2-3
Roar of the Crowd	Hold Your Peace/Time Tested	M	9	U	M	5	3-4
Rob An Plunder	Pirate's Bounty/Reflected Glory	C	9	U	C	4	2-3
Robellino ENG	Roberto/Pronto	D	6	C+*	C	2	3-4
Roberto	Hail to Reason/Nashua	D	2*	A*	C	1	2-3
Roberto Reason	Roberto/Princequillo	U	7	M	U	3	3-4
Robin des Bois	Nureyev/Key to the Mint	D	6	C	M	2	3-4
Robin des Pins*	Nureyev/Key to the Mint	D	7	C	C	3	3-4
Robyn Dancer	Crafty Prospector/Sword Dancer	C+	6	B	CT	3	2-3
Rocamadour IRE		M	7	U	U	4	3-4
Rockamundo^^	Key to the Mint/Nijinsky II	U	8	M	M	2	3-4

Stallion	Sire/Broodmare Sire	FTS	CL	TRF	OT	SI	AB
Rock City *ENG*	Ballad Rock/Petingo	C	6	C	M	3	2-3
Rock Hill^	Mr. Prospector/Nijinsky II	M	8	M	M	4	3-4
Rock Lives	Rock Talk/Joust	D	8	U	C	4	2-3
Rock of Cashel	Noholme II/Newtown Wonder	D	8	C-	F	2	3-4
Rock Point	Believe It/Hoist the Flag	C-	7	C-	C	3	3-4
Rock Royalty	Native Royalty/Fleet Nasrullah	D	8	D	F	4	3-4
Rock Talk	Rasper II/Polynesian	C	5	C+*	C	2	3-4
Rocky Marriage	Riva Ridge/Candy Spots	D	7	D	C-	3	3-4
Rocky Mountain	Alydar/Jacinto	D	7	C	D	4	3-4
Roi Dagobert	Sicambre/Cranach	D	6	C	C	3	3-4
Roi Danzig *IRE*	Danzig/Sir Ivor	D	7	C	M	3*	3-4
Rokeby*	Lomond/Habitat	M	7	M	M	4	2-3
Rolfe	Tom Rolfe/Sir Gaylord	D	7	C*	C	3	3-4
Rolfson	Tom Rolfe/Olden Times	F	8	D	CT	3	3-4
Rollicking	Rambunctious/Martins Rullah	D	7	C-*	C+	4	2-3
Rollick 'N Roll	Rollicking/Chompion	U	7	U	M	4	3-4
Rollin on Over	Brent's Prince/In the Pocket	C-	9	D	F	4	3-4
Rolls Aly	Alydar/Traffic Mark	C-	8	D	C	3	3-4
Roman Bend	Proudest Roman/Grey Dawn II	U	9	M	U	2	3-4
Roman Diplomat	Roberto/Chieftain	D	6	C+Y	C-	3*	2-3
Roman Majesty	His Majesty/Majestic Prince	C	8	D	D	3	3-4
Roman Reasoning	Bold Reasoning/Roman	C-	6	F	C	4	3-4
Romantic Lead	Silent Screen/Sir Gaylord	D	7	D	CT	4	3-4
Romantic Prince *IRE*	Henbit/Crowned Prince	M	7	M	M	3	2-3
Romeo	T.V. Lark/Tiger Wander	D	7	D	CT	3	3-4
Ron Bon	Halo/Proudest Roman	U	8	M	M	4	3-4
Ron's Victory *ENG*			7	M		4	3-4
Roo Art	Buckaroo/Ribot	F	8	D	C	3	3-4
Rooney's Champ	Fappiano/Secretariat	M	10	U	M	4	3-4
Root Boy*	Baederwood/King's Bishop	C	6	U	C+	4	2-3
Rory's Jester	Crown Jester/Rory's Rocket		7	L		3	3-4
Roscius	Stage Door Johnny/Sir Ivor	U	7	L	M	3	3-4
Rougemont	Seattle Slew/Bold Bidder	C-	8	U	C	4	2-3
Rough Iron	Nodouble/T.V. Lark	C-	8	D	C	3	3-4
Rough Pearl	Tom Rolfe/Ruffled Feathers	M	8	C	M	1	3-4
Roulette Wheel	Key to the Mint/Sir Gaylord	D	9	D	C	4	3-4
Round Table	Princequillo/Sir Cosmo	C-	3*	B	C-	4	2-3
Rouse the Louse	Irish River/Restless Native	D	7	C+	C	3	3-4
Rousillon *JPN*	Riverman/Marshua's Dancer	F	6	C	D	3*	3-4
Roving Minstrel	Diplomat Way/Poona II	U	9	C	U	3	3-4
Roxbury Park	Mr. Prospector/Filberto	D	8	F	C	4	3-4
Roy *CHI*	Fappiano/Never Bend	M	6	L	M	4	2-3
Royal Academy *IRE*	Nijinsky II/Crimson Satan	C-	7	C	C-	4*	2-3
Royal And Regal	Vaguely Noble/Native Dancer	D	7	C	C	3	3-4
Royal Chocolate	Amber Morn/Prince John	D	8	D	D	4	3-4

Stallion	Sire/Broodmare Sire	FTS	CL	TRF	OT	SI	AB
Royal Design	Never Bend/Gallant Man	D	9	M	D	4	3-4
Royal Egyptian	Theatrical/Verbatim	L	9	L	M	3*	2-3
Royal Gardner	Landscaper/Son Ange	U	8	U	U	3	3-4
Royal Manner	Native Royalty/Tompion	D	8	D	C	4	3-4
Royal Match *ENG*	Sovereign Path/Skymaster		7	C-		3	3-4
Royal N Trouble	Royal and Regal/Our Native	U	10	M	M	3	3-4
Royal Pavilion	Native Royalty/Bonjour	C-	7	F	C	4	3-4
Royal Pennant	Raja Baba/Hoist the Flag	C	8	U	C	3	2-3
Royal Roberto	Roberto/Royal Note	C	7	C	C	3	3-4
Royal Sherry	Bold Reason/Amber Morn	D	7	C-	D	2	3-4
Royal Ski	Raja Baba/Involvement	C-	8	C-	C-	3	3-4
Royal Value	Regal Embrace/Vice Regal	M	8	U	U	5	3-4
Ruben's Art	Rube the Great/Arts and Letters	U	10	U	C-	3	3-4
Rubiano	Fappiano/Nijinsky II	C+	5	C	CT	3	2-3
Ruffinal	Tom Rolfe/Nasrullah	D	9	C	C	2	3-4
Rugged Angel	Mr. Prospector/Vice Regent	M	8	M	M	4*	2-3
Ruhlmann	Mr. Leader/Chieftain	C	7	C-	C+	3	2-4
Ruler's Conquest	Iron Ruler/Royal Consort	U	9	U	M	5	3-4
Ruling Gold	Gold and Myrrh/Distinctive	C-	8	D	C	4	3-4
Rumbo	Ruffinal/Windy Sands	D	9	C*	D	4	3-4
Runaway Groom	Blushing Groom/Call the Witness	C	6	CY	C+T	3*	2-3
Runderbar *IND*	Run Dusty Run/Clem Pac	C-	8	U	D	4	3-4
Run Johnny Run	Graustark/Round Table	D	8	D	D	3	3-4
Running Gold	Slew o'Gold/Prince John	U	8	U	DT	3	3-4
Run of Luck	Coursing/Berseem	D	8	C*	C	3	3-4
Run Paul Run	Mambo/Ingrained	M	9	M	M	4	3-4
Run the Gantlet	Tom Rolfe/First Landing	D	7	C	C	1	3-4
Run to Daylight	Grey Dawn II/Dewan	U	8	M	L	3	3-4
Run Turn *PR*	Charming Turn/Iron Ruler	C-	7	M	C	3	2-3
Rupert's Wing	Redwing Bold/Springside	C-	9	C-	C	3	3-4
Ruritania	Graustark/Djebe	D	6	C	C-	1	3-4
Ruthie's Native	Native Royalty/Citation	C-	7	C	D	4	3-4
Ryeko	Wajima/The Pie King	U	10	U	M	5	3-4
Sabona	Exclusive Native/Hail to Reason	C	6	C+	C	3	3-4
Sabrehill *ENG*	Diesis/Alleged	U	5	M	M	1	3-4
Sadler's Wells *IRE*	Northern Dancer/Bold Reason	D	1	A	D	1	2-3
Safawan *ENG*			7	C		2	3-4
Sagace *FR*	Luthier/Chaparral	D	6	C	C	1	3-4
Sail Me Again	Relaunch/Revoked	M	6	M	M	4	3-4
Saint Ballado*	Halo/Herbager	C+	5	C-	C-	3*	2-3
Saint Estephe *FR*	Top Ville/Traffic	D	5	L	M	1	3-4
Salem Drive	Darby Creek Road/Northfields	C-	7	C	C	1*	3-4
Salem End Road	Big Burn/Hail the Prince	C-	8	D	C+	5	2-3
Sallust *BRZ*			6	C*		2	3-4
Salse *ENG*	Topsider/Prince John	C-	6	C+	C-	3*	3-4

Stallion	Sire/Broodmare Sire	FTS	CL	TRF	OT	SI	AB
Salt Dome	Blushing Groom/Crimson Satan	D	9	C-	C-	3	2-3
Salt Lake	Deputy Minister/Queen City Lad	C+	6	M	C+	4	2-3
Salt Marsh	Tom Rolfe/Sailor	D	8	D	D	3	3-4
Salty Shoes	Staff Writer/Captain Courageous	C-	8	M	C	4	2-3
Salutely	Hoist the Flag/Amerigo	C-	5	C	C	1	3-4
Sam Again	It's Freezing/Somebody II	M	9	U	M	4	3-4
Samarid	Blushing Groom/Rheffic	U	8	M	M	4	3-4
Same Direction	Vice Regent/Sallymont	D	7	F	D	4	3-4
San Feliou *FR*			7	C*		3	3-4
Sanglamore *FR*	Sharpen Up/Irish River	M	7	C	M	2	3-4
Santiago Peak	Alydar/Secretariat	D	10	D	D	4	3-4
Saratoga Express	Saratoga Six/Blade	L	9	U	L	4	3-4
Saratoga Legend	Saratoga Six/Full Pocket	U	10	U	M	4	3-4
Saratoga Six	Alydar/Irish Castle	C+	7	C-	BT	4	2-3
Sarawak	Northern Dancer/Bold Bidder	D	8	C	C-	4	3-4
Saros	Sassafras/Floribunda	D	7	C	C	3	3-4
Sassafras *FR*	Sheshoon/Ratification	D	6*	C+*	F	3*	3-4
Satan's Flame	Crimson Satan/Kentucky Pride	D	9	F	D	5	3-4
Satan's Gem	Crimson Satan/Jacinto	M	9	U	M	5	3-4
Satellite Signal^	Valid Appeal/Elocutionist	L	8	U	M	4	2-3
Sauceboat	Key to the Mint/My Babu	D	6*	C+*	C-	3*	3-4
Saulingo			7	C*		3	3-4
Saumarez *FR*	Rainbow Quest/Welsh Pageant	U	6	M	M	1	3-4
Saunders	Nijinsky II/Princequillo	D	8	D	D	3	3-4
Savings	Buckfinder/Star Kingdom	C	7	D	C	3	3-4
Savona Tower	Somethingfabulous/Dimaggio	M	9	M	M	4	3-4
Sawbones	The Axe II/Tom Fool	F	7	D	C	3	3-4
Scarlet Ibis	Cormorant/Cornish Prince	C	7	D	C	3	3-4
Scenic *IRE*	Sadler's Wells/Foolish Pleasure	U	6	C	M	1	3-4
Schaufuss	Nureyev/Gallant Romeo	D	8	C-	D	3	3-4
Schembechler	Damascus/What a Pleasure	U	9	M	M	4	3-4
Scherando^^	Dimaggio/Kinsman Hope	M	8	U	M	5	3-4
School Hero	Crozier/Noholme II	C-	8	U	C-	5	3-4
Schossberg^	Broad Brush/Balzac	M	7	U	M	2	2-3
Score Twenty Four	Golden Eagle II/Traffic Judge	D	10	D	C	3	3-4
Scottsville^	Deputy Minister/The Axe II	M	8	U	M	3	3-4
Scouts Oath	Scout Leader/Gainsworth	D	8	D	D	4	3-4
Screaming Fife	Roberto/Santa Claus	D	10	D	C	3	3-4
Screen King	Silent Screen/Nashua	D	7	D	C	3	3-4
Screen Trend	Silent Screen/Prove it	U	8	U	M	4	3-4
Scroll	Nijinsky II/Princequillo	D	9	D	D	2	3-4
Sea Aglo	Sea Bird/Royal Serenade	C	8	D	C+	3	2-3
Sea Bird	Dan Cupid/Sicambre	D	6	D	C	3*	3-4
Seafood	Proud Clarion/Crewman	D	8	D	C	4	3-4
Sea Hero^^	Polish Navy/Graustark	M	5	M	M	1*	2-3

Stallion	Sire/Broodmare Sire	FTS	CL	TRF	OT	SI	AB
Search For Gold	Raise a Native/Nashua	D	8	C*	C	4	3-4
Seat of Power	Bold Ruler/My Babu	C-	7	C*	C	3	3-4
Seattle Battle	Seattle Slew/Raise a Native	C-	8	C	C	4	3-4
Seattle Bound	Seattle Slew/Raise a Native	M	9	U	L	4	3-4
Seattle Dancer *JPN*	Nijinsky II/Poker	D	7	C+Y	D	I	3-4
Seattle Knight	Seattle Slew/Prince John	D	8	M	M	3	3-4
Seattle Sleet*	Seattle Slew/The Minstrel	M	7	M	M	4	2-3
Seattle Slew	Bold Reasoning/Poker	C	4	C+*	C	3*	3-4
Seattle Song	Seattle Slew/Prince Blessed	F	6	C	C-	3*	3-4
Seattle Sun	Seattle Slew/Solazo	M	10	M	M	4	2-3
Sea Wall^	Storm Bird/Sassafras	U	7	L	M	3	3-4
Second Set *ENG*	Alzao/Go Marching	U	6	L	M	3	2-3
Secretariat	Bold Ruler/Princequillo	D	2	B	C	2	3-4
Secretary of State	Secretariat/Native Charger	D	8	C-*	D	3	3-4
Secretary of War	Secretariat/Dunce	D	8	D	D	3	2-3
Secret Claim	Mr. Prospector/Secretariat	D	6	D	C	3	3-4
Secret Counsel	Secretariat/Hail to Reason	D	9	C	C	3	3-4
Secret Hello	Private Account/Silent Screen	C	6	U	CT	3	2-3
Secreto *JPN*	Northern Dancer/Secretariat	D	8	C-	C-	3	3-4
Secret Odds^	Secreto/Kaskaskia	M	7	M	M	4	2-3
Secret Prince	Cornish Prince/Lanvin	F	8	F	C	2	3-4
Secret Slew	Seattle Slew/Ack Ack	D	7	D	C	4	2-3
Seeking the Gold	Mr. Prospector/Buckpasser	C+	5	C	C+T	4*	2-3
Sefapiano*	Fappiano/Lt. Stevens	M	6	U	L	4	2-3
Sejm *PR*	Danzig/Cyane	C	6	C	C	3	2-3
Selari			7	C+*		3	3-4
Selkirk *ENG*	Sharpen Up/Nebblio	U	5	C+Y	M	I	2-3
Selous Scout	Effervescing/Roman Line	C-	7	D	C	3	3-4
Semaj	Zen/Ambernash	F	8	U	C-	4	3-4
Semenenko *CHI*	Vaguely Noble/Dante	D	5	CY	C	3	3-4
Semillero	Proposal/Sertorious	D	8	D	F	3	3-4
Semi Northern	Northern Dancer/Semi-Pro	D	7	C	F	2	3-4
Seneca Jones*	Alydar/Bold Forbes	L	7	U	L	4	2-3
Senor Speedy*	Fast Gold/General Assembly	U	8	M	M	3	2-3
Sensational Luck	Apalachee/What Luck	D	7	C-	C-	2	3-4
Sensitive Prince	Majestic Prince/Sensitivo	C-	7	C-	C+	2	3-4
Sentimental Slew	Seattle Slew/Never Bend	D	8	C+	C-	3	3-4
Sentinel Star	Shamgo/Bold Commander	D	8	U	C-	3	3-4
Separate Realities	Drone/One Count	F	8	F	D	3	3-4
Septieme Ciel *FR*	Seattle Slew/Green Dancer	B	6	B	C	4*	2-3
Serraj	Zen/Ambernash	U	9	U	M	4	3-4
Set Free	Majestic Prince/Pago Pago	D	9	M	D	4	3-4
Settlement Day *AUS*	Buckpasser/Swaps	D	7	D	DT	3	3-4
Sevastopol	Nijinsky II/New Providence	D	8	C-*	D	3	3-4
Sewickley	Star de Naskra/Dr. Fager	C	6	C	C-	3	3-4

Stallion	Sire/Broodmare Sire	FTS	CL	TRF	OT	SI	AB
Sexton Blake *IRE*	Blakeney/Abernant	D	6	CY*	M	I	3-4
Sezyou	Valid Appeal/Dr. Fager	C	7	D	C	4	2-3
Shaadi *JPN*	Danzig/Hoist the Flag	D	7	C	D	4*	2-3
Shadeed	Nijinsky II/Damascus	C-	8	C	D	3	3-4
Shadow in the Dark	Seattle Slew/Mr. Prospector	D	8	U	C-	3	3-4
Shahrastani *JPN*	Nijinsky II/Thatch	D	7	C	F	I	3-4
Shalom Dancer	Fire Dance/Run for Nurse	D	8	U	D	4	2-3
Sham	Pretense/Princequillo	D	5	C-*	CT	2	3-4
Shamgo	Sham/Final Ruling	F	8	D	D	3	3-4
Shamrock Ridge	Cox's Ridge/Our Native	U	8	M	M	3	3-4
Shamtastic	Sham/No Robbery	D	9	C-	C	3	3-4
Shananie	In Reality/Cohoes	C	7	C	C+	3	2-3
Shanekite	Hoist Bar/Any Old Time	C	8	C-	C	4	2-3
Shardari *IR*	Top Ville/Zeddaan	F	7	C*	M	I	3-4
Shareef Dancer *IRE*	Northern Dancer/Sir Ivor	D	7	C*	M	2	3-4
Sharif	Damascus/Bold Ruler	C	10	C-	C	5	3-4
Sharpen Up *ENG*	Atan/Rockefella	C	4*	BY	C	I*	2-3
Sharper One	Drum Fire/Drone	C	8	F	C+	4	2-3
Sharp Frosty	Sharpen Up/Diplomat Way	C-	7	M	C	3	2-3
Sharp Hoofer	Blade/Crozier	C-	8	U	C	3	2-3
Sharpman			7	C*		I	3-4
Sharpo *ENG*	Sharpen Up/Falcon	C	7	C*	M	3	3-4
Sharp Reason	Turn-to Reason/Our Babu	F	8	F	C-	4	3-4
Sharp Terdankim	Sharpen Up/Raise a Native	C-	9	U	C-	4	2-3
Sharp Victor	Sharpen Up/Sir Ivor	D	7	C+	D	3	3-4
Sharrood *ENG*	Caro/Cougar II	C	7	C	C	I	3-4
Shawklit Won	Air Forbes Won/Groshawk	F	7	D	C	4*	3-4
Shecky Greene	Noholme II/Model Cadet	C	7	C	C+	4	2-3
Sheikh Albadou *ENG*	Green Desert/Welsh Pageant	C	7	C	C	3	2-3
Shelly's Charmer	Secretariat/Icecapade	C-	7	M	C-	3	3-4
Shelter Half	Tentam/Sir Gaylord	C-	7	C	C	4	2-3
Shenadoah River	Dewan/Sea o'Erin	D	7	C-	D	3*	2-3
Shergar's Best	Shergar/Secretariat	D	7	C+	C	3	3-4
Shernazar *IRE*	Busted/Val de Loir	F	7	C	U	I	3-4
Shifty Sheik	Damascus/Ambehaving	C-	9	F	C	3	3-4
Shimatoree	Marshua Dancer/Tudor Minstrel	D	7	D	C+	3	3-4
Shining Steel *ENG*	Kris/Mill Reef	M	5	C-	M	4*	2-3
Shipping Magnate	What Luck/Royal Dorimar	C-	7	F	D	4	3-4
Shirley Heights *ENG*	Mill Reef/Hardicanute	D	5*	C*	C	I	3-4
Shirley's Champion	Noholme II/Have Tux	C	7	C*	C	5	3-4
Shoot Again	Resound/Mamboreta	D	9	D	F	5	3-4
Shot Gun Scott	Exuberant/Rambunctious	C-	6	C-	C	3	2-3
Shotiche	Northern Dancer/Cyane	F	7	C-	C-	2	2-3
Showbrook *FR*	Exhibitioner/Godswalk Forli	M	6	M	M	5	2-3
Show Dancer	Sovereign Dancer/Sir Gaylord	C-	7	C-	C-	4	2-3

Stallion	Sire/Broodmare Sire	FTS	CL	TRF	OT	SI	AB
Show'em Slew	Seattle Slew/Spanish Riddle	C-	7	C	D	3	3-4
Shuailaan^	Roberto/Alydar	U	7	L	M	2	3-4
Shuttleman*	Pappa Riccio/Timeless Moment	M	6	M	M	4	2-3
Shy Groom IRE	Blushing Groom/Dancer's Image	F	7	C-	C	3*	3-4
Shy Guy	Blushing Groom/Turn-to	D	10	D	C	4	3-4
Siberian Express	Caro/Warfare	C-	7	C	C	3*	2-4
Sicilian Law	Wardlaw/Bronzerullah	M	8	U	M	4	3-4
Sicyos FR	Lyphard/Habitat	C-	7	C	C-	4*	3-4
Sifounas	Secretariat/Aristophanes	D	10	D	F	4	3-4
Silent Cal	Hold Your Peace/Arrogate	F	8	C-	F	4	3-4
Silent Code	Speak John/Khaled	F	10	D	D	3	3-4
Silent Dignity	Damascus/Court Martial	D	8	C-	C-	2	3-4
Silent Fox	Exclusive Native/Crafty Admiral	D	8	D	C	3	3-4
Silent King	Screen King/Jet Action	C	10	D	C-	3	3-4
Silent Landing	Silent Screen/First Landing	D	9	U	C-	4	3-4
Silent Reality	In Reality/Never Bend	M	7	M	L	4	3-4
Silent Review	Silent Screen/Reviewer	C	7	C	C	2	3-4
Silent Screen	Prince John/Better Self	C	6	C+*	C	3	3-4
Silent Slander	Quiet Fling/Tentam	U	8	U	U	4	3-4
Silent Tempest*	Storm Bird/GreyDawn II	U	8	M	M	3	3-4
Silken Reality^^	In Reality/Never Bend	M	8	M	L	4	2-3
Silk or Satin	Impressive/Olden Times	C-	10	C	C	5	3-4
Sillery FR	Blushing Groom/Bellypha	M	7	L	M	1	2-3
Silver Badge	Poker/Hail to Reason	D	7	D	C-	4	3-4
Silver Buck	Buckpasser/Hail to Reason	C	6	C	C-	2	2-3
Silver Deputy	Deputy Minister/Mr. Prospector	C+	4	C	C	3	2-3
Silver Ending JPN	Silver Hawk/Hawaii	M	6	L	U	3	2-3
Silver Florin	Ingrained/Windy City II	U	8	U	L	4	3-4
Silver Ghost	Mr. Prospector/Halo	C+	6	C	C+T	4	2-3
Silver Hawk	Roberto/Amerigo	D	6	B-	D	1	3-4
Silver Nitrate	Vitriolic/Native Charger	D	9	C	D	2	3-4
Silver of Silver^^	Silver Buck/Gold Stage	M	8	U	M	4	3-4
Silver Survivor^^		C	6	M	CT	3	3-4
Silveyville	Petrone/Successor	C	8	D	C	3	3-4
Simply Great FR	Mill Reef/Chaparral	F	6	C-	M	3*	3-4
Simply Majestic	Majestic Light/King Emperor	D	8	C	C	3	3-4
Singh America	Singh/Mongo	F	9	M	C	4	3-4
Single Solo	Nodouble/Solo Landing	U	10	M	L	4	3-4
Sing Sing	Stop the Music/No Robbery	C	8	D	D	4	3-4
Singular	Nodouble/Cohoes	D	6	C*	C	1	3-4
Sir Ap	Conquistador Cielo/Smarten	M	8	M	L	3	2-3
Sir Dancer	Jig Dancer/Linmold	F	9	F	D	4	3-4
Sir Eric	Alydar/Reviewer	M	6	U	L	4	3-4
Sir Francis Fru	Distinctive Pro/Hail to Reason	L	7	U	C-	4	3-4
Sir Harry Lewis ENG	Alleged/Mr. Prospector	D	6	CY	C-	2	3-4

Stallion	Sire/Broodmare Sire	FTS	CL	Trf	OT	SI	AB
Sir Ivor	Sir Gaylord/Mr. Trouble	D	3*	C+Y*	C	1	3-4
Sir Ivor Again	Sir Ivor/Fleet Nasrullah	F	8	C	D	3	3-4
Sir Jinsky	Nijinsky II/Tim Tam	D	7	D	C-	2	3-4
Sir Keys	Son Ange/Damascus	D	9	U	D	4	3-4
Sirlad *IR*			7	CY*		1	3-4
Sir Leon	Private Account/Ballymoss	D	7	C-	B	3	2-3
Sir Macamillion	Macarthur Park/Bobby's Legacy	U	7	U	U	4	3-4
Sir Mala Mala	Seattle Slew/Tom Rolfe	D	8	D	D	3	3-4
Sir Naskra	Naskra/Mito	D	6	D	CT	3	3-4
Sir Richard Lewis	Carr de Naskra/Mr. Prospector	C+	7	U	C-	4	2-3
Sir Session	Sir Ivor/Hoist the Flag	D	8	D	C	4	2-3
Sir Sizzling Jim	Jim J./Tudorka	D	8	U	C	4	3-4
Sir Spectator	Sir Ivor/Crewman	U	8	U	U	4	3-4
Sir Stout	Nostrum/Royal Vale	U	9	U	U	5	3-4
Sirtaki	Raja Baba/Nijinsky II	U	10	U	M	4	3-4
Sir Tristram *NZ*	Sir Ivor/Round Table		5	C+		3	3-4
Sir Wiggle			7	C*		3	3-4
Sir Wimborne	Sir Ivor/Tom Fool	D	7	C-*	D	3	3-4
Sitzmark	J.O. Tobin/Dunce	C-	7	D	CT	3	2-3
Six Speed	Saratoga Six/Tilt Up	C-	9	M	C	4	3-4
Siyah Kalem	Mr. Prospector/Graustark	C-	8	C-	C	4	2-3
Ski Chief *FR*	Chief's Crown/Royal Ski	M	5	M	M	4*	3-4
Skip Out Front	Bynoderm/Highbinder	U	10	U	M	4	3-4
Skip Trial	Bailjumper/Promised Land	C	5	D	CT	3*	2-3
Ski Resort	Delta Judge/Hawaii	D	8	M	C	4	3-4
Sky Classic	Nijinsky II/Nodouble	C+	6	BY	C	3*	3-4
Sky Command	Relaunch/Kinsman	C-	10	U	C	5	2-3
Sky Filou *NZ*			7	C		4	3-4
Sky Lawyer *FR*	Sea Lawyer/Prudent	C-	6	C		1	3-4
Skywalker	Relaunch/Boldnesian	C	5	B	B	3	3-4
Sky White	Relaunch/Windy Tide	M	8	M	L	4	2-3
Slady Castle	Tudor Melody/Blue Train	F	7	C	C	4	3-4
Slewabration	Seattle Slew/Swaps	D	10	U	C-	4	3-4
Slewacide	Seattle Slew/Buckpasser	C	7	C-	CT	3	3-4
Slew Baby	Settle Slew/Eddie Schmidt	C-	6	M	C-	4	3-4
Slew City Slew	Seattle Slew/Berkeley Prince	C	5	C	AT	2	2-3
Slew Dancer	Seattle Slew/Northern Dancer	M	8	M	T	3	3-4
Slewdledo	Seattle Slew/Cyane	C	7	C-	C+	4	2-3
Slewdonza	Seattle Slew/Bold Bidder	C-	8	D	C-	3	3-4
Slew d'Orsay	Seattle Slew/Minera	D	10	U	D	4	3-4
Slew Express	Seattle Slew/L'Enjoleur	D	10	M	D	3	3-4
Slew Machine *SDA*	Seattle Slew/Sassafras	D	8	C+	C	3	3-4
Slew of Angels	Slew o'Gold/Quadrangle	D	9	U	C	4	3-4
Slew o'Gold	Seattle Slew/Buckpasser	C-	7	C-	C	3*	3-4
Slew o'the North	Seattle Slew/Jabneh	D	9	C-	D	3	3-4

Stallion	Sire/Broodmare Sire	FTS	CL	TRF	OT	SI	AB
Slew Pilot	Seattle Slew/Nodouble	D	9	M	D	4	3-4
Slewpy	Seattle Slew/Prince John	C	7	C+	C	3	2-3
Slew's Folly	Seattle Slew/Tom Fool	D	10	F	F	3	3-4
Slew's Royalty	Seattle Slew/Swaps	C+	7	C	C	4	2-3
Slew the Bride	Seattle Slew/Al Hattab	C-	9	C-	C-	3	3-4
Slew the Coup	Seattle Slew/Buckpasser	D	9	C-	CT	3	3-4
Slew the Knight	Seattle Slew/Prince John	C-	7	D	C	3	3-4
Slew the Slewor*	Slew o'Gold/Lyphard	C+	8	C	D	3	2-4
Slew the Surgeon	Slew the Bride/Surgeon Sam	C	7	U	C	4	2-3
Slewvescent	Seattle Slew/Herbager	D	8	C	C	2	3-4
Slick	Alydar/Jacinto	C-	6	D	C	3	2-3
Sligh Jet	Tri Jet/Exclusive Native	D	7	M	C	4	3-4
Slip Anchor ENG	Shirley Heights/Birkhahn	F	5	C*	C	1	3-4
Sluggard	Drone/Hitting Away	D	9	D	C	4	3-4
Smart Alec^^	Smarten/Le Haar	L	7	U	L	4	2-3
Smarten	Cyane/Quibu	C+	5*	CY	CT	3*	2-3
Smart Magician^^	Clever Trick/Going Straight	M	8	M	M	4	2-3
Smart Style	Foolish Pleasure/Quadrangle	D	8	D	C	3	3-4
Smart Talk	Speak John/Gallant Man	D	9	F	C	4	3-4
Smelly	Judge Smells/Summing	D	6	U	C-	4	3-4
Smile	In Reality/Boldnesian	C	7	CY	C	4	3-4
Smokester	Never Tabled/Transworld	C+	5	C	C	3	2-3
Smoking Gun	Northern Dancer/Sir Ivor	F	10	F	D	2	3-4
Snake Doctor	Fit to Fight/Drone	M	9	U	L	4	3-4
Snake Oil Man	Raise a Native/Tom Fool	C+	9	U	C+	5	2-3
Snar	Sir Ivor/Olden Times	D	6	D	C	4	3-4
Sneaky Solictor PR*	Crafty Prospector/	L	8	U	M	4	2-3
Snow Chief	Reflected Glory/Snow Sporting	C-	8	F	CT	3	3-4
Snowgun	Flush/Ramsinga	M	8	M	M	5	3-4
Snow Knight			7	M*		4	3-4
Snow Satyr			7	M*		2	3-4
Sobat	Relaunch/Graustark	M	8	M	M	4	3-4
Sobig NZ			7	C+*		4	3-4
Society Max	Mr. Prospector/Hoist the Flag	C-	7	D	C+	4	3-4
Soda Springs	Herbager/Bold Ruler	F	9	U	D	4	3-4
Soft and Sly	On the Sly/Promised land	M	9	U	M	4	3-4
Solar City	Northern Dancer/Halo	C	6	D	C+	4	3-4
Solarstern GER			7	C		3	3-4
Solford GER	Nijinsky II/Cavan	D	7	D	C	2	3-4
Solid Print	Vaguely Noble/Court Martial	F	8	U	D	4	3-4
Solo Chorus*	Dixieland Band/Cyane	L	8	M	L	4	3-4
Solo Guy	Solo Landing/Royal Levee	D	8	U	C-	4	3-4
Somebody's Great	Villamor/Great Nephew	C-	9	U	C-	5	3-4
Somekindofmiracle	Distinctive Pro/Caro	C	8	M	C	4	3-4
Somethingfabulous	Northern Dancer/Princequillo	D	8	C-	C	3	3-4

Stallion	Sire/Broodmare Sire	FTS	CL	TRF	OT	SI	AB
Something Lucky	Somethingfabulous/Lucky Fleet	C	8	D	C	5	3-4
Son Ange	Raise a Native/Tom Fool	D	7	F	D	3	3-4
Sonaskra	Naskra/Raise a Native	D	9	U	C-	4	3-4
Song of Delta	Sing Along/Great Day	D	9	U	C-	5	3-4
Sonic Shuttle	Fleet Discovery/Honeys Alibi	C-	8	D	C-	4	3-4
Sonny's Solo Halo	Halo/Solo Landing	C-	9	M	D	3*	2-3
Son of Briartic	Briartic/Round Table	C	7	C+	B	3	2-3
Son of Repute	Northern Dancer/Vaguely Noble	D	8	M	C	3	3-4
So Private	Private Account/Avatar	U	8	U	M	3	3-4
Sorrento FR	Stratege/Priolo	D	7	C	D	I	3-4
Sort	Nijinsky II/Forli	D	9	C	C	2	3-4
So Splendid			7	C*		3	3-4
Soukab ENG	Good Gounsel/Tom Rolfe	D	7	C	C	I	3-4
Sound Reason NZ			7	C		3	3-4
Southern Halo	Halo/Northern Dancer	D	6	C	C	3*	3-4
Southern Rhythm^	Dixieland Band/Mr. Prospector	L	6	M	L	4*	2-3
Southern Sultan VEN	Stage Door Johnny/Hail to Reason	D	8	C	C	3	3-4
Sovereignall^^	Sovereign RulerAssemblyman	M	8	M	M	4	2-3
Sovereign Dancer	Northern Dancer/Bold Ruler	C-	5*	C+	CT	3*	3-4
Sovereign Don ARG	Sovereign Dancer/Hold Your Peace	C	5	D	C	3	2-3
Sovereign Exchange	Sovereign Dancer/Best Turn	D	9	D	C	4	3-4
Sovereign Immunity	Native Royalty/No Robbery	U	8	M	U	2	3-4
Sovereign Romance	Sovereign Dancer/In Reality	U	8	M	M	3*	3-4
Sovereign Ruler	Sovereign Dancer/Roi Dagobert	U	9	U	U	4	3-4
Sovereignty	Affirmed/Never Bend	D	8	U	CT	4	3-4
Soviet Lad AUS	Nureyev/Val de Loir	D	7	C	D	4*	2-3
Soviet Star JPN	Nureyev/Venture	D	5	C	M	3	3-4
Soy Numero Uno	Damascus/Crafty Admiral	D	7	D	C-	4	3-4
Space Cup	Saratoga Six/Run For Nurse	M	10	U	M	4	3-4
Space Rider	Tri Jet/Crozier	M	9	M	M	4	3-4
Space Station	Mr. Prospector/Graustark	F	10	C-	D	4*	3-4
Spacewinner	Nashua/Princequillo	D	8	D	C	3	3-4
Spanish Drums	Top Command/Drone	C	8	D	C	3	3-4
Spanish Way	Roberto/Olympia	F	8	D	D	I	3-4
Spare Card	Paris Dust/Mito	D	8	D	C	4	3-4
Sparkling Blade	Plucky Blade/Mister Judge	U	9	U	U	5	3-4
Sparkly	Halo/Amerigo	D	7	U	D	3	2-3
Spartacus			7	C*		3	3-4
Speak	Mr. Prospector/Honest Pleasure	M	7	M	M	3	3-4
Speak John	Prince John/Tornado	C-	6	C+	C	3	3-4
Speak the Verb	Verbatim/Kauai King	D	9	C-	C-	2	3-4
Spearhead	Vice Regent/Tatan	D	9	D	U	4	3-4
Special Blend	Staff Writer/Key to the Kingdom	M	9	M	U	4	3-4
Special Lineage	Alydar/Barbizon	D	9	C	C	5	3-4
Spectacular Bid	Bold Bidder/Promised Land	D	6*	CY*	C	3*	3-4

Stallion	Sire/Broodmare Sire	FTS	CL	TRF	OT	SI	AB
Spectacular Round	Spectacular Bid/Never Bend	U	10	M	M	3	3-4
Speedy Cure *	Cure the Blues/Tudor Grey	M	9	U	L	3	3-4
Speedy Prospect	Mr. Prospector/Nashua	D	8	C+*	C	3	3-4
Spellbound	Lyphard's Wish/Elocutionist	C-	7	C	D	3	3-4
Spend a Buck	Buckaroo/Speak John	C-	7	C-	C	3	3-4
Spicy Monarch	Believe the Queen/Sham	D	7	D	D	3	3-4
Spicy Story	Blushing Groom/Nijinsky II	F	8	D	C	4*	3-4
Spirited Boy	Monetary Crisis/Manifesto	D	8	U	D	5	2-3
Spirit Rock	Selari/Jet Pilot	F	8	D	C	4	3-4
Splendid Courage	Raise a Native/Gallant Man	D	8	C	C	4	3-4
Splendid Hour	Gummo/The Pie King	F	7	U	C	4	2-3
Splendid Son	Cyane/Boldnesian	D	9	D	C-	4	2-3
Split Run^	Relaunch/Secretariat	L	8	M	L	4	2-3
Sportful	Crozier/Quibu	D	9	C	C	4	3-4
Sportin' Life	Nijinsky II/Round Table	D	7	C	D	3*	3-4
Sports View	Cox's Ridge/Tom Rolfe	C	7	C+	C-	2	3-4
Spotter Bay	Coastal/Iron Ruler	D	10	C	C-	5	3-4
Spread the Rumor	Forli/Damascus	C-	8	C*	C-	4	3-4
Spring Double	Double Jay/Hyperion	C-	7	C-	C-	3	3-4
Springhill IRE	Sallust/Trouville	C	8	C+*	C	3*	2-3
Spruce Bouquet	Big Spruce/Sailor	D	8	B	C-	3	3-4
Spunky Rascal	Devil's Bag/Bold Bidder	U	8	U	M	4	3-4
Spy Signal	Hoist the Flag/Swaps	F	8	C	C	3	3-4
Squad Car	Police Car/Winning Shot	M	8	M	M	4	2-3
Squadron Leader^	Storm Bird/Bold Ruler	U	7	L	M	3	2-3
Squan Lake	Alydar/Exceller	M	10	M	L	4	3-4
Squill AUS	Stop the Music/Riverman	F	8	D	M	1	3-4
Squire	Graustark/Hail to Reason	D	9	D	C-	1	3-4
Sri Pekan^	Red Ransom/Son Ange	U	6	L	M	2	3-4
S.S. Hot Sauce	Sauceboat/Le Fabuleux	D	8	M	C	4	3-4
Stack	Nijinsky II/Tom Rolfe	C-	7	C+	U	2	3-4
Stacked Pack	Majestic Light/Buckpasser	C-	6	C	C	3	3-4
Staff Riot	Staff Writer/Tom Rolfe	D	8	C-	C	4	3-4
Staff Writer	Northern Dancer/Swaps	C	7	C	C-	4	3-4
Stage Boss	Stage Director/Bull Page	D	10	M	C-	4	3-4
Stage Colony*	Pleasant Colony/Stage Door Johnny	U	8	M	M	1	3-4
Stage Door Johnny	Prince John/Ballymoss	F	5*	B*	C	1	3-4
Stage Door Key	Stage Door Johnny/Arts & Letters	D	9	C-	F	3*	3-4
Stallwood ARG	El Centauro/Sigma Septima	C-	6	C-	F	2	3-4
Stalwart	Hoist The Flag/Iron Ruler	C	6	C*	CT	3	2-3
Standstead	Gummo/First Landing	C-	9	D	C	4	3-4
Star Appeal	Applani/Nectar	U	7	C*	M	1	3-4
Star Choice	In Reality/Tirreno	F	8	C-	C	3*	3-4
Star de Naskra	Naskra/Clandestine	C+	7	C-	C	3	2-3
Starfields IRE	Northfields/Hugh Lupus	D	8	M	F	3	3-4

Stallion	Sire/Broodmare Sire	FTS	CL	TRF	OT	SI	AB
Star Gallant	My Gallant/Bold Hitter	D	6	C-	C	4	3-4
Stark Dancer	Graustark/Northern Dancer	D	10	U	D	3	3-4
Stark Duster	Stark Broke/Lees Boy	M	10	U	U	5	3-4
Star of the Crop*	Relaunch/What a Pleasure	D	7	M	C+	4	2-3
Stars n' Stripes	True Colors/Crozier	U	8	U	M	4	3-4
Star Way NZ			7	C*		4	3-4
State Dinner	Buckpasser/Barbizon	D	8	C-	C	3	3-4
Stately Cielo*	ConquistadorCielo/Nijinsky II	U	8	M	M	3	3-4
Stately Don JPN	Nureyev/Le Fabuleux	F	7	C	D	2	3-4
Statoblest IRE	Ahonoora/Skymaster	C	6	C	M	4	2-3
Staunch Avenger	Staunchness/Revoked	C-	8	F	C	5	2-3
Stay the Course VEN	Majestic Light/Indian Hemp	D	7	C	C-	2	3-4
Steady Growth	Briartic/Crepello	D	6	C	D	3	3-4
Steelinctive ENG	Steel Heart/Distinctive	D	8	D	D	3	3-4
Steel Robbing	No Robbery/On-and-On	D	8	U	D	4	3-4
Steinlen	Habitat/Jim French	D	7	C-	C-	3	3-4
Sterling Key	Key to the Mint/Swaps	U	10	U	U	4	3-4
Steven's Best	Lt. Stevens/Reneged	U	8	U	C	4	3-4
St. Forbes	Bold Forbes/The Axe II	F	10	F	F	3*	3-4
St. Jovite	Pleasant Colony/Northfields	D	7	C+	D	1	3-4
Stone Manor	Knightly Manner/Besomer	D	8	C	D	4	3-4
Stonewalk	Knightly Manner/Besomer	D	7	C-*	C	3	3-4
Stopgap			7	C-*		3	3-4
Stop the Bells	Stop the Music/Jacinto	D	9	U	C-	4	3-4
Stop the Fighting	Cure the Blues/Aggresor II	D	7	U	C	4	3-4
Stop the Music	Hail to Reason/Tom Fool	C	4*	B*	C	3*	<u>3-4</u>
Storm a Head	Storm Bird/Damascus	M	8	U	M	4	3-4
Storm Bird	Northern Dancer/New Providence	C	5*	C	D	2	3-4
Storm Boot*	Storm Cat/Mr. Prospector	C-	7	D	C+	4	2-3
Storm Brewing	Storm Bird/Stage Door Johnny	D	8	C	DT	3	3-4
Storm Cat	Storm Bird/Secretariat	C+	1	C+	A	4*	2-3
Stormin' Again	Vice Regent/Cyane	D	9	M	D	4	3-4
Storm of Angels	Storm Cat/Deputy Minister	L	8	L	M	4*	2-3
Stormy Boy	Colonel Power/Rocket Pocket	M	9	U	M	3	3-4
Straight Flush	Riva Ridge/Princequillo	D	10	D	D	3	3-4
Stratford	Hoist the Flag/Nantallah	M	10	M	M	4	3-4
Strawberry Road	Whiskey Road/Rich Gift	C	5	B-	CT	1*	3-4
Strike Gold	Mr. Prospector/Roi Dagobert	C+	8	D	CT	4	3-4
Strike the Anvil	Bolinas Boy/Imbros	C-	6	C	D	3	3-4
Strike the Gold TUR *	Alydar/Hatchet Man	D	7	C	C-T	3*	<u>2-3</u>
Strodes Creek^	Halo/Topsider	U	6	M	M	2	3-4
Strolling Along^^	Danzig/Alydar	L	7	M	L	3*	2-3
Strong Performance	Jig Time/Blazing Count	D	8	M	C	4	3-4
Stuka^^	Jade Hunter/Caerleon	M	7	M	M	3*	<u>2-3</u>
Stutz Blackhawk	Mr. Prospector/Amber Morn	D	6	D	CT	3*	<u>2-3</u>

Stallion	Sire/Broodmare Sire	FTS	CL	TRF	OT	SI	AB
Stylish King	Roberto/Exclusive Native		7	C		3	3-4
Suave Dancer *ENG*	Green Dancer/ Alleged		6	C		1	3-4
Sucha Pleasure	What a Pleasure/Hail to Reason	C	8	D	D	3	3-4
Sugarland Run			7	C		1	3-4
Sultry Song*	Cox's Ridge/Buckfinder	C-	5	C	C	3*	3-4
Summer Advocate	Advocator/Swaps	D	8	D	C	4	3-4
Summer Squall	Storm Bird/Secretariat	C-	6	C<u>Y</u>	CT	1*	2-3
Summer Time Guy	Gummo/Crozier	F	9	C+*	D	4	3-4
Summing	Verbatim/Groton	D	8	C-	C-	3	3-4
Sun Catcher	Search for Gold/Sir Gaylord	F	9	F	D	4	3-4
Sundae *ARG*	Dancing Moss/Idle Hour	C-	6	C	C-	3	3-4
Sunday Silence *JPN*	Halo/Secretariat	M	4	M	L	3*	2-4
Sun Hunter	Boldnesian/Pappa Fourway	D	8	U	C	5	3-4
Sun Master	Foolish Pleasure/Prince John	C	7	C	C+	3	3-4
Sunny Clime	In Reality/Newtown Wonder	C+	6	C	C	4	<u>2</u>-3
Sunny Feet	Sunny Clime/Noholme II	C	8	U	C	5	2-3
Sunny North *SAF*	Northern Dancer/In Reality	C-	7	C	C	4	<u>2</u>-3
Sunny's Halo	Halo/Sunny	C	7	C-	C+	3	2-4
Sun Power	Great Sun/Noble Jay	F	7	D	C	4	<u>2</u>-3
Sunshine Forever *JPN*	Roberto/Graustark	D	6	C+	D	3*	3-4
Sun War Dancer	Northern Dancer/Val de Loir	D	7	C	D	4*	3-4
Sun Worship *IRE*			7	C-		3	3-4
Super Abound	SuperbityDamascus	U	8	L	M	4	3-4
Superbity	Groshawk/Rough'nTumble	D	8	C*	C	2	2-3
Super Concorde	Bold Reasoning/Primera	C-	7	C+*	D	3	2-<u>3</u>
Super Gun	Super Smile/Gunshot	M	8	U	M	5	2-<u>3</u>
Super Hit	Nalees Man/Pia Star	U	9	U	M	3	3-4
Superlative *ENG*	Nebbiolo/Hook Money	D	7	C-	M	4	3-4
Super Moment *SWS*	Big Spruce/Shantung	D	7	C*	D	3*	3-4
Super Native	Be My Native/Super Concorde	U	9	M	M	3	3-4
Superoyale	Raise a Native/Never Bend	C	7	D	D	4	2-3
Superpower *ENG*	Superlative/Northfields	C-	7	C-	M	4	2-3
Supreme Alarm	Sovereign Dancer/Blazing Count	U	9	M	M	<u>4</u>	3-4
Supremo^	Gone West/Danzig	L	6	<u>L</u>	M	4*	2-3
Sure Blade *ENG*	Double Lock/ Home Guard	F	6	C	M	3*	3-4
Sure to Fire	Sure Fire/Donut King	U	10	U	U	4	3-4
Surreal	Reviewer/Crimson Satan	C-	8	F	C-	3	2-<u>3</u>
Surumu *GER*	Literat/Reliance		4	C*		1	3-4
Sutter's Prospect	Mr. Prospector/Nijinsky II	C	8	D	C	4	2-4
Suzanne's Star	Son Ange/Greek Game	C-	9	D	C	3	3-4
Swaps			7	C*		3	3-4
Swaps Fire	Sweet Swaps/Play with Fire	D	9	D	D	4	3-4
Swedaus^	Proud Birdie/Determined Cosmic	U	7	U	M	4	3-4
Sweet Candy *VEN*	Bold and Brave/Blue Prince	C-	5	C-	C	5	3-4
Sweetwater Springs	Tantoul/Ridan	U	10	U	M	5	3-4

Stallion	Sire/Broodmare Sire	FTS	CL	TRF	OT	SI	AB
Swelegant	L'Enjoleur/Mito	F	8	D	C-	5	3-4
Swinging Sway	Bask/Bold Reasoning	M	9	U	M	5	3-4
Swing Till Dawn	Grey Dawn II/The Axe	D	8	C	C-	3	3-4
Swiss Trick	Damascus/Buckpasser	D	8	C-	C	3*	3-4
Switcheroo AUS			7	C*		3	3-4
Switch Partners	Great Sun/Turn-to	D	6	D	C-	4	3-4
Swoon	Secretariat/Sea Hawk	D	9	C-	DT	3	3-4
Sword Dance	Nijinsky II/Secretariat	C	6	B	C-	I*	2-3
S.W. Wildcard	Sawbones/No Dividends	M	9	U	M	4	2-3
Synastry	Seattle Slew/Nashua	C	8	C	C	4	2-3
Syncopate	Marshua's Dancer/Prince John	C	7	C+*	D	3	3-4
Tabasco Cat^	Storm Cat/Sauceboat	M	5	M	M	3*	2-3
Table Express	Table Run/Saltville	C	9	M	C	5	3-4
Table Run	Round Table/Fleet Nasrullah	C	7	C+*	C	3	2-3
Tabun Bogdo	Seattle Slew/Caro	F	9	D	C-	3	3-4
Tactical Advantage^^	Forty Niner/Roberto	B	5	M	C	4*	2-3
Tagish	Mr. Prospector/Faraway Son	D	8	U	C	4*	3-4
Tahitian King	Luthier/Decathlon	C-	8	C-	F	3	3-4
Taj Alriyadh	Seattle Slew/El Relicario	D	7	M	CT	3	3-4
Tajawa	Gallapiat/Nashua	M	8	U	M	4	2-3
Take Action	Ack Ack/Raja Baba	D	8	D	D	4	3-4
Take Me Out^^	Cure the Blues/Tom Rolfe	L	7	M	M	3	2-3
Take the Floor	Cornish Prince/Promised Land	D	9	C-*	C-	3	3-4
Take the Plunge	Roanoke Island/Rock Talk	U	9	U	M	3	3-4
Talc	Rock Talk/Rash Prince	C	5	CY	C+	3*	2-3
Talinum SWE	Alydar/Riverman	C-	7	D	C+T	3	3-4
Talkin Man^	With Approval/Miswaki	M	6	M	M	2	2-3
Tall Ships	Olden Times/Restless Native	C-	10	C-	C	1	3-4
Tally Ho the Fox	Never Bend/Hail to Reason	C-	8	D	C	3	3-4
Tammany	Mr. Prospector/Drone	C	7	U	D	4	2-4
Tamourad	Blushing Groom/Sanctus	M	9	M	M	4	3-4
Tampa Trouble			7	M*		I*	3-4
Tandem	Benny Bob/Bold Sultan	M	8	U	M	4	2-3
Tank	Tank's Prospect/Exclusive Native	M	7	U	M	4*	3-4
Tank's Number*	Tank's Prospect/Native Charger	L	7	U	M	3	2-3
Tank's Prospect	Mr. Prospector/Pretense	C-	7	D	C-	3	3-4
Tanthem	Tentam/Nashua	C	7	C	C	3	3-4
Tantoul	Tatan/Hill Prince	D	8	D	C	4	3-4
Tap on Wood ENG			7	C*		4	3-4
Tapping Wood VEN	Roberto/Tudor Melody	F	9	F*	C-	3	3-4
Tap Shoes BRZ	Riva Ridge/Bold Bidder	D	8	C-	C	3	3-4
Tara's Time NZ			7	C		2	3-4
Targowice	Round Table/Bold Ruler	D	6	C*	D	I*	3-4
Tarr Road	Grey Dawn II/Chieftain	U	7	U	LT	3	3-4
Tarsal	Tom Rolfe/Royal Union	D	8	C-	C-	4	3-4

Stallion	Sire/Broodmare Sire	FTS	CL	TRF	OT	SI	AB
Tartar Chief			7	C+*		5	3-4
Tasso *IND*	Fappiano/What a Pleasure	D	6	C+	C-	3	3-4
Tasting	Nureyev/Secretariat	C	9	L	M	4	3-4
Tate Gallery *IRE*	Northern Dancer/Bold Reason	F	6	C+	C	3*	3-4
Taufan *IRE*	Stop the Music/Sadair	C-	7	C	C	4*	3-4
Taxachusetts	Gallant Romeo/Hasty Road	C-	8	D	C-	4	3-4
Tax Collection	Private Account/Reviewer	M	10	U	L	4	3-4
Tayfun	Lord Tomboy/Correlation	U	9	U	M	3	3-4
Taylor	Taylor's Falls/Roman Line	U	9	U	M	5	3-4
Taylor Road	Proudest Roman/Groton	U	8	U	M	5	3-4
Taylor's Falls	In Reality/Newtown Wonder	D	7	C+*	C+	3	2-3
Taylor's Special	Hawkin's Special/Espea	C-	8	F	C-	4	3-4
Technology*	Time for a Change/One for All	C	6	U	C-	2	2-3
Teddy's Courage	Exclusive Native/Dead Ahead	F	7	C*	C	4	3-4
Tejano *IND*	Caro/Exclusive Native	D	7	D	C	3*	3-4
Telemarket^^	Phone Trick/Quadratic	L	8	U	M	4	2-3
Tell	Round Table/Nasrullah	C-	8	C*	D	3	3-4
Tella Fib	Bold Laddie/Tell	C	9	D	C	4	3-4
Tell the Tale	Tell/Mongo	C-	10	C	D	4	3-4
Tel Quel *FR*	Akarad/Birdbrook	U	6	M	M	1	3-4
Temerity Prince	Cornish Prince/Native Dancer	D	8	D	C	4	3-4
Temperance Hill *THI*	Stop the Music/Etonian	D	7	C-*	C	3*	3-4
Tempest Ways	Crozier/Daryl's Joy	D	8	C	M	3	3-4
Temptor	Vice Regent/Bunty's Flight	M	7	M	M	3*	3-4
Tenby *IR*	Caerleon/Kalaglow	U	6	C	M	3*	3-4
Tender King IR	Prince Tenderfoot/Alcide	M	7	M	M	3	3-4
Ten Gold Pots	Tentam/Search for Gold	C-	7	C-	C	3	3-4
Ten Keys	Sir Ivor Again/Exceedingly	M	7	C-	C-	1	3-4
Tentam	Intentionally/Tim Tam	C+	6*	C	C+	3	2-<u>3</u>
Tentiltwo	Damascus/Graustark	D	8	D	C	4	3-4
Tent Up	Shelter Half/Nashwood	M	8	M	M	3	3-4
Tequillo			7	C*		2	3-4
Terresto	Intentionally/Fair Ruler	C	7	C	C+	4	2-<u>3</u>
Texas City	Mr. Prospector/Buckpasser	C	7	U	DT	4	2-<u>3</u>
Texas Dancer	Native Dancer/Beau Gar	C-	8	D	C+	4	3-4
Texian	Majestic Light/Raja Baba	U	7	MY	U	4	3-4
Tex R. Rabbit	Text/Symmetric	M	8	M	U	4	3-4
Text	Speak John/Gunshot	C-	8	C*	C-	3	3-4
Teychas	Lyphard/Varano	D	9	M	C-	3	3-4
Thaliard	Habitat/Sing Sing	M	6	C*	M	3	3-4
Thatching *IRE*	Thatch/Abernant	C-	6	C+*	C	3*	3-4
That's a Nice	Hey Good Lookin/Palestinian	C-	7	C+	D	2	3-4
T.H. Bend	Full Out/Bold Reason	C	9	U	C	4	3-4
The Astonisher	Bold and Brave/Our Babu	C-	9	D	C	4	3-4
Theatre Critic*	Sadler's Wells/Habitat	M	8	L	U	1	3-4

Stallion	Sire/Broodmare Sire	FTS	CL	TRF	OT	SI	AB
Theatrical	Nureyev/Sassafras	B	5	AY	CT	I*	2-4
Theatrical Charmer *ENG*	Sadler's Wells/Vaguely Noble	D	7	C-	M	I	3-4
The Axe II	Mahmoud/Shut Out	D	6	C-*	C	2	3-4
The Bart *HNG*	Le Fabuleux/St Crespin III	F	7	C*	D	2	3-4
The Breeze	Crafty Drone/Umbrella Fella	D	8	C-	C	3	3-4
The Captain	Stevward/Francis S.	D	10	U	C	5	3-4
The Carpenter	Gummo/Fulcrum	D	8	D	DT	4	3-4
The Cool Virginian	Icecapade/Royal Gem II	D	6	D	C-	3	3-4
The Corps	Drone/Lt. Stevens	M	9	U	M	4	2-3
The Crowd Roars	Secretariat/Lt. Stevens	U	10	M	M	4	3-4
The Flips Comin	Flip Sal/Big Bluffer	M	9	U	M	4	2-3
The Gifted One	Time for a Change/His Majesty	M	10	M	M	3	3-4
The Great Shark *CHI*	Storm Bird/Correspondent	D	7	C	C	3*	3-4
The Hague	Transworld/Reform	F	9	U	C-	3	3-4
The Irish Lord	Bold Ruler/Double Jay	C-	8	D	C	4	3-4
The Knack II			7	C		3	3-4
The Jandy Man		C+	8	U	M	4	3-4
The Miller	Mill Reef/Sir Ivor	D	9	C	C-	3	3-4
The Minstrel	Northern Dancer/Victoria Park	C	3*	C+*	D	4*	2-3
Then Again *ENG*	Jaazeiro/Reform	D	8	C-	M	4	2-3
The Name's Jimmy^^	Encino/Grey Dawn II	U	8	L	M	3	3-4
The Prime Minister	Deputy Minister/Illustrious	C+	6	C+	D	3	3-4
The Pruner	Herbager/Better Self	D	7	C*	D	2	3-4
The Very Best	Best Turn/Venture 7th	C-	9	U	C	4	3-4
The Vid	World Appeal/Rising Market	M	8	M	M	3	3-4
The Wedding Guest	Hold Your Peace/Olden Times	D	8	D	C	3	2-3
The Wicked North^^	Far North/Good Behaving	C-	7	M	D	2	3-4
The Wonder *FR*	Wittgenstein/Lanark	D	7	C	M	3	3-4
Third World	Restless Native/Bryan G.	C	8	C-	C	4	2-3
Thirty Eight Paces	Nodouble/Dancing Count	D	7	C	C	3	3-4
Thirty Six Red	Slew o' Gold/Stage Door Johnny	C-	6	C+	C+	3	3-4
Thorn Dance	Northern Dancer/Bold Forbes	C-	8	C	C	4	3-4
Thowra *ENG*	Sadler's Wells/Vaguely Noble	F	7	C-	M	I	3-4
Three Martinis	Third Martini/One Count	C-	8	C	C+	5	2-3
Thug^	Kris S./To the Quick	U	8	M	M	3*	3-4
Thumbsucker	Great Sun/Royal Intent	C-	9	D	C-	4	3-4
Thunder Gulch^	Gulch/Storm Bird	M	5	M	M	3*	2-3
Thunder Puddles	Speak John/Delta Judge	D	7	C	C-	I	3-4
Thunder Rumble^^	Thunder Puddles/Lyphard	U	8	M	M	3	3-4
Tiffany Ice	Icecapade/Chieftain	C-	8	D	CT	4	3-4
Tilt the Odds	Tilt Up/Handsome Boy	C	8	U	M	5	2-3
Tilt the Stars *VEN*	Danzig/Halo	C	6	C+Y	C	4*	2-3
Tilt Up	Olden Times/Tudor Melody	C-	6*	C*	C	4	2-3
Timber Native	Hula Chief/American Native	D	10	U	D	5	3-4
Time for a Change	Damascus/Reviewer	C+	6	C	C+	3	2-4

Stallion	Sire/Broodmare Sire	FTS	CL	TRF	OT	SI	AB
Timeless Moment	Damascus/Native Dancer	C-	6*	C+*	C	3	2-3
Timeless Native	Timeless Moment/Executioner	C	8	C	C+	4	2-3
Timeless Story	Timeless Moment/Slady Castle	M	9	U	M	4	2-3
Timeless Times *ENG*	Timeless Moment/Noholme II	C	7	C	M	4	2-3
Timely One	Bold Hour/First Balcony	F	7	U	C	4	3-4
Time to Explode	Explodent/Olden Times	C	7	C	C	3	2-3
Tim Tam Aly	Alydar/Tim Tam	F	8	F	C	3	3-4
Tim the Tiger	Nashua/Court Martial	C-	7	F	D	5	2-3
Tina's Pet *ENG*	Mummy's Pet/Wills Somers	F	7	C-	M	5	3-4
Tirol *IR*	Thatching/Great Nephew	C-	7	C	M	3	3-4
Tisab	Loom/Nashua	D	10	F	F	4	3-4
Titanic	Alydar/Lt. Stevens	D	8	C	C-	3	3-4
Tithingman *ARG*			7	M*		4	3-4
T.K. Chance	Sain Et Sauf/Better Bee	M	8	M	M	4	3-4
Tobin Bronze	Arctic Explorer/Masthead	D	8	C	C	3	3-4
To B. or Not	Don B./Fair Truckle	D	9	C	D	4	3-4
To Freedom*	Blue Ensign/Diplomat Way	D	8	M	C	3	2-3
Tokatee	Seattle Slew/Northern Dancer	D	7	C	M	3	3-4
Told	Tell/Boldnesian	D	8	D	D	5	3-4
Toll Key *PR*	Nodouble/Buckpasser	F	10	D	D	4	3-4
Tolstoy	Nijinsky II/Key to the Mint	F	9	C-	F	3	3-4
Tom Buck	Tom Rolfe/Buckpasser	C-	8	U	C	4	2-3
Tom Cobbley*	Seattle Slew/Song	D	8	D	C	5	3-4
Tommy the Hawk	Judgable/Donut King	D	10	D	C	4	3-4
Tom Rolfe	Ribot/Roman	D	5*	CY*	C	3*	3-4
Tom Tulle	Tom Rolfe/War Admiral	D	8	C	C	3	3-4
Tong Po *AUS*	Private Account/Hoist the Flag	D	7	F	C	3	3-4
Tonkaton	Raise a Native/Chieftain	C	8	D*	C	4	3-4
Tonzarun	Arts and Letters/Buckpasser	D	8	F	C	3	3-4
Toomuchholme	Noholme II/Delville Wood	F	7	D	C	4	3-4
Toooverprime	Red Alert/Dancer's Image	F	9	D	C	4	3-4
Top Avenger	Staunch Avenger/Dunce	C	8	F	C	5	2-3
Top Brick	Top Command/Mr. Brick	U	10	U	M	4	3-4
Top Cash	Stalwart/Hold Your Peace	C-	8	M	C	4	3-4
Top Command	Bold Ruler/Prince Bio	C	7	C*	C	3	3-4
Top Horn			6	C*		1	3-4
Topsider	Northern Dancer/Round Table	C	5*	C+	C	3	2-3
Top Ville *ENG*	High Top/Charlottesville	F	6*	C+	C	3*	3-4
Toronto	Sir Ivor/Larkspur	F	8	C	F	3*	3-4
Toronto Trip	Tentam/Victoria Park	D	7	D	D	4	3-4
Torsion	Never Bend/Prince John	C-	6*	BY*	C	2	3-4
Tossofthecoin^	Magesterial/Drone	M	7	M	M	3	3-4
Total Departure	Greek Answer/Manifesto	C-	9	D	F	4	3-4
Totality	In Reality/Boldnesian	C-	8	D	C-	5	2-3
Total Pleasure	What a Pleasure/Dark Star	D	10	D	D	4	3-4

Stallion	Sire/Broodmare Sire	FTS	CL	TRF	OT	SI	AB
To the Quick	Raise a Native/Princequillo	C-	9	D	C+	3*	3-4
Touching Wood *NZ*			7	C*		3*	3-4
Tough Knight	Knights Choice/Capt. Courageous	C+	8	D	C+	5	2-3
Tour d'or	Medaille d'Or/Turn to Mars	C-	6	C+Y	C	3	3-4
Touring Dancer	Sovereign Dancer/Song	C-	7	M	C	4	3-4
Track Barron	Buckfinder/Sir Gaylord	C-	8	C-	C-	2	3-4
Track Dance	Green Dancer/L'Enjoleur	C-	7	C+	C-	3	2-4
Track Rebel*	Devil's Bag/Bolinas Boy	C-	9	D	D	4	3-4
Traffic Breaker	In Reality/Traffic Judge	C-	8	D	C	4	3-4
Traffic Cop	Traffic Judge/Count Fleet	C	7	C	C+	3*	3-4
Tragic Role *ENG*	Nureyev/Graustark	C-	6	C	C	3*	2-3
Tralos *VEN*	Roberto/Briartic	D	7	C	D	3	3-4
Transworld	Prince John/Hornbeam	D	7	C+	D	1	3-4
Trapeze Dancer	Northern Dancer/Tim Tam	F	8	M	F	3	3-4
Trapp Mountain	Cox's Ridge/Round Table	D	7	D	C-	3	2-3
Travelling Music	Spring Double/Silent Screen	C-	7	D	C	4	3-4
Travelling Victor	Hail to Victory/Travelling Dust	D	7	U	C	4	2-3
Treasure Kay *IRE*	Mummy's Pet/Welsh Saint	C-	7	C	M	4	3-4
Tree of Knowledge	Dr. Fager/Nasrullah	D	9	D*	C	5	3-4
Treetopper^	Woodman/Full Out	M	8	U	M	3	3-4
Trempolino	Sharpen Up/Vice Regal	C	6	C	C	1*	2-4
Trick Me	Phone Trick/Alleged	C	7	U	DT	4	3-4
Trick Question	Lyphard/Prince John	M	10	M	M	3	3-4
Tricky Creek	Clever Trick/His Majesty	C	6	D	C+	3	2-3
Tricky Fun*	Phone Trick/Hempen	C-	9	U	C	5	2-3
Tricky Six^^	Saratoga Six/Clever Trick	L	8	U	L	4	2-3
Tricky Tab	Clever Trick/Al Hattab	M	7	M	M	3	2-3
Tridesseus	Northern Dancer/Ribot	D	8	C	D	2	3-4
Tri Jet	Jester/Olympia	C+	5*	CY	C	4*	2-3
Triocala	Tri Jet/Francis S.	C	7	D	C	4	3-4
Triomphe	Hoist the Flag/Tom Fool	D	7	C-	C	3	3-4
Triple Bend	Never Bend/Gun Shot	F	8	D	C	4	3-4
Triple Sec	Tri Jet/Duck Dance	C	8	D	C-	4	2-3
Tri Swaps	Tri Jet/Swaps	C	8	C	C	4	3-4
Trojan Fen *IRE*			7	C*		3	3-4
Trooper Seven	Table Run/Holandes II	C	9	C	C	4	3-4
Trophy Man	Strike the Anvil/Tumiga	D	8	D	D	4	2-3
Tropular *FR*	Troy/Lorenzaccio	D	7	C	M	4	3-4
Troy *ENG*	Petingo/		6	C*		2	3-4
Truce Maker	Ack Ack/Gallant Man	D	7	C+	C+	3	3-4
Truculent	Val de L'orne/Luthier	D	6	C-	D	1	3-4
True Colors	Hoist the Flag/Princequillo	C-	6	C+	D	3	2-3
True Knight	Chateaugay/Olympia	D	8	C*	C	2	3-4
Truk^^	Secreto/Alydar	U	9	M	M	2	3-4
Trulo	Halo/Bold Bidder	D	10	U	D	3	3-4

Stallion	Sire/Broodmare Sire	FTS	CL	TRF	OT	SI	AB
Truly Met	Mehmet/Caro	M	8	L	M	3	3-4
Trumpeteer	Raise a Native/Damascus	D	8	U	C	4	3-4
Truxton King	Bold Ruler/Swaps	F	8	C*	C	3	3-4
Try My Best	Northern Dancer/Buckpasser	C-	7	C-	F	3*	3-4
Tsunami Slew *BRZ*	Seattle Slew/Barbizon	D	7	C+*	C-	3*	3-4
Tuckerstown	Tom Rolfe/Nasrullah	C	10	D	F	3	3-4
Tudor Grey			7	C+*	C+	4	3-4
Tunerup	The Pruner/Rocky Royal	C	5*	C+	C	3*	2-3
Tumiga			7	C*		3	3-4
Tunic	Nijinsky II/Buckpasser	F	10	D	F	3	3-4
Tunnel of Love	Groton/Cornish Prince	C-	9	F	C	5	3-4
Turbulent Kris^^	Kris S./My Dad George	M	7	M	M	3	2-3
Turf Career			7	M*	C-	4	3-4
Turgeon *FR*	Caro/Targowice	U	6	M	M	I	3-4
Turkey Shoot	Seattle Slew/Swaps	D	7	F	C	3	3-4
Turkoman	Alydar/Table Play	D	6	C	C+	3*	3-4
Turn and Cheer	Best Turn/Fleet Nasrullah	D	8	D	D	4	3-4
Turn and Count			7	C*		3	3-4
Turnberry	Raja Baba/Dogon	M	10	M	M	5	3-4
Turnbuckle	Best Turn/Greek Song	F	9	U	C	3	3-4
Turn to Mars	Turn-to/Nashua	C-	8	D	C	4	3-4
Turn to Reason	Hail to Reason/Mahmoud	D	7	C*	C-	3*	3-4
T.V. Alliance	T.V. Commercial/Staunchness	C-	8	C	C	4	3-4
T.V. Commercial	T.V. Lark/Alibhai	C-	6	C*	C+	2	2-3
T.V. Lark	Indian Hemp/Heelfly	C-	6	C*	C+	3*	2-3
Twice Burned	Singh/Buckpasser	D	9	F	C	4	3-4
Twice Worthy	Ambiopoise/Vandale	F	7	C+	F	3	3-4
Twilight Agenda	Devil's Bag/Grenfall	D	7	CY	D	2	2-3
Twining^^	Forty Niner/Never Bend	L	5	M	L	4*	2-3
Twoballsidepocket	Full Pocket/Double Jay	C-	9	D	C+	4	3-4
Two Davids	Olden Times/In Reality	C-	8	C-	C	4	2-3
Two Punch	Mr. Prospector/Grey Dawn II	C+	5	F	CT	4	2-3
Two's A Plenty	Three Martinis/Dark Star	C-	7	C-	C-	3	2-3
Tyrant	Bold Ruler/My Babu	C	6	C*	D	3	3-4
Tyrone Terrific	Lyphard/Bold Ruler	D	10	C	D	5	3-4
Ulan	Danzig/Gallant Man	M	10	M	M	4*	3-4
Ultimate Pleasure	Foolish Pleasure/Hawaii	C-	7	C	D	3*	3-4
Ultimate Pride	Lyphard/Princequillo	D	7	C*	D	3*	3-4
Ultramate	Nijinsky II/Hoist the Flag	D	9	C	D	I	3-4
Unable	Northern Dancer/Pago Pago	C	9	C-	C	4	3-4
Unaccounted For^	Private Account/The Minstrel	U	6	M	L	2	3-4
Unanimous Vote *IRE*	Roi Danzig/Sailust	U	8	M	M	3	3-4
Unbridled	Fappiano/Le Fabuleux	C+	5	C+	C+	3*	3-4
Unconscious	Prince Royal II/Mount Marcy	D	7	C*	C	3*	3-4
Under Tack	Crozier/Sailor	C-	8	F	C-	4	3-4

Stallion	Sire/Broodmare Sire	FTS	CL	TRF	OT	SI	AB
Un Desperado *FR*	Top Ville/Baldric	D	7	C	M	3*	3-4
Undulating^^	Alydar/Tilt Up	M	9	U	L	4	2-3
Unduplicated		M	6	L	M	3	3-4
Unfold	Raja Baba/Hoist the Flag	D	8	D	D	4	3-4
Unfuwain *ENG*	Northern Dancer/Bustino	D	6	C-	M	1	3-4
Unite	Raise a Native/Gleaming	C-	6	C	C	3	2-3
United Holme	Noholme II/Drawby	D	8	D	C	4	3-4
Universal	Raise a Native/Hail to Reason	D	8	C*	C	3	3-4
Unmistaken	What a Pleasure/Barbizon	M	9	U	U	4	3-4
Uno Roberto	Roberto/Secretariat	D	8	C	D	3	3-4
Unpredictable	Tri Jet/Ambehaving	D	9	D	CT	4	3-4
Unreal Currency	Unreal Zeal/Free State	C-	9	U	D	4	2-3
Unreal Zeal	Mr. Prospector/Dr. Fager	C+	6	C	C+	4	2-3
Un Reitre *ARG*	Nonoalco/Val de Loir	M	7	D	CT	3	3-4
Unzipped	Naked Sky/Specialmante	C	7	C	C+	3	2-3
Up and At'em *IRE*	Forzando/Song	M	7	L	M	4	2-3
Upmost	Roberto/Third Martini	D	8	D	C-	3	2-3
Upper Case	Round Table/Bold Ruler	C-	7	C+	C	3	3-4
Upper Nile	Nijinsky II/Round Table	D	7	C+	C	3	3-4
Uprising	Raise a Native/Hoist the Flag	D	10	U	C-	5	3-4
U.S. Flag	Hoist the Flag/Sir Gaylord	C-	7	C-	C+	4	3-4
Uzi	Rich Cream/Dr. Fager	F	8	D	C	3*	3-4
Vaal Reef *IND*	Raise a Native/Nashua	D	7	D	C	4	3-4
Vaguely Noble	Vienna/Nearco	D	5*	C+*	C-	1	3-4
Vaigly Great *IT*	Great Nephew/Derring-do	D	7	C-	M	4	3-4
Valanjou *FR*	Pampabird/Rex Magna	M	6	M	M	1	3-4
Valdali *IRE*	Darshaan/Val de Loire	C-	7	C	M	1	3-4
Val de Loir *FR*	Vieux Manoir/Sunny Boy	D	5*	B*	C	1	3-4
Val de L'orne	Val de Loir/Armistice	D	5	C+*	C-	3*	3-4
Valdez	Exclusive Native/Graustark	C-	7	C*	C	4	3-4
Valiant Lark	Buffalo Lark/Delta Judge	D	7	C+	C-	3	3-4
Valiant Nature^	His Majesty/Lyphard	M	6	L	M	3*	2-3
Valid Appeal	In Reality/Moslem Chief	A	3*	C	BT	4*	2-3
Valid Likeness *PR*	VaidAppeal/Creme dela Creme	C+	7	U	C+	4	2-3
Valid Wager^^	Valid Appeal/Bold Bidder	L	7	M	L	4	2-3
Valioso	Conquistador Cielo/Sir Gaylord	D	8	M	C	4	2-3
Valley Crossing^^	Private Account/His Majesty	U	7	M	M	3*	3-4
Van Go	Full Out/Victoria Park	C-	7	U	C	4	3-4
Vanlandingham	Cox's Ridge/Star Envoy	F	8	D	C-	3	3-4
Varennes	L'Enjoleur/Tyrant	U	10	M	M	4	3-4
Varick *AUS*	Mr. Prospector/Fleet Nasrullah	D	7	C+	C	3	3-4
Variety Road	Kennedy Road/Macarthur Park	C	8	D	D	3	3-4
Vayrann *FR*	Brigadier Gerard/Val de Loir	D	7	C	M	3*	3-4
Velvet Cap			7	C-*		5	3-4
Vencedor	Flag Raiser/Fulcrum	D	8	C	C	4	3-4

Stallion	Sire/Broodmare Sire	FTS	CL	TRF	OT	SI	AB
Vendor*	Alydar/Le Fabuleux	U	9	M	M	3*	3-4
Venetian Jester	Tom Fool/Princequillo	D	7	D	C-	4	3-4
Vent du Nord		C	7	C-*	C+	3	3-4
Ventriloquist	Lyphard/Stage Door Johnny	D	9	C-	D	1	3-4
Verbago	Verbatim/My Babu	U	10	M	M	5	3-4
Verbatim	Speak John/Never Say Die	D	5*	C+Y	C	<u>1</u>	2-3
Verge	Alydar/Damascus	C	6	D	C	4	3-4
Verification	Exceller/Buckpasser	C-	8	D	C	2	3-4
Vermont*	Chief's Crown/High Echelon	C	6	C	C+	<u>4</u>	<u>2-3</u>
Vernon Castle	Seattle Slew/Prince John	F	8	D	C	2	3-4
Veronica's Sir	Graustark/Prince John	F	8	D	F	3	3-4
Verzy	Vice Regent/New Providence	C-	7	C	C-	4	2-<u>3</u>
Viceregal	Northern Dancer/Menetrier	C	4*	C	C	2	3-4
Vice Regent	Northern Dancer/Menetrier	D	2*	B*	C	3*	2-3
Vicksburg	Mr. Prospector/Sea Bird	D	6	B	C	3	3-4
Victorian Prince	Victorian Era/Windfields	D	8	C-	C	3	3-4
Victoria Park	Chop Chop/Windfields	C-	6	C*	D	3	3-4
Victorious	Explodent/Majestic Prince	D	7	C-	C	2	3-4
Victor's Gent	Pukka Gent/Hagley	D	9	U	C-	5	3-4
Victory Stride	Northern Dancer/Victoria Park	C-	8	D	C-	4	2-3
Video Ranger	Cox's Ridge/Nijinsky II	D	7	D	D	3	3-4
Vigors	Grey Dawn II/El Relicario	F	5	CY	C	2	3-4
Villamor	Native Dancer/Your Host	C	7	C	C	4	3-4
Vilzak	Green Dancer/Hilarious	D	7	C-	D	2	3-4
Virginia Rapids^	Riverman/Sir Ivor	U	7	L	M	3	3-4
Virilify			7	C*		3	3-4
Vision *JPN*	Nijinsky II/Round Table	D	7	C*	M	4*	3-4
Vitriolic	Bold Ruler/Ambiorix	C	7	C*	C	4	3-4
Vittorioso	Olden Times/Native Charger	D	8	C	D	2	3-4
Viva Deputy	Deputy Minister/Secretariat	M	7	L	M	2	2-3
Vying Victor*	Flying Paster/Sir Ivor	M	7	M	M	3	2-3
Waajib *JPN*	Try My Best/Sassafras	D	7	C	D	3*	3-4
Wabasha	In Reality/Secretariat	M	8	M	L	3	2-<u>3</u>
Wa Bert^	Waquoit/Cyane	M	7	U	L	2	2-3
Wait Till Monday	Maelstrom Lake/SuperConcorde	U	10	M	M	4	3-4
Waitinginthewings	Winged T./Bupers	F	9	U	D	4	3-4
Wajima	Bold Ruler/Le Haar	C-	7	C-*	C	<u>4</u>	3-4
Waki Warrior^^	Miswaki/Bold Forbes	<u>L</u>	7	M	M	4	2-3
Walesa	Danzig/Gallant Man	M	7	M	L	4	2-<u>3</u>
Walker's	Jaipur/Swaps	C-	9	D	C	3	2-3
Wallenda^^	Gulch/Liloy	M	6	M	M	2	3-4
Wall Street Dancer*	Sovereign Dancer/Prince John	C	7	M	C	3*	2-3
Walsingham		M	7		M	4	3-4
Wander Kind	Hold Your Peace/Bupers	D	7	C-	C	3	2-3
Wanpum^^	Knights Choice/Agitate	L	9	U	L	5	2-3

Stallion	Sire/Broodmare Sire	FTS	CL	TRF	OT	SI	AB
Waquoit	Relaunch/Grey Dawn II	C-	5	C	C+	3*	3-4
War	Majestic Light/Victoria Park	D	7	C+	D	3	3-4
War Deputy^^	Deputy Minister/Sir Ivor	M	7	M	M	3	2-3
Wardlaw *SAF*	Decidedly/King of the Tudors	D	6	C	C	2	2-3
Ward Off Trouble	Wardlaw/Francis S.	D	5	B	C	2	3-4
Warfield*	Roberto/Reviewer	U	8	M	M	3	3-4
Warner Jones	Mr. Prospector/Pitskelly	M	8	M	M	3	3-4
Warning *JPN*	Known Fact/Roberto	C	7	C	D	3	2-3
War Rollick	Rollicking/Wise Exchange	C-	8	F	D	5	2-3
Warrshan *ENG*	Northern Dancer/Graustark	C-	6	C	M	3*	2-3
Wasa	Dust Commander/Intentionally	U	10	U	M	4	3-4
Washington County	Buckpasser/Sensitivo	C-	7	F	C	4	3-4
Water Bank	Naskra/Crewman	C	8	C*	C	4	3-4
Water Gate	Political Coverup/Bargain Ticket	U	7	U	U	4	3-4
Water Moccasin	Topsider/Hawaii	D	8	C	C	4	3-4
Water Power	In Reality/Hail to Reason	C-	8	D	C	4	2-3
Waterway Drive	Poker/Royal Serenade	U	9	M	M	4	3-4
Wavering Monarch	Majestic Light/Buckpasser	C-	5*	C	C	3*	3-4
Wayne's Crane	L'Enjoleur/Gallant Romeo	C+	7	D	B	5	2-3
Wayward Ace	Elocutionist/Mr. Brick	M	8	C+	M	1	3-4
Way West^	Gone West/Targowice	M	7	L	M	4	3-4
W.D. Jacks	Matsadoon/Young Emperor	D	9	C-	C	4	3-4
Weekend Guest	Mr. Prospector/Round Table	M	8	M	M	4	2-3
Weldnaas *ENG*	Deisis/Gallant Romeo	C	7	C-	M	3*	3-4
Well Decorated	Raja Baba/Majestic Prince	C	7	C*	CT	4	2-3
Well Selected	Well Decorated/Explodent	M	7	M	C-	4	3-4
Well Written	Bold Bidder/Creme dela Creme	U	10	U	M	4	3-4
Welsh Idol *ENG*	Welsh Pageant/Fortino	C-	7	M	C	4	3-4
Welsh Saint *ENG*			6	C+*		2	3-4
Weshaam	Fappiano/What a Pleasure	C	7	F	C	4	3-4
West by West^^	Gone West/Cox Ridge	L	6	M	L	4*	2-3
Western Miner*	Gone West/Buffalo Lark	M	8	M	L	3	3-4
Western Playboy	Play Fellow/Daniel Boone	D	6	U	D	2	3-4
Western Trick	Seattle Slew/Buckpasser	C	8	D	C	3	2-4
Westheimer *SPN*	Blushing Groom/Northern Dancer	D	7	C	C-	3	2-3
Whadjathink	Seattle Song/Great Nephew	C-	7	DY	C	2	3-4
Wharf^	Storm Bird/Riverman	U	7	L	M	3	3-4
What a Cooker	Smile/Ramsinga	M	7	M	M	4	2-3
What a Gent	What Luck/Nasrullah	D	8	F	DT	5	3-4
What a Hoist	Hoist the Flag/Cyane	F	8	U	C	4	2-3
What a Pleasure	Bold Ruler/Mahmoud	C-	7	C	C	3	3-4
What a Spell	What Luck/Dance Spell	C	7	U	C	4	3-4
Whatever For	Caro/Hail to Reason	D	7	C	C	1	3-4
What Luck	Bold Ruler/Double Jay	C-	6	C*	C	3	3-4
What's Dat			7	C*		4	3-4

Stallion	Sire/Broodmare Sire	FTS	CL	TRF	OT	SI	AB
Wheatley Hall	Norcliffe/Miracle Hill	C-	6	C+	C-	3	3-4
Wheaton^	Alydar/Secretariat	U	9	U	M	3	3-4
Whiskey Road	Nijinsky II/Sailor	D	6	C*	C	1	3-4
White Bridle AUS	Seattle Slew/His Majesty	D	6	D	C-	2	3-4
White Fir	Swaps/First Landing	D	9	U	C	4	2-3
White Mischief	Roberto/Intentionally	C-	6	B	D	2	2-3
Whitesburg	Crimson Satan/Prince Bio	C	7	C*	C	3	3-4
Whitney Tower^	Storm Bird/Shecky Greene	M	7	M	M	4	2-3
Whiz Along*	Cormorant/Northern Answer	M	8	M	M	3	3-4
Who's Fleet	Villamor/Hafiz	F	8	F	DT	5	2-3
Who's For Dinner	Native Charger/Intentionally	F	8	C-	C	2	3-4
Wiking	Arab/Sprinter	L	8		L	5	3-4
Wild Again	Icecapade/Khaled	C+	4	C+	C+T	4*	2-3
Wild Catch	Pass Catcher/Victoria Park	D	8	C-	C	5	3-4
Wild Gale^	Wild Again/Little Current	M	7	L	M	3	3-4
Wild Injun	Exclusive Native/Warfare	F	10	F	F	4	3-4
Wild Jose	Jose Kanu C./Board Ship	M	10	U	M	5	2-3
Wild Zone^	Wild Again/The Minstrel	M	7	L	M	3	3-4
Willard Scott	Roanoke Island/Quadrangle	D	9	U	C-	4	3-4
William Lawrence	Fappiano/Minnesota Mac	M	10	U	M	4	3-4
Williamstown^^	Seattle Slew/Northjet	M	8	M	M	3	2-3
Willing Worker	Compliance/Brave Emperor	M	10	M	M	4	3-4
Willow Hour	Bold Hour/Pia Star	D	9	F	C	3	3-4
Will Win	Raise a Native/Our Michael	C-	8	F	C	5	3-4
Winango	Restless Native/Piano Jim	D	7	D	D	3	3-4
Wind & Wuthering	No Robbery/John's Joy	D	9	C	D	3	3-4
Wind Chill	It's Freezing/Bold Hour	M	7	M	M	4	3-4
Wind Flyer	Full Pocket/Cyane	C-	7	D	C	4	3-4
Windlord	Secretariat/Pappa Fourway	F	8	U	F	4	3-4
Windy Sands	Your Host/Polynesian	C	7	C*	C+	4	3-4
Windy Tide	Windy Sands/Depth Charge	F	8	C-*	C	4	3-4
Winged T.	Tom Fool/Phalanx	D	7	D	C+	4	3-4
Wing Out	Boldnesian/Toulouse Lautrec	C-	8	C	C	3	3-4
Wing's Pleasure	Quiet Pleasure/Emblem II	U	10	U	U	5	3-4
Winner's Pleasure	Princely Pleasure/Silky Sullivan	D	9	D	D	4	3-4
Winnerwald	Private Account/Promised Land	U	8	M	M	3	3-4
Winning Hit	Bold Ruler/Ambiorix	C-	8	D	C	4	2-3
Winrightt	Distinctive/Sir Khalito	C	6	D	C	4	2-3
Winter Halo^^	Halo/Grey Dawnll	U	7	M	M	3*	3-4
Wintersett	Gummo/Acroterion	C	9	D	C	4	3-4
Wipe 'em Out	Annihilate 'em/What a Pleasure		8		M	3	3-4
Wise Exchange	Promised Land/Coastal	D	7	C*	C	3*	3-4
Wise Times IND	Mr. Leader/He's a Pistol	D	6	D	C+	4	3-4
With Approval	Caro/Buckpasser	C-	5	BY	C	1	3-4
With Caution	Raja Baba/Prince Dare	C-	9	D	C	5	3-4

Stallion	Sire/Broodmare Sire	FTS	CL	TRF	OT	SI	AB
Wolf TUR^^	Domineau/Rigel II	M	8	M	M	3	3-4
Wolfire	Wolf Power/Northern Fling	M	8	M	M	4	3-4
Wolfhound ENG	Nureyev/Buckpasser	U	7	L	M	4	3-4
Wolf Power SAF	Flirting Around/Casablanca	C	6	C+Y	CT	3	2-4
Wollaston	Lord Gaylord/Le Fabuleux	U	8	C	M	4*	3-4
Wonder Dancer	Raise a Native/Hail to Reason	C-	8	M	CT	4	3-4
Wonder Lark	Verbatim/T.V. Lark	D	10	D	F	4	2-3
Woodland Lad	Woodland Pines/Atomic	D	10	C	D	3	3-4
Woodman	Mr. Prospector/Buckpasser	D	7	CY	C-	3*	3-4
Word Pirate	Verbatim/Groshawk	U	8	M	M	3	3-4
World Appeal	Valid Appeal/Restless Wind	C-	6	C	C	3	2-3
World Court	Damascus/Wolver Hollow	U	7	U	M	4	3-4
Worthington Hills	Mr. Prospector/Buckpasser	D	8	C	M	2	3-4
Worthy Endevor	Ruken/Port Wine	F	10	F	F	5	3-4
Wynslew	Seattle Slew/Shantung	D	7	D	C	3*	3-4
Xenix	Halo/Prince John	U	9	M	M	3*	3-4
Xoda	The Axe II/Aberant	D	8	C*	C	2	3-4
Xray^	Allen's Prospect/Cornish Prince	M	8	U	L	4	2-3
Yallah ENG	Bold Lad/Habitat	M	7	M	M	4	3-4
Yankee Fan	Our Native/Cimmarron	M	7	M	M	4	3-4
Yarnallton Native	Raise a Native/T.V. Lark	F	9	F	C	4	3-4
Yaros^	Rare Brick/Cox's Ridge	M	7	U	M	3	2-3
Yeats AUS	Nijinsky II/Forli	D	7	C+*	C	4*	3-4
Yes I'm Blue	Marfa/No Fooling	C	8	M	M	4	3-4
Yesterdays Hero	Olden Times/Round Table	C-	8	C	C	4	2-3
Youmadeyourpoint	Diamond Prospect/Grundy	C	7	C	D	3	2-3
Young Commander	Lt. Stevens/Blue Prince	F	10	D	D	4	3-4
Young Ralph	Olden Times/Stage Door Johnny	D	7	C+	C	4	3-4
Young Tribute	High Tribute/Naskra	D	7	D	D	4	3-4
You and I^	Kris S./Ups	L	6	M	M	4	2-3
Your Dancer	Gaelic Dancer/The Pie King	F	9	F	D	4	3-4
Youth BRZ	Ack Ack/Dark Star	C-	7	C*	C	3*	3-4
Yukon	Northern Dancer/Nashua	C-	7	D	C-	4*	3-4
Yukon Eagle	Majestic Prince/Mongo	D	7	C*	C	3*	3-4
Zafarrancho	Farnesio/Martinet	D	6	C	CT	3	2-3
Zafonic ENG	Gone West/The Minstrel	L	6	L	M	4*	2-3
Zaizoom GER	Al Nasr/Turn-to	D	8	D	D	3	3-4
Zalazl JPN	Roberto/Northern Dancer	U	7	D	M	1	3-4
Zalipour	Rexson/Cyane	M	7	M	M	3	3-4
Zamboni	Icecapade/Eddie Schmidt	C-	8	C	C+	4	3-4
Zanthe	T.V. Lark/Turk's Delight	C	8	C+*	C	4	3-4
Zarbyev	Nureyev/Blushing Groom	C-	8	C+	C	3	2-3
Zeeruler	Lucky North/Exceller	M	8	M	M	3	3-4
Zen	Damascus/Tulyar	C-	6	C	C+	4	3-4
Zero for Conduct^^	Danzig/Stage Door Johnny	M	7	L	M	3*	2-3

Stallion	Sire/Broodmare Sire	FTS	CL	TRF	OT	SI	AB
Zevi	Cornish Prince/Carry Back	C-	8	D	C+	5	2-3
Ziad	Key to the Mint/Jacinto	D	6	C*	DT	3	3-4
Zie World	Transworld/Proudest Roman	D	8	C	C+	1	3-4
Ziggy's Boy	Danzig/Sunrise Flight	C-	8	D	C	4	2-4
Zignew^^	Danzig/Prince John	M	7	L	M	3*	2-3
Zilzal ENG	Nureyev/Le Fabuleux	C	6	B	D	3*	2-3
Zingalong	Raise a Native/Nasrullah	C-	8	D	C	4	3-4
Zinov	Drone/Crafty Admiral	D	9	C	C	3	3-4
Zodiac	Speak John/Northern Dancer	D	9	D	F	4	3-4
Zoffany AUS	Our Native/Grey Dawn II	C	7	C	C	2	3-4
Zonic	Swaps/Thinking Cap	F	9	C	F	4	3-4
Zoning	Hoist the Flag/Round Table	F	7	F	C+	2	3-4
Zoot Alors	Raise a Native/Saint Crespin	C	9	F	C	5	3-4
Zuppardo's Future	In Reality/Vice Regent	M	9	M	M	4	3-4
Zuppardo's Love	Icecapade/Jester	D	9	C	C	4	3-4
Zuppardo's Prince	Cornish Prince/Primate	C	7	D	BT	4	2-3
Zuppardo's Prospect	Miswaki/Bold Commander	M	8	M	M	4	3-4

Academy Award	3.5K	Compelling Sound	3K	Festin	2.5K
Affirmed	25K	Compliance	5K	Fit to Fight	10K
Alaskan Frost	1K	Conquistador Cielo	20K	Flying Continental	3.5K
Allen's Prospect	7.5K	Cool Halo	1.5K	Fly So Free	10K
Alwuhush	12.5K	Cool Victor	3K	Fly Till Dawn	4K
Alydeed	7.5K	Copelan	10K	Formal Dinner	2.5K
Alysheba	5K	Cormorant	6.5K	Fort Chaffee	5K
Alzao	15K	Cozzene	15K	Fortunate Prospect	10K
American Chance	5K	Crafty Prospector	25K	Forty Niner	70K
Anjiz	4K	Crusader Sword	5K	Fred Astaire	2.5K
A.P. Indy	75K	Cryptoclearance	25K	French Deputy^	17K
Apalachee	5K	Cure the Blues	15K	Furiously	5K
Ascot Knight	5K	Danzig	150K	Future Storm	5K
Batonnier	5K	Danzig Connection	7.5K	Geiger Counter	7.5K
Beau Genius	10K	Darn That Alarm	7.5K	Gilded Time	12K
Belong To Me	5K	Dayjur	50K	Glitterman	5K
Bertrando	10K	Deerhound	3K	Go For Gin^	15K
Bet Big	3K	Defrere^	6.5K	Gold Legend	2.5K
Black Tie Affair	15K	Dehere	25K	Goldwater	2.5K
Blushing John	15K	Demons Begone	5K	Gone West	75K
Bold Rukus	9K	De Niro^	5K	Gray Slewpy	3.5K
Boone's Mill^	5K	Deputy Minister	60K	Green Dancer	25K
Boundary	7.5K	Devil His Due^	20K	Groovy	5K
Broad Brush	25K	Devil's Bag	25K	Gulch	40K
Brocco	10K	Diablo	2.5K	Half A Year	3K
Buckaroo	7.5K	Diazo	4K	Halo	20K
Bucksplasher	5K	Diesis	30K	Hansel	15K
Caller I.D.	6K	Dignitas	3K	Harlan	5K
Candi's Gold	3.5K	Discover	2K	High Brite	3.5K
Capote	30K	Distinctive Pro	10K	Holy Bull	25K
Carnivalay	6K	Dixie Brass	5K	Homebuilder	5K
Carr de Naskra	6.5K	Dixieland Band	40K	Honor Grades	5K
Carson City	20K	Dixieland Brass	3K	Housebuster	20K
Caveat	7.5K	Dixieland Heat^	3K	Houston	5K
Cherokee Colony	3.5K	Double Negative	2.5K	Hula Blaze	2.5K
Cherokee Run^	7.5K	Dr. Adagio	2.5K	Ice Age	3K
Chief's Crown	20K	Dynaformer	18K	Incinerator	5K
Chief Honcho	3K	Eastern Echo	5K	In Excess	3K
Chimes Band^	7.5K	El Gran Senor	30K	Inspired Prospect	3K
Chromite	2.5K	End Sweep	6K	Interco	3.5K
Citidancer	10K	Exbourne	3.5K	Irish Open	2.5K
Claramount	2.5K	Explodent	5K	Irish River	35K
Clever Trick	15K	Falstaff	3.5K	Irish Tower	7.5K
Colonial Affair	15K	Fast Play	3.5K	Is It True	3.5K
Colony Light	3K	Fatih	2.5K	Island Whirl	3K

Jade Hunter	25K	Mountain Cat	7.5K	Prized	15K
Jazzing Around	4K	Mr. Greeley^	15K	Proper Reality	1K
Jeblar	7.5K	Mr. Prospector	200K	Prospectors Gamble	6K
Jolie's Halo	10K	Mt. Livermore	30K	Prospector's Halo	1.5K
Judge Smells	3.5K	Naevus	4K	Prospector's Music	2.5K
Katowice	2.5K	Nasty and Bold	2.5K	Proud Birdie	5K
Kingmambo	50K	Nelson	3K	Proud Truth	7.5K
Kipper Kelly	1.5K	Nines Wild	2K	Quest for Fame	10K
Kissin Kris^	5K	Noactor	5K	Quiet American	10K
Kleven	2.5K	Norquestor	4K	Rahy	50K
Known Fact	8K	Northern Baby	10K	Rainbow Quest	60K
Kokand	1.2K	Northern Flagship	15K	Raise A Man	15K
Kris S.	40K	Northern Prospect	3K	Rajab	2K
Lear Fan	18K	Northern Score	2.5K	Rare Brick	3K
Leo Castelli	4K	Notebook	7.5K	Rare Performer	3K
Lil E. Tee	7.5K	Now Listen	2.5K	Reach for More	1K
Line in the Sand	5K	Numerous^	10K	Really Awesome	1K
Lively One	5K	Nureyev	100K	Red Ransom	30K
Local Talent	4K	Ogygian	12.5K	Red Wing Bold	3.5K
Lord at War	15K	Oh Say	1.5K	Regal Classic	4K
Lord Avie	10K	Olympic Native	3.5K	Regal Intention	2K
Lost Code	10K	Olympio	7.5K	Regal Remark	2K
Lucky North	2.5K	Opening Verse	7.5K	Regal Search	3.5K
Lyphard	75K	Order	2K	Reign Road	3K
Majestic Light	12.5K	Our Emblem	10K	Relaunch	35K
Major Impact	3.5K	Out of Place	3.5K	Repriced	3.5K
Man From Eldorado	2.5K	Pancho Villa	5K	Restless Con	2.5K
Manila	10K	Pembroke^	5K	Risen Star	5K
Manlove	3K	Pentelicus	7.5K	Riverman	75K
Marfa	4K	Personal Hope	7.5K	River Special	7.5K
Marked Tree^	1.5K	Peteski	10K	Rizzi^	3.5K
Marquetry	10K	Phone Trick	15K	Robin des Pins	6K
M Double M	1.5K	Pick Up the Phone	2K	Robyn Dancer	4K
Meadowlake	20K	Pine Bluff	15K	Roman Diplomat	3K
Mercedes Won	3.5K	Pirate's Bounty	8K	Roy	10K
Metfield	7.5K	Pistols and Roses	3.5K	Rubiano	20K
Mi Cielo	4K	Pleasant Colony	60K	Ruhlmann	5K
Miner's Mark	20K	Pleasant Tap	15K	Runaway Groom	10K
Mining	10K	Polish Numbers	15K	Sabona	4K
Missionary Ridge	10K	Polish Precedent	30K	Saint Ballado	20K
Mister Bailey's^	10K	Premiership	7.5K	Salt Lake	7.5K
Miswaki	35K	Present Value	2.5K	Saratoga Six	5K
Moon Up T.C.	1K	Press Card	4K	Saros	3.5K
Montbrook	3K	Private School	2K	Scarlet Ibis	2.5K
Moscow Ballet	7.5K	Private Terms	10K	Sea Hero	10K

Seattle Dancer	7.5K	Strawberry Road	15K	Vigors	5K
Seattle Sleet	3K	Strike Gold	3.5K	Virginia Rapids^	6K
Seattle Slew	100K	Strodes Creek^	5K	Wallenda	7.5K
Seattle Song	5K	Stuka	3K	Waquoit	5K
Secret Claim	1K	Sultry Song	7.5K	War Deputy	2K
Secret hello	5K	Summer Squall	25K	Wavering Monarch	7.5K
Seeking the Gold	100K	Sunny Clime	2.5K	Wayne's Crane	2.5K
Sejm	2.5K	Sunny North	5K	Way West^	3.5K
Senor Speedy	3.5K	Supremo^	5K	Well Decorated	5K
Septieme Ciel	15K	Swing Till Dawn	3.5K	Weshaam	1K
Shadeed	10K	Sword Dance	5K	West by West	7.5K
Shanekite	5K	Synastry	2K	Whitney Tower^	2.5K
Sheik Albadou	10K	Tabasco Cat^	25K	Wild Again	35K
Silver Buck	6K	Tactical Advantage	4K	Williamstown	7.5K
Silver Deputy	10K	Take Me Out	2K	With Approval	15K
Silver Ghost	12K	Talinum	3.5K	Wolf Power	5K
Silver Hawk	40K	Talkin Man^	7.5K	Woodman	50K
Simply Majestic	5K	Tasso	3K	World Appeal	2K
Siyah Kalem	2.5K	Tejano	5K	You and I^	10K
Sky Classic	15K	Temperence Hill	2.5K	Zafonic	50K
Skywalker	7.5K	Theatre Critic	5K	Ziggy's Boy	2.5K
Slew City Slew	7.5K	Theatrical	65K	Zilzal	20K
Slewdledo	1.5K	The Prime Minister	5K		
Slew o'Gold	15K	Thirty Six Red	7.5K		
Slewpy	7.5K	Thunder Gulch^	40K		
Slew's Royalty	3K	Time For A Change	20K		
Slew the Bride	1.5K	To Freedom	2K		
Slew the Slewor	2.5K	Top Avenger	3.5K		
Smarten	5K	Trempolino	20K		
Smile	4K	Tricky Creek	3.5K		
Smokester	10K	Tricky Fun	2K		
Son of Briartic	6.5K	Tricky Six	1K		
Spectacular Bid	9.5K	Tsunami Slew	3.5K		
Speedy Cure	1.5K	Turkey Shoot	2.5K		
Spend A Buck	5K	Turkoman	5K		
Squadron Leader^	2.5K	Twilight Agenda	7.5K		
Stage Colony	2K	Twining	10K		
Star de Naskra	10K	Two Punch	10K		
Stately Cielo	2.5K	Unaccounted For^	10K		
Steinlen	7.5K	Unbridled	25K		
St. Jovite	25K	Unreal Zeal	3.5K		
Stop The Music	10K	Valiant Nature^	7.5K		
Storm Bird	45K	Valid Appeal	20K		
Storm Boot	2K	Valley Crossing	5K		
Storm Cat	125K	Vermont	3K		

Also from City Miner Books

New
VALUE HANDICAPPING:
THE ART OF MAKING YOUR OWN LINE AND IDENTIFYING OVERLAYS
by Mark Cramer   168 pages $25.00

Most horseplayers underachieve because they play too many races and are obsessed with picking winners as opposed to identifying and backing only those horses that are underbet in proportion to their chances of winning. In this pioneering book Cramer shows handicappers how to create their own personal odds lines and then use them to identify which, if any, horses are overlayed and worth betting in any given race.

"I know of no other handicapper who is as insightful in both mechanics and the spirit of crafting a personal betting line as Mark Cramer." — Dave Litfin

DEBUT WINNERS OF 1998
edited by Mike Helm $25.00

An indispensible tool for playing first-time starters in maiden races that integrates Mike Helm's *Sire Ratings* with longshot trainer/owner angles. Includes every debut winner from the top fifty tracks around the country. Each winner is chronologically analyzed according to the time of year and class level at which it won, its sire, gender, post-position, winning distance and time, odds and connections. Bound to give any horseplayer who uses it an edge on the rest of the public by identifying seasonal pattern matches from 1998 that are likely to be repeated throughout 1999. Also includes an introduction with useful tips for playing maiden races.

FRESHMEN SIRES OF 1999
edited by Mike Helm $25.00

An inside look at the freshmen sires of 1999 including such hot prospects as Chimes Band, Boone's Mill, Go For Gin. Mr. Greeley, Pembroke, Tobasco Cat, Thunder Gulch, and You and I. Each freshman sire profile includes a horse-for-course angle indicating where he broke his maiden and won his most important races, as well as what you can expect from his progeny the first time they start, stretch out, switch to turf or run on an off-track. Also updates how last year's freshman crop performed and alerts horseplayers to any significant changes in how the progeny of older sires are performing.

EXPLORING PEDIGREE: HANDICAPPING'S NEWEST FRONTIER
by Mike Helm   224 pages $29.95

This best selling title gives horseplayers the tools to intelligently evaluate debut runners in maiden races, as well as young horses stretching out, switching to the turf or trying an off-track for the first time. Over 50 races are analyzed in such a way that the pedigree factor is integrated with speed and pace analysis, trainer angles and toteboard action. Praised by Tom Ainslie, Mark Cramer, Howard Sarton, Dave Litfin and many others as the definitive text on pedigree handicapping.

SCARED MONEY
by Mark Cramer   144 pages $19.95

An engaging collection of racetrack stories that explores the strategic changes in betting psychology, money management and everyday decision-making that are necessary to become a consistent winner.

Also from City Miner Books

REAL-LIFE HANDICAPPING: AN ECLECTIC HORSEPLAYER'S YEAR AT THE TRACK
by Dave Litfin   192 pages $25.00

Takes horseplayers on a year-long, handicapping odyssey. Shows horseplayers how to exploit the results charts and workout tabs in the *Daily Racing Form* to uncover hidden pace advantages and ready layoff horses, how to use pedigree information, and how to intelligently structure bets when playing the exotics. Required reading not only those who play the New York circuit, but anyone interested in sharpening their handicapping and decision-making skills.

MUDDERS & TURFERS
L. Tomlinson $49.00

A pocket-size booklet that takes a numerical approach to rating sires for how their progeny do on turf and off-tracks. Used by both Mark Cramer and Dave Litfin along with Mike Helm's *Sire Ratings*.

ULTIMATE TRAINER PATTERN POCKET GUIDE 1999-2000
Bill Olmsted $50.00

Features more than 4800 trainers and their most profitable maneuvers. Alphabetically-arranged, every trainer is rated (or not) according to how well they do with 7 day wheelbacks, first/second time off a claim, layoffs, first-time starters, distance and surface changes, shippers, drops in class and much more.

ORDERING INFORMATION

NEW!   24 hour fax ordering: (510) 841-1566

Name_____

Address_____

City_____

State/Zip Code_____

Phone (optional)_____

www.wenet.net/~cminer/

e-mail: cminer@wenet.net

For phone orders call (510) 841-1511

Credit Card Orders:

Card #:_____

Expiration Date: _____

Please Circle: VISA   MasterCard

Please check items wanted:

Value Handicapping	$25.00	_____
Debut Winners of 1998	$25.00	_____
Debut Winners of 1997	$15.00	_____
Freshmen Sires of 1999	$25.00	_____
Exploring Pedigree	$29.95	_____
Scared Money	$19.95	_____
Mudders & Turfers	$49.00	_____
Real-Life Handicapping	$25.00	_____
Sire Ratings: 1999-2000	$35.00	
Trainer Pattern Guide 1999-2000	$50.00	_____
Sub-total		_____
CA residents add 8.25% sales tax		_____
Shipping ($3 per item)		_____
Total		_____

Mail check or money order to: City Miner Books, P.O. Box 176, Berkeley, CA 94701

sr99/00